inequality.com

Dedications

KOH: To my father, Derek O'Hara, who did not live long enough to see the Internet in full bloom, but cared passionately about justice.

DS: For Matthew.

inequality.com
Power, Poverty and the Digital Divide

Kieron O'Hara and David Stevens

ONEWORLD

OXFORD

INEQUALITY.COM
POWER, POVERTY AND THE DIGITAL DIVIDE

Oneworld Publications
(Sales and Editorial)
185 Banbury Road
Oxford OX2 7AR
England
http://www.oneworld-publications.com

ISBN-10: 1–85168–450–6
ISBN-13: 978–1–85168–450–2

Cover design by Liz Powell
Typeset by Forewords, Oxford
Printed and bound in India for Imprint Digital

1004895023

Contents

CONTENTS

Acknowledgements

Funding for the research for this book was provided by an Economic and Social Research Council (ESRC) grant (award no. RES-000-22-0563). As such it forms part of the wider funded project 'Justice On-line: Distributing Cyberspace Fairly'. The authors would like to thank the ESRC, and all those at Polaris House, for their support. Thanks also to Peter Elford, Adrian Pickering and John Darlington.

Kieron O'Hara was supported by the Advanced Knowledge Technologies (AKT) Interdisciplinary Research Collaboration (IRC), which is sponsored by the UK Engineering and Physical Sciences Research Council (EPSRC) under grant no. GR/N15764/01. The AKT IRC comprises the Universities of Aberdeen, Edinburgh, Sheffield, Southampton and The Open University. The views expressed in this book are personal, and not necessarily endorsed by other consortium members.

Parts of chapter 5 have been taken from David Stevens, 'Reasonableness and Inequality in Rawls's Defence of Global Justice', Acta Politica, 38, 2003, pp. 231–53. Some of the discussion in chapter 6 has been taken from Kieron O'Hara, 'The Internet: A Tool for Democratic Pluralism?', Science as Culture, 11, 2002, pp. 287–98.

Many thanks for helpful discussions and comments at various times and in various contexts from Christopher Brewster, Matthew Clayton, Brian Collins, Daniel Dyal, Wendy Hall, Erik Jones, Rameesh Kailasam, Peter Lacy, Mark Neocleous, Nigel Shadbolt, Cass Sunstein, Yorick Wilks, Chris Woodard, many members of the AKT IRC, the EPSRC Memories for Life network (http://www.memoriesforlife.org) and participants in the UK Office of Science of Technology Foresight programme on Cyber Trust and Crime Prevention.

We owe a special debt of thanks to Mark Neocleous for reading and commenting at length on a draft of the entire manuscript.

Preface

Technology has developed at such a pace that it is often difficult to make sense of the things going on around us. Do your children look at you aghast when you can't perform what for them is the simplest of functions on a home computer or a mobile phone? Do you get confused by the mass of new technologies available in the entertainment market? iPods, WiFi, TiVo, 3G?

Keeping abreast of technological change is difficult enough. Understanding it is even more problematic. When the very fabric of our social existence is constantly being altered, redefined or completely uprooted, we can feel a certain sense of dislocation. The whirl of technological advance can pull us down, as though there is no solid base upon which to stand. The old, familiar concepts and ideas that we used to order and understand our world no longer seem to apply to the new situations or the new technologies.

However, we believe that it is possible to map the contours and features of the new Information Society; that there are fixed points from which to take bearings in this unfamiliar country – landmarks to help guide us on our journey. These landmarks come from history, and from the more abstract but familiar disciplines of social science and philosophy. The challenge is to apply these to the new terrain. Once we do so, that new terrain looks far less hostile, far less foreboding and much more familiar than we might have initially imagined.

Our subject matter is no less than information and communications technology (ICT) itself. Out of all the new technologies spawned in the last forty years, it is, without doubt, the field of ICT that has had the greatest social, economic and political impact. It is the ICT revolution that has contributed significantly to our disorientation. But is this truly a brave new world? ICT makes things happen faster, and therefore enables more things to happen in a given period. And it should never be forgotten that a sufficiently large quantitative change will eventually become a qualitative change. Equally, many of the problems, dilemmas and issues that we face now have been encountered in various guises throughout history. The details may have changed or altered, but the underlying stories have remained relevantly similar. In this book we draw upon an array of writers and thinkers from the history of philosophy, science and political thought to illustrate the connections between our present circumstances and the historical arc of human society. Karl Marx, Adam Smith, Thomas Hobbes, Plato, John Stuart Mill, John Locke, Alexis de Tocqueville and the framers of the American constitution have all wrestled with problems that bear a striking resemblance to those faced by the world at the moment.

ICT does not, for the most part, raise any fundamentally new social and political issues. It therefore does not require us to jettison our moral, ethical or political framework, as numerous commentators have suggested, though it might require us to rethink parts of it. Traditional questions of social justice, personal ethics, the place of liberty and the role of community all reappear in this new terrain, but with a fresh slant, in a more nuanced fashion or with new urgency. As different technologies emerge, the problem is not how to replace our existing norms which have been rendered obsolete, but rather how to understand the new terrain in order to apply those existing norms to it.

Is this simply business as usual, then? Does ICT provide no more of a challenge than just tinkering with old theories, concepts and ideas so as to make them fit newer contexts? Definitely not. The explanatory and analytical tools of modern social science and philosophy help us make sense of these new contexts, and give us methods of addressing them. But the process is not unidirectional. Sometimes new technologies can make the rethinking of our moral and political norms and concepts necessary. The relationship between ethics (broadly construed) and technology travels in both directions.

We sit somewhere between the two extremes of either viewing recent technological advances as nothing new at all, and therefore not worth troubling ourselves with unduly, or as so radically transformative that all our previous thinking has to be thrown out of the window. Technology – and particularly ICT – does pose severe challenges which may, sometimes, require us to rethink received wisdom or to be inventive, but we also have some useful tools and established landmarks to help us work our way through them. This might not be as radical or eye-catching as other recent views such as postmodernism, but the historical record suggests that such radical theories are rarely correct, and even more rarely useful.

The Internet excels in the provision of information to knowledge-poor populations. But, bearing in mind the freedom of speech and the difficulty of regulating the Internet, how can we ensure the veracity of that information? Do we, indeed, have a responsibility to put correct information online? Do we have a responsibility for maintaining repositories of knowledge? (The cost of maintaining existing knowledge bases in order to ensure continuing relevance and truth is surprisingly high.) Is there any need for, or indeed method of, regulating?

In this book we explore these questions and more, outlining the problems and sometimes bravely suggesting their solutions. In the first chapter we note how many of these issues are closely tied together at their foundations, and how such problems have been recurring themes in the history of human society. In the next three chapters, we set out a framework for understanding the online world. Chapter 2 looks more closely at the currect state of ICT, and its likely course of development over the next few years. Chapter 3 argues the importance of ICT to the ordinary citizen, while chapter 4 shows how we might think about justly distributing something as important as ICT to citizens.

However, life is never simple, even online. The next four chapters look at particular areas of online political life, in order to lay out some of the complexities of the new political arena. Chapter 5 introduces an international dimension, and looks at the issues of globalisation and development. Chapter 6 narrows the focus and examines what ingredients we need for democracy to flourish, while chapter 7 looks specifically at how technology affects the mechanics of the political world, with so-called e-governance and e-democracy. Chapter 8 looks even more narrowly into the personal space of the individual citizen, and tries to weigh up the complex issues relating to privacy in the online world.

Finally, chapter 9 draws some of the various threads together. By then, we hope to have established three things. First, we should have shown, by the judicious use of arguments from classic philosophers, that the Internet and related technologies, conceived as a political space, do not raise a host of new, unfamiliar questions. Traditional formulations of the great political problems remain important and relevant, even in the whizzy techno-age.

Secondly, we should also have shown that the concepts that these luminaries dealt with – whose application in truth is hard enough in the offline world – are often greatly underdetermined online. Ideas such as equality, privacy and liberty are argued over all the time, but we have a general sense that two people can more or less agree on their meaning offline – at least, enough to have a meaningful argument. But equally, we have to be constantly on our guard that we are not talking past each other, or talking nonsense. In the online world, the meanings of these notions are rather less obvious, and consequently the dangers of meaningless argument, nonsense or dialogues of the deaf are that much greater.

Thirdly, although we look at fairly specific issues related to international politics (chapter 5), national politics (chapters 6 and 7) and the politics of the individual (chapter 8), nevertheless we should have said enough to suggest very strongly what politics shifted online will look like in the not-so-distant future. The issues we describe now may seem somewhat arcane, or remote from the usual political experience. But by 2020, the world will have been transformed; if you think technology is proliferating rapidly now, you ain't seen nothing yet.

We certainly don't want to pretend that we know the shape of this future. In this book we extrapolate from current developments to try to guess future developments, but we are well aware of the limitations of that strategy. As Ged Davis of Shell International put it, 'a trend is a trend is a trend until it bends'. The future will contain surprising events and new developments that are impossible to foresee. But we claim that the online political world will dramatise many, if not all, of the questions of justice that we talk about in this book. To find answers to those questions, we need to return to the masters and mistresses of political theory – Marx, Smith, Arendt et al. – and try to reinterpret the new world within their frameworks, and reinterpret those frameworks in the context of the new world we have created.

Much as we try to do nowadays.

1:⟩
Introduction – the New Habitat

Politics and spaces: what is a space?

Let us begin with a truism: politics goes on in the world. Defining politics may not be very easy, but whether the point of politics is to change the world, to supervise the control and transfer of resources, to decide between rival visions of the regulation of pre-existing societies or merely the artful concealment of power by the cloak of authority, it requires an arena and some actors.

If the actors never meet, if they cannot influence each other, then there would be no politics, no political argument. The arena is where the actors meet, and therefore must enable the actors to interact in some way – a way which is likely to create disputes, for otherwise there would be little point in being, and less inclination to be, political.

In this chapter we sketch a number of issues that point up the political aspects of the Internet, including the issues of identity, security, access to and control of the new information technologies. We certainly do not pretend that these are the only relevant political issues here. All we wish to establish at this early stage is that the Internet is an arena for political action, and that as such the question of policing and maintaining the space becomes a political one.

Politics, ultimately, is about the resolution of disputes via compromise or force, rather than through technocratic means which illicitly assume that independent criteria for a 'best' solution already exist, and that therefore all that is required is expert implementation. This is particularly important online because technocrats are every-where; indeed, the space was created by technocrats. Technocratic solutions can be imposed on the Internet user community, but, by restricting the actions that are performable online, such solutions prejudge the political issues.

Where disputes are to be resolved, and behaviour managed, questions of fairness and justice immediately raise their heads. How are we to ensure that decisions made online are just? And what, in relation to online action, constitutes justice? Are there differences between those online actions which have chiefly online effects and those which make a difference in the real world? Can we, in the latter case, import our real world ideas of justice into the online world, or should we follow the alternative complex route of marking out new guidelines for the new territory? Does the Internet really provide an entirely new terrain for political action, one which differs so much from what has gone before that a complete rethinking of our moral framework is required? Or can the concepts of justice and ethics that operate in our own world be extended to cover this new and challenging space adequately?

What are the conditions of online justice? How do we deal with identity? Or privacy? Or security? Or freedom of speech? Are there requirements for access to particular levels of hardware or software? Are certain capabilities necessary for full use of the Internet?

In this book, we argue that certain political ideas apply to the online world as represented by the Internet (and related technologies). The idea of thinking about technology in political terms is not new; after all, that is what the Luddites did when they worried, correctly, about the new textile technologies undermining their incomes. And surely the supreme technological achievement of humankind – landing and walking on the moon – was first and foremost a political act, designed to show that capitalism was superior to communism. New technologies are always provoking political disputes, from the genetic modification of food to nanotechnology. Whoever thought the Internet would be any different?

Who indeed? But it *is* different, in a very subtle way. As a bundle of technologies, the Internet impinges on our lives in much the same way as other technologies; it makes some people rich and others poor, it enhances some people's lives and irritates the hell out of others. This being the case, one might well expect disputes to arise out of its deployment. All well and good, but that's not quite the point.

The Internet is different from other technologies in that it not only exists in the world, it also constitutes a type of world itself. In other words, the Internet is an arena for political action. This means that there must be actors within it, who interact in ways analogous to those of real actors in the real world.

What might such an interaction consist of? First, the actors in any space used for politics must be able to communicate with each other, to send and receive messages. These messages need not necessarily be understood, but they must be interpretable. Also, the interactions must have the potential to change the actors in some way: it must be possible for an actor to become altered during the course of an interaction. This alteration need not be very large, but it must have real consequences; for example, it may only be that the actor's beliefs about the world have changed, or the resources under the actor's control have changed in quantity. And thirdly, the actors should, to some extent, be both independent of and vulnerable to each other. This has the effect that, for most interactions of most actors, the actors cannot control the interaction and will be uncertain about its outcome.

Spaces that have these qualities can become political arenas because there is always the potential for dispute and cooperation. The classic political dilemmas will emerge from rich enough societies. Self-interest will bring rewards, but may 1) lead to others being deprived; and 2) prevent the mutual rewards of trust and cooperation from being achieved. And the perennial moral and political issues of justice and fairness will inevitably be raised. Where resources are being argued over and where benefits have to be distributed, the actors would have the option to attempt political settlement of the spoils. This would involve at a minimum the creation of agreed decision-making processes. If the Internet really is a space in this (political) sense, then it too will raise questions of justice and fairness. This is because of the issues of self-interest in its design and operation that it creates. Arguments over who should receive the benefits and who should bear the burdens of the development of the Internet and related technologies are already raging. An agreed upon decision-making process in this context looks increasingly necessary.

According to the seventeenth-century political theorist Thomas Hobbes, the development of such agreed processes was a rational response to the inevitable problems of a free-for-all.[1] Naturally, Hobbes focused his own analysis on the development of political processes in the real world; he imagined the means whereby political authority (i.e. the state) would grow up in a precivilised society (what he called the 'state of nature'), in effect as a means of keeping the peace by a combination of fairness and muscle.

Hobbes's 'state of nature' is an imaginary society with many of the properties of the real world in which we live; we can guess the sanctions that would be placed on the people in it (typically violent and painful). In this book, we describe another society that is different from our own. The sanctions available to the authorities are different, as are many of its properties (personal identity is much less fixed than it is in the real world). This may seem strange, but the abstraction of Hobbes's thought experiment enables him to look at his own existing society with a rather more discerning eye.

Abstraction is a useful tool for thinking about a problem. Indeed, the only way to see what it means to develop a space in which politics is conducted is to abstract away from the messy details of the actual political spaces which we inhabit, and whose scruffiness was well described and lauded by Bernard Crick some years ago.[2] Without abstraction it would often be impossible to see beyond the chaotic detail of everyday life or politics and to understand, explain or even cure a particular problem.

In more recent times, the political theorist Hannah Arendt investigated the properties of a political space; its essential property, for her, is that it 'gathers us together and yet prevents our falling over each other'.[3] In other words, a political space is a bit like a table, in that it relates the people who are sitting around it while simultaneously separating them. This space is a common, shared world that also allows people their own independent existence.

This public, political space is a world of appearances.[4] The space can be seen, heard and felt by all the people participating in it, which allows experiences to be shared and enables action to be cooperative. In such a world, participants can be individuated by their identities, and these identities can be evaluated. Arendt claims that such a space is created whenever political action takes place; equally, we might add that such a space, existing already, creates the potential for political action in that space.

Furthermore, the political space is common to us, and distinct from our own private space. We should not think of it as a natural thing. Rather, it is something that is created by us and for us, an artificial construct created partly to house political action, and which ultimately transcends ordinary human capabilities and lifespans. For thinkers such as Hobbes the construction of this political space was to be welcomed – it helped to extract individuals from the anarchic conflict of all against all. For others, such as Karl Marx, it represents something to be overcome, something from which we require emancipation in order fully to realise our true nature as human beings.[5] Yet, however we view this political space, whether as something to celebrate or something to lament, its existence is impossible to deny. We might expect (some) political spaces to pre-date us and others to survive us when we die. It is our participation in such spaces that takes us beyond the sphere of mere self-interest; after all, we would have very little self-interest in ensuring that a political space is functional, and that justice and fairness are to be obtained within it, if our participation in that space were relatively limited. Our private interests are somewhat different from our public interests.

Arendt's description of a public, political space, is very abstract; Hobbes's is imaginary. But the political space determined by technology is certainly not imaginary; neither is it abstract, as it is with us now. The Internet, like it or not, exists. It is a constructed space, and a political one at that. Political actions and decisions are being taken within it all the time, even now, and increasingly so. These actions and decisions entail disputes, arguments and distribution of resources, and questions of ethics and of justice. Who should reap the benefits of the new technologies? Who should bear the burdens? Who should control the distribution of those benefits and burdens? What restrictions on liberties are justified by the distribution of technology? These are all pressing questions. The resolution of such disputes and the investigation of such distributional and ethical questions are the very subject matter of this book.

Technologies

What are these technologies we are talking about? Since the industrial revolution, the impact of technology on our lives has increased dramatically decade on decade, and the political aspects of this have not been overlooked – from the nineteenth-century Luddites to today's Greens. Economist William Baumol estimates that nearly 90% of current US GDP is due to technological innovations developed since 1870.[6]

Why is technology so transformative, and why is it the focus of such political and economic interest? Technologies are artificial methods for solving problems. For a technology to be worth developing, it has to be an improvement on existing methods in some way.

Not in every way; diesel trains, for example, are an improvement on steam trains in terms of speed, power and cost, but not at all aesthetically. On balance, it tends to be economic factors that drive us to develop technology, but not always; sometimes we just want things to look nicer or be less hassle.

How does a technology transform things? In very rough terms, what a technology does is to make a complex task, one that typically needs an expert to perform it, routine. This has a number of effects. First of all, it means that the owners of a technology, instead of being at the beck and call of a few select, expensive practitioners, can ask more people to work for them. The technology enables many more people to do the job; or to do it at a particular cost; or with a particular reliability; or at a particular speed. Think, for instance, of the mechanised production of textiles. The invention of the power loom by Edmund Cartwright in 1785 allowed the production of cloth at a rate that far exceeded the traditional hands-and-feet method. Operating the steam-powered loom required less skill than traditional weaving, meaning that more people could do it. This, in turn, reduced labour costs because highly trained weavers were no longer required.

All this means that the cost of getting the job done falls: as more people are able to do the job, the supply of 'experts' increases and this increased competition drives their costs down. This is good for many people. The person who wants the job done saves money and time; there are many more employment opportunities in the population at large; and the lower cost of getting the job done means that more people can afford it, and can benefit from it. Materially, we are infinitely better off than we were even two or three decades ago; an average person in a twenty-first-century Western European democracy leads a more comfortable (indeed, luxurious) life than did the Queen of Sheba. Standing at the advent of the Industrial Revolution in eighteenth-century Britain, political economist Adam Smith recognised this phenomenon of the material benefits of technological progress, even for those at the very bottom of society – the labouring poor. Here we see historical parallels and precedents for current technological impacts.

> Compared, indeed, with the more extravagant luxury of the great, his [the labourer's] accommodation must no doubt appear extremely simple and easy; and yet it may be true, perhaps, that the accommodation of an European prince does not always so much exceed that of an industrious and frugal peasant, as the accommodation of the latter exceeds that of many an African king, the absolute master of the lives and liberties of ten thousand naked savages.[7]

Technology is politically controversial because it brings with it a whole range of costs and benefits for individuals (and groups). Some benefit from a new technology, others do not. This creates trade-offs and political wrangling. For example, the experts who benefited from the scarcity of practitioners before the technology was introduced will lose their livelihoods. The Luddites, skilled weavers who resisted the mechanisation of their craft – by inventions such as Cartwright's power loom – in the early nineteenth century, are often caricatured as boorish conservatives cravenly trying to halt the march of progress. Actually they were no such thing; their economic analysis of what the new technology would do to their standard of living was quite correct.

Similarly, the rich who could afford the expertly produced goods and services find that they have to share their consumption patterns with poorer people. Central heating, television, membership of the local golf club, clean and tidy houses, cars, dishwashers: all of these have, at some point, been badges of success used by the upwardly mobile. Yet these are now within reach of anyone in regular employment.

Thirdly, by routinising skills, technology removes the uniqueness of the hand-crafted product. It is impossible to make something is as wonderful as a Chippendale chair using a machine.

Modern machine-made furniture is bland and identical. But equally, most people can afford modern furniture, whereas a Chippendale is beyond the pockets of all but the very wealthy. Similarly, an off-the-peg suit will never fit as perfectly as a tailor-made one. But for most, Seventh Avenue is much more affordable than Savile Row.

Fourthly, the introduction of technology often means change: changes in working or leisure practices, and alterations in patterns of consumption, including of raw materials. This can be unsettling to those of a conservative disposition; it may also result in pressures on the environment.

So technologies are certainly not unmixed blessings. As a political problem, they tend to be more controversial than even this account suggests, because the many who gain from the introduction of technology tend to gain relatively little, while the few who lose tend to lose a lot. Technological progress brings long-term gains, but this is often at the expense of significant losses to those who had little in the first place. Typically one finds the losers shouting more loudly than the beneficiaries, even though the benefits for society as a whole are usually greater. Sometimes, however, those who lose also lose their voice to complain and become further oppressed.[8] Measuring benefits and burdens from the viewpoint of society as a whole is an ethically troubling enterprise. It obscures the fact that persons are separate beings who should not be used as means to greater ends, and that we can do great injustices to people if we do not take their interests into account on an individual basis. The philosophical position of utilitarianism has traditionally courted this type of criticism, and we will see why this is so in chapter 3.

Information and communication technology

The technology that is most transformative in today's society is information and communication technology (ICT). The technology that comes under the ICT rubric does not impact on physical objects directly; instead, it moves and processes information. The people whose jobs ICT replaces are clerical staff and managers – people who used their brains rather than their brawn. ICT enables decisions to be taken, it assembles data, it stores information, it passes messages around efficiently. Other technology has transformed the shop floor; ICT is now starting on the back office.

Because ICT's focus is on information, it has a different layer of significance in society. ICT produces stuff with content. Information has a meaning, or at least an interpretation, and can inform all sorts of decisions.

What sort of technologies are we talking about? Most of us spend at least some of our time interacting directly with ICTs; even those of us who do not own computers still interact with them, for example when calling automatic call centres. Let us list some of the ICTs that are most familiar, or that will be prominent in the next few years. (Some of the less familiar technologies will be discussed in the next chapter.)

- *Email.* This is the automatic and relatively secure transfer of messages. It has the advantage that composition and sending is much simpler than letter writing (no envelopes, stamps or postboxes), and receiving is more convenient than telephoning, as one can read one's email at one's leisure. However, the tiny cost of email has led to the development of the 'spam' industry, the sending out of unsolicited emails for commercial or criminal gain.

- *Networks.* Originally, computers were giant, expensive things that sat on one floor of an office building, and everyone used a workstation that used the centrally held computing and infor-mation storage resources. Now, the development of the personal computer means that we have the benefit of flexibility. Our own computers, with their own hard disks, can also interact with other computers, file storage systems, etc. And so sets of computers can be linked in networks, to give individual PCs much greater power than they could have on their own.

- *Mobile phones.* Telephones used to be attached to your house. Now, you can carry your phone around with you. Not only that, you can use it for much more than voice mail: photographs, games and email, for instance.

- *The World Wide Web (WWW, or the Web).* A network of 'web pages' presenting information in multimedia formats, with links from page to page often created associatively, to allow multiple ways of navigating through the content.

- *Chatrooms.* Similar to email, public sites where users can type messages to each other and receive answers in real time.

- *e-Commerce.* The WWW, credit cards and mail order come together to create e-commerce, online commerce which is prevalent not only from businesses to consumers, but also between businesses – and indeed, via sites such as eBay, between individuals.

- *Pervasive computing.* Computers are tiny, and they are everywhere. Most watches contains more computing power than the spaceships of a few decades ago. Not so long ago, to keep a car on the road you had to carry around half the components of the engine as spares; now a car is so computerised that only specialists have much chance of repairing them. The use of such tiny computers is bound to spread, to anywhere that might potentially benefit from information processing power.

- *Grids.* Computing power can be 'collected' from networked machines and sold to individuals as a commodity. Such a service is often called grid computing, by analogy to the electricity grid – where one doesn't create one's own electricity, but simply downloads as much as one needs from a centralised supply source.

- *P2P.* Peer-to-peer computing involves people creating networks by linking together their computers. Order emerges spontaneously. The most notorious example of a P2P system is Napster, the now-legal music downloading system.

- *Web services.* Over the WWW, one can buy specific Web-based services. For example, businesses can hire agencies to process all their credit card orders.

- *The Semantic Web.* This extension of the WWW gives the creator of content more expressive power, enabling much greater intelligence by the computer while navigating through the Web. More tasks previously performed by humans, requiring intelligence on the part of the agent, can be automated partly or wholly.

The Internet and the World Wide Web

Technologies such as these have transformed both work life and leisure time. They have dramatically altered the way we relate to others, both remotely and locally. They have brought new kinds of crime into being, new forms of art, new assumptions about the world, new sources of empowerment, new sources of complexity and new types of confusion. This power has come from a number of sources, including the impressive engineering methods that have meant that the ability of a computer chip of a given size to compute has approximately doubled every eighteen months for the last forty years or so. But the main cause of the transformative power of ICT is the Internet.

Sometimes it is the very unspectacular technologies that have the most far-reaching effects. Movable type, the stirrup and penicillin hardly compare to space rockets – or, indeed, computers – for complexity, but humanity has been transformed by all three. The Internet is one such technology. It may be very humdrum and mundane, yet it is remarkably powerful for all that. As former Microsoft guru Nathan Myhrvold wrote in the mid-1990s:

Centuries before the revolutionary democratic theories of Jefferson were adopted, a powerful new information technology liberated Europe and its people: the Gutenberg printing press. This 15th century technology gave the world an information distribution vehicle that influenced the very evolution of humankind. This dissemination process raised the education level of the masses and opened new worlds of invention. It put the control of content and its use literally in the hands of readers. It directly delivered the world's ideas and resources to the individual, carrying insight across sociological as well as geographical boundaries. This advent of mass communications revolutionized politics, religion, science, and literature and redefined the quality of life for all. This dramatic impact wasn't driven by the availability of content but by the means of distribution. Great philosophical, mathematical, and religious works existed long before the printing press. Yet it was the ability to access information that rewrote the world. The same has occurred with each major advancement in information dissemination: the telephone, movies, radio, and television all reshaped the world. Today, we're on the brink of another life-altering transformation.[9]

We don't want to go into massive and obsessive detail about technologies in this book. But it is one of our axioms that theorising in a field about which one knows nothing is at best pointless, at worst damaging. Hence we want to explain what the Internet is and how it works, in order that, when we come onto the more political discussions later on, we can do so in the context of a realistic appraisal of its potential.

The Internet is simply a network of computer networks; what makes it the Internet, as opposed to any old network, is that it is connected using the *Internet Protocol* (IP). IP helps the network transfer information from computer to computer. The problem it was devised to solve, in the 1960s, was the security and integrity of

America's communication systems in the event of catastrophic nuclear war. In the event of a serious strike on, say, New York, the danger would be that all communications that required hard wires going through the region would break down.

How to get round that difficulty? The first thing to note is an important property of networks. Suppose we have a set of computers connected in a network as in figure 1, and suppose the aim was to get important information from computer A to computer B. There is a direct link from A to B, but only one; and that is very vulnerable. There are, however, many indirect links from A to B, e.g. A–D–I–B or A–F–E–I–J–G–D–L–B. If the information could be passed from computer to computer in such an indirect way, so that no enemy could know which particular route was in operation at any particular time, then it would be much harder for that enemy to prevent the transfer of information from A to B. And if a key computer – computer

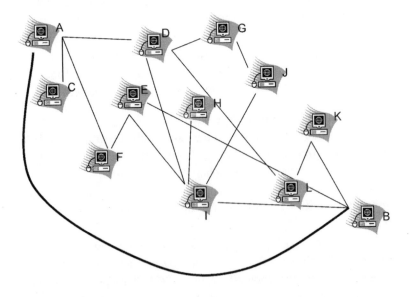

Figure 1: Getting information from A to B.

I, say – was knocked out, then the network contains other routes that could bypass I, such as A–F–E–B. How would such a route be worked out? Well, it need not be. Each computer needs only to know which computers it is connected to, and have a rough idea of how the computers are interconnected. If one computer, e.g. F, receives a message from A to go to B, it can look to see 1) which computers it is currently connected to; 2) which of those are likely to be closest to B (it need not necessarily be correct in this judgement); and 3) which of those connections are currently busy and which are relatively free of traffic. It can then send the message to the most plausible connected computer. This is most likely to be E, but sometimes (if the connection to E is blocked or busy) the best option might well be to go back to A and on via a different route. The result is that the network functions, even though no one knows the state of the whole network; all that is required is that each individual computer in the network understands its local environment.

It is precisely this sort of indirect networking that IP facilitates. The trick is to make the decision as to which route to take as late as possible. What IP does is this. First of all, it enables computer A to slice up the file containing the information into smaller pieces, called *packets*. A then sends out the packets individually down the telephone lines to other computers; it chooses which computer to send the packets to at the very moment of sending. Those other computers, aware of the ultimate destination for the packets they receive (computer B), send the packets forward to other computers that they reckon are nearer to computer B. Again, the decision as to where to send the packets is made at sending time. This last-minute decision is called *dynamic routing*. Dynamic routing is the key to the Internet; it is what makes the sending of information reliable, quick and efficient. Information attached to the packets tells B when it has all the packets, and how to reassemble them into a copy of the original file. The packets are tracked using the *Transmission Control*

Protocol (TCP), and the combination of the two protocols, TCP/IP, is the Internet standard.

This rather prosaic technology underlies the whole of the Internet, including email, chatrooms and newsgroups. Perhaps the most interesting part of the Internet, the part that has been almost entirely responsible for the astonishing online growth of the past decade or so, is the WWW. This is basically the multimedia part of the Web, and consists largely of pages written in a language called the *Hypertext Markup Language* (HTML), which in effect tells your computer how to arrange the objects on the page on the screen when it displays them.

All the files containing the HTML code are kept on computers called *servers*. The clever bit of the WWW is to pretend that all pages are kept on a single giant computer, rather than lots of smaller ones; it does this by assigning to each page a *web address*. Addresses are created using a consistent system of *uniform resource identifiers* (URIs), such as http://www.oneworld-publications.com, the address of the website of Oneworld Publications.

Given all these pages – there are literally billions of documents on the WWW – the key, as with any information storage system, is to be able to retrieve the documents you want. In ye olden days, one would have to remember the Web addresses, and type them in manually. But two clever innovations have made things easier and faster.

First, there is the *hyperlink*. Hyperlinks are links, often highlighted in blue, that take you from the page being read to another page; they allow you to follow concepts you are interested in, so that you can then find more pages on the same or similar topics. This brings in the flexibility and context-sensitivity of associative memory. HTML allows you to insert hyperlinks to other interesting web pages when you are writing pages of your own.

The second innovation is the *search engine*. These are big bits of software that trawl round the WWW, finding and storing web pages in a cache. When you query the search engine – the usual method is to type in *keywords* – the engine then retrieves all the pages that contain those words. Depending on how well chosen your keywords are, you can narrow the list of retrieved pages. For example, the market leader in search engines, Google, can find 6390 pages containing the words 'Kieron' and 'O'Hara', about 3,400,000 pages containing 'David' and 'Stevens', 494,000 containing 'David', 'Stevens' and 'politics', and 7640 with 'David', 'Stevens', 'politics' and 'Nottingham'. By the time the four key words are used, David Stevens's homepage is the first page to be listed by the Google search.

Hyperlinks and search engines enable you to find your way around the WWW; hyperlinks take you on a nonlinear journey as dictated by the authors of the pages you are reading, while search engines put you in control.

The Internet as a space

So the Internet is a giant store of information – the amount of information on the WWW alone would fill something of the order of ten billion books the size of this one – which provides some more or less fancy ways of navigating through that giant quantity. In that sense, what we basically have is a library, or, more prosaically, a filing cabinet. But the Internet seems to raise hard political questions that libraries and filing cabinets do not.[10] What is it about the Internet that gives it this property?

At the beginning of this chapter we discussed the nature of a space. We set out three key factors relating to the definition of a space: the actors within a space should be able to communicate, to change the circumstances of other actors and to act independently. A library, in one sense, is a space under this definition; it is a building and therefore can be the location of action. People can communicate and interact within it, exactly as they can in a warehouse or a telephone kiosk. However, the informational world contained in the library's books is not a space. Apart from the reading function (in some sense, when I read Swift's *Gulliver's Travels*, Swift communicates with me; but he is unable to tailor his message for the individual reader, I am unable to communicate with Swift, and furthermore I am unable to communicate, through the library services, with other readers), no communication goes on. Readers cannot affect each other.

Unlike with books, on the Internet all sorts of interactions between actors are possible. People can communicate, they can converse, they can buy and sell goods. Exchanges are made, information passed around and friendships made. Even votes can be cast; events on the Internet can cause the overthrow of governments.

We will go into more detail about the Internet as a space later. For now, it is enough to note that the Internet has many different properties to real, physical space (the space that we all know and understand). First of all, the Internet is constructed, and can be altered completely. It could even disappear, though this is unlikely. On the other hand, recall that Hannah Arendt's argument that a political space is artificial, and depends on the significance placed on the objects that comprise it; it is a cultural achievement. From which it follows that the political space can disappear, as a political space if not a space itself, if the significance of the objects changes.

To continue our theme of historical precedent, Karl Marx believed that the political space would disappear once capitalism was replaced by communism. The state that was necessary for bourgeois rule under the capitalist mode of production would wither away because it was unnecessary for a communist society. The political concerns and interests of individuals under communism would be reabsorbed into their everyday social life. There would be no separation between the interests of the citizen and the interests of the individual. Whilst Marx's predictions of a communist society seem largely unfulfilled (even societies that claim to have been communist have relied heavily on the existence of state apparatus), his underlying observation remains: the space of the political is a human construct rather than a natural phenomenon. In this, Marx is in agreement with many philosophers of all political persuasions.

Secondly, events online can have real effects in real space. Votes are counted, mail-order products arrive on real doorsteps. But they require a mechanism for agency with a hybrid online/offline constitution. A business's ordering and delivery system needs to have an interface between the online and offline worlds so that online events can have real-world effects. Even events in computer games have real-world consequences.[11] Online games like *World of Warcraft* or *EverQuest*, which have hundreds of thousands or even millions of subscribers, generate substantial offline economies, and provide a persistent online theatre in which quite complex moral judgements have to be made.

Thirdly, because the Internet is made out of information, anything online can be copied and reproduced as often as you like for negligible cost. Items can be deleted and then restored to 'life'.

Fourthly, distance is of little object on the Internet. In the real world, you have the greatest effect in the space close to you; the further away you are, the more difficult it becomes (though not impossible) to cause things to happen. But online, there is no limit to where you can strike. Firewalls, password protection and other security systems may put certain areas of the Internet out of bounds to you, but they are 'artificial' limits to your effectiveness; they are more akin to fences or security guards that prevent you from gaining the access you could gain easily enough were they not there.

The Internet and identity

Arendt claimed that the nature of a space allows identities to be negotiated and disclosed. So: who are the actors on the Internet that carry out the actions in the space? Obviously, many of the actors are ourselves. But this is not the entire picture. Many actors on the

Internet are in fact completely artificial. They are so-called *autonomous agents*, pieces of software designed to do particular tasks automatically, with minimal human intervention.

For example, imagine a piece of software designed to trawl through the Internet to look for the cheapest holiday arrangements, let's say the cheapest flights it can find. A human would start the search process going by saying when he or she wanted to fly from where to where. But the actual details of the search, how the software agent moves through the Internet and how it compares prices, are unknown to the human. Even the programmer might only have a very tenuous grasp of how the agent works.

Indeed, many software agents do not even require human intervention. Suppose our artificial travel agent had found a few prices for flights in different currencies, and wanted to compare them. It might itself call for another agent that compares currency prices at the latest rates. So a second artificial autonomous agent is called into action – but this time without any direct human influence. Much of the Internet fauna is artificial in this way, yet acts very independently of human agents in the real world.

And even human agency online is not unproblematic. An old saying has it that on the Internet, no one knows you're a dog. This is actually very important to the ethos of the Internet. When two people are interacting, they do not see each other's physical form, or hear voices or accents. There may be some clues to real-world identity by such identifiers as vocabulary. But that is basically it.

This means that the Internet has become a favoured form of communication for many who feel somehow alienated from society, or even from their own bodies. We all know the stereotype of the pale, spotty, bespectacled nerd with the black T-shirt and the complete set of *Star Trek* on DVD who never leaves his bedroom but conducts all sorts of relationships with people on different continents. Such people, who may well be figures of offline fun, find themselves at ease when online.

The Internet allows you fairly easily to adopt false identities. In such well-structured environments as MUDs (Multi-User Domains), people can play games and adopt roles as various fantasy figures, elves, fairies, hobbits, trolls, wizards or what have you. In these interactions, the characters in the game come together, and their duels are just as 'real' online as my paying a bill from my online bank account; they both consist in the communication of bits of information between computers connected to the Internet. The only difference is that the financial transaction has some important effects in the real world related to my abilities to purchase goods.

More plausible identities are also allowed. For instance, the service provider America Online (AOL) allows you to take on five different identities; in other words, it creates for you, and allows you to use, five names for your online transactions. These are often doled out to different members of one's own family, but actually one person can adopt all of them. These identities then are the online face of the human actor.

Such identities can enable many people to do things they could not do offline. Small, powerless people can question giant corporations and bring them to account. Racial or gender prejudice can be sidestepped. In effect, if one wants to be, one can be divorced from one's body online. Offline, we can adopt various identities, but ultimately we are traceable via our physiognomies, gender and physical location. Online, one can pretend to be anyone: a man can be a woman, a woman a man, a white person black or a black person white.

This fluidity of identity is one of the selling points of the Internet, especially for enthusiasts. But, needless to say, it has its sinister side. One obvious example concerns areas where security is strongly associated with the identification of authorised users, such as banking, or some medical applications where confidentiality and privacy are important. Armed with the right password, someone could masquerade as the correct owner of the account. This is actually less of a problem than is often made out; the offline world suffers much more fraud than the online world. But it is clearly an issue that needs to be monitored.

Another example concerns the predatory so-called 'grooming' process, whereby adults pretend to be someone they are not, in chatrooms and the like, in order to attract people – often young people – into sexual relationships, which may be inappropriate if consensual, or sometimes even forced. Nowhere other than online can a shabby, middle-aged man pretend to be a fourteen-year-old streetwise boy. The ability of such a man to avoid presenting evidence of his deception until a meeting has been arranged away from the prying eyes of parents is the stuff of nightmares for many families.

Action and information

An action online is basically the shifting of information from one virtual location to another. In the real world, we can track that with two sets of events. The first is down to the technical engineering of electrical signals being transferred, and the storage of representations in a computer memory. These electrical events literally make up the virtual space we are talking about, but, taken simply as electrical events, they are devoid of significance. It is only when considering the virtual nature of the space that the movement of information makes any sense.

The second is the interface with the real world. Shifting information from place to place on a computer, or down a telephone line, can actually cause grand movements in the real world. As we noted, one can do quintessentially offline things online: vote, buy goods, read the paper, chat people up.

There are many examples of how the online and offline worlds interact. The most obvious with regard to the WWW is that one can publish. Most newspapers have an online edition. Admittedly, these are harder to take on the train with you, but on the other hand they have useful properties compared with the paper equivalent, such as being searchable, having archives and having hyperlinks to other sites. So, for example, if I was interested in the news about a particular politician, I could search to find today's articles, look for related articles from previous weeks and years, and even find the politician's own website or sites set up to give opposing views.

But publishing goes far beyond that. The economic barriers to entry to offline publishing are twofold. First, although publishing is very cheap nowadays (thanks to computer technology), it is still fairly expensive to get a decent-looking product. Anyone who has been handed a tatty flier by protesters outside an embassy, a shop or Parliament knows how unconvincing such a leaflet is, however sensible the message. Three hundred years ago the pamphlet was the state-of-the-art medium for political communication, thanks to the printing press.[12] Modern printing and publishing technologies have seen off the pamphlet as a serious form of political communication.

Secondly, the distribution of hard copy is very expensive; a small or voluntary publishing outfit may well be reduced to standing around handing out their publications to people, asking to include their material with parish magazines or going through the tedium of posting them door to door. Sometimes there are political barriers to entry too; in countries that curtail freedom of speech, publishing can put one's liberty, and sometimes even one's life, at risk.

The Internet transforms all that. In general, professional-looking websites, where the hyperlinks all work and the words are spelt right, are trusted more than amateurish ones. But creating a website is simple, and the skills required to make it look really flash are not actually that great. And once one has created a fantastic-looking website, that is the extent of the costs; the site is up and running, and will look as good in ten years' time as it does now. With online journals, however costly the initial edition is, future editions can use it as a template. Hence the cost of good-looking publishing falls dramatically. And the cost of distribution is even smaller; once you have a website on the Internet, you have potential access to anyone who is connected – which is at least one person in eight worldwide. The political barriers to entry can also be counteracted online, although repressive governments are getting better at censoring the Internet.

This ability to publish, and the inverse ability to find information, also have effects on the conduct of democracy. One can trace events happening, one can watch decisions being made. Many of us do this quite straightforwardly in the non-political arena; for example, when we buy goods online we might actually take many of the distribution decisions that in the offline world the retailer would be expected to make (e.g. deciding when a delivery will take place). But one can also keep an eye on governments online. Many democracies must release, by law, large amounts of information. Information on paper is hard to monitor, and reading it involves physically travelling to libraries – possibly many of them. But even if the information is not collected in one place online, citizens can get at all the information they need while remaining in the office, or at home in the spare room. Effective monitoring of government requires not just the gathering of information, but the juxtaposition of relevant information from different sources that between them shed light on what is happening. This is much easier to do online than off. Offline, you shuffle paper; online, you shuffle the informational content directly.

Indeed, as computer power has grown, and with it our understanding of how intelligence operates in the chaotic world of the Internet, searching for information has become automated to a surprisingly large extent. The Internet and the WWW are fairly new, and, like all new territory, they needed to be mapped. Our mathematicians and information scientists have begun to understand their topography and contours, and we are beginning to move around online more effectively. Computers, on which the Internet sits, are increasingly able to find things themselves. The fairly simple interface of Google conceals some quite impressive reasoning about the Web. This automation of routine and not-so-routine clerical work will also aid the citizen.

Governments have not been slow to realise that the provision of information to its citizens is easier and cheaper online. The information simply has to be released – the citizens will actually do much of the work, such as form-filling, for themselves, rather than waiting for civil servants to do it, as is the case in much of the paper-based offline world. Benefits and other government services will be supplied increasingly via the Internet.

It is also important to understand the risks as computing power grows and more forms of information processing, communication, storage and retrieval make their way online. First, problems arise regarding the authenticity or accuracy of material on the Internet. If virtually anyone can publish anything for public consumption without the filtering process of editors and publishing houses, then all manner of misinformation is likely to arise. For instance, by featuring on the Internet, fringe medical treatments can appear to have a more central position in the treatment of certain ailments and illnesses than they in fact do. The non-specialist 'Googler' lacks any immediate way of telling which treatments have greater acceptability within the wider medical community and which are money-spinning schemes invented by the greedy or mad. The consequences are, of course, potentially catastrophic for individuals.

Secondly, although much more information is being stored now, some traditionally stored material is being all but lost. For example, written letters are now a communication form largely of the past. Yet, for biographers, archives of written letters were an incredibly important resource. Email has risen as a replacement, but it is very much a temporary communication medium. We might converse with others a lot more via email than we ever did in traditional written form, but emails are rarely stored for posterity.

Thirdly, the flip side of the vast amount of storage is that there are no spatial restrictions to force you to clear out old, out-of-date stuff. As the Web ages, much that is online has simply fallen out of relevance; laws, statistics, companies and politics change. However, the Web pages that refer to them need not. There is some sort of moral obligation to keep one's pages up to date, but this is a tedious chore, and you have to be pretty motivated to do it.

That is not to say that this is a flaw in the Internet. A vast decentralised information Web has many good properties that other more structured spaces do not possess. The imposition of a centralised editor or knowledge verifier would cripple the Web by creating a major bottleneck. But the reader should be aware – as in daily life – that not everyone tells the truth.

Information is now a resource. It has always been valuable, but the Internet has provided us with a technology that can really exploit information. 'Information' has two senses. The first is information as is usually understood, information describing the world, e.g. information that the population of the United Kingdom at the 2001 census was 58,789,194, or that foreign direct investment into the UK fell from $120 billion to $14.5 billion between 2000 and 2003. This sort of information, describing the offline world, is an essential resource for holding a government correctly to account.

Information in the engineering sense is a series of signals – in a computer, bits, 1s and 0s that are interpretable. This sort of information constitutes the online world. Resources of this sort might well include one's online identity, the software one has access to, the agents that will do one's bidding and the files that one stores on one's home computer, or increasingly farms out to information storage companies. As the real world integrates with the online world more and more, and the distinction between them begins to blur, the possession of online resources, access to them, and the ability to manipulate and exchange them will become more important. We will have to ask whether citizens can play a full part in the democratic deliberations of their polity without adequate access to the Internet.

The architecture of online space and limits to action

The actions that one can take online depend on the system within which one is working. In other words – unlike spaces in the real world – the spaces online are entirely constructed. The construction and design will therefore determine what can be done online (bad construction or bad design may allow online behaviour that was unintended, such as hacking or spamming).[13] Given that actions in Internet space increasingly affect politics in the real world, it follows that the construction, design and maintenance of the Internet will have correspondingly increasing political dimensions.

So, for example, one important aspect of the Internet is fluidity of identity, which many enthusiasts find very attractive. No one, as we noted above, can prove you are a dog. On the other hand, there are many circumstances where it is actually quite useful to prove you are *not* a dog. If I want my bank to pay my bills, and I ask it to do so online, then for that purpose I want good security that means that any instructions obeyed by my bank are ultimately traceable back to me.

This leads to a – perhaps *the* – biggest dispute over the Internet and its values. The founders of the Internet, mainly scientists and computer scientists, have a strong commitment to freedom. First of all, they have an interest in knowledge sharing, in getting academic papers before they are published, in finding stores of data, etc. But more than that, the idea of the Internet as an unregulated space, where the harm that people can do is limited and where freedom of speech flourishes, is clearly very attractive, especially to very ideal-istic people.

On the other hand, as more and more non-academics and non-geeks come on board, there is a larger constituency that does not share their ideals. Newer Internet users tend to be more interested in the arts, entertainment and commerce, as well as enjoying spicy activities that are either illegal, embarrassing or difficult offline, such as gambling and pornography. Such people often want to exchange money or other resources online, and so the anarchic structure of the Internet does not really suit them. Indeed, the Web often appears to be little more than a big shop window. Commerce has started to dominate online, but this is the reason for its growth. Similar growth and dispersal would not have occurred had the Internet remained a tool for furthering academic interest. But the new users of the Internet are more interested in security, privacy (these two are often at odds) and a firm identity that can be traced.

Governments also like control. So Internet service providers, such as British Telecom or AOL, store up traces of one's surfing activity. Information is collected about where you have been, what files you have downloaded, who you are contacting and, indeed, what you are saying. This information might be quite damning or embarrassing, or may reveal patterns of subversion.

Hence there is quite a battle for the heart and soul of the Internet, with anarchistic hackers often ranged against representatives of big business. Who precisely should run the Internet, because who runs the Internet determines what actions can be performed in the spaces it defines?

Regulating the Internet

No one controls the Internet, although there are some organisations that oversee particular aspects of it, e.g. the World Wide Web Consortium (W3C), which controls technical standards on the WWW, and the Internet Engineering Task Force (IETF), which is in charge of technical standards Web-wide. But the most controversial body is ICANN.

ICANN, the Internet Corporation for Assigned Names and Numbers, was created in 1998, by a representative body of the Internet's users from business, science, academe and individuals, to take over the functions of ensuring that all the Internet's addresses remain unique – basically, they dole out addresses. As a non-profit organisation in the private sector, ICANN's original function was to take over the management of the Internet from the US government, after the cold war requirements of the Internet were overtaken by its rapid and surprising growth.

The technical challenges that ICANN face are less significant than the political challenges. For a start, although the Internet is highly decentralised, the address system is very hierarchical, which makes it easier to navigate. Only a small number of servers, known as 'root servers', hold the vital information of where a computer needs to go to get the address of another.

Furthermore, now that the Internet is increasingly used for business, there is money in memorable addresses. Trademark owners generally invest a lot of money in brand management; but if a firm – O'Hara Products, say – has marketed its brand, it may well be appalled to find someone else owning the Web address www.ohara.com. Such cybersquatting, as it is known – the practice of registering domain addresses in the hopes that someone else will buy the rights to use them – has become a very large and disputed business. The industry of registering domain names generates something of the order of $1 billion annually.

There are also geographical interests: most countries have a two-letter suffix to addresses associated with them. The only exception to this rule is the United States, for the same reason that Britain does not put its name on its postage stamps – it was a pioneer. So, for instance, the homepage of Southampton University is http://www.soton.ac.uk, with the 'uk' standing for the United Kingdom. But the borders, or the integrity, of many countries are disputed (Spain, Russia, India and Indonesia are four prominent examples of major nations with strong separatist disputes raging). The European Union would like to create an 'eu' suffix.

ICANN tries, like most Internet bodies, to govern by consensus rather than fiat. But it is perceived by many to be American-biased (it still reports to the US Government's Department of Commerce), dominated by the corporate sector and too secretive. Most govern-ments would like a larger slice of the action themselves, and there are moves afoot at the time of writing to shift governance of the Internet to the United Nations, as with the international telephone system. The business community, on the other hand, prefers the current regime, and worries that a bureaucratic government-dominated organisation would slow down the rapid pace of innovation. The UN Working Group on Internet Governance was set up to explore these issues.[14]

The next few years will be crucial to the future of the Internet. The current system is undoubtedly US-dominated, and run in the US's best interests. But the US's overseeing of the Internet has undoubtedly contributed massively to the tremendous development of the Internet over the intervening years; the regime has generally been benign and 'hands off'. On the other hand, the UN Working Group contains representatives from Saudi Arabia, China and Cuba, all of which are actively involved in research into ways to restrict the access of users to certain censored parts of the Internet. The issues are not clear-cut.

The US had hinted that it would accept transferring ICANN to a self-regulatory industry group, but few seemed willing to accept that compromise. In the end, before the UN group reported, and in line with a general unilateralism in US foreign policy, the Bush adminis-tration announced on 30 June 2005 that it would retain control of ICANN. But President Bush's credibility in the international forum was so low by late 2005 that this solution, though welcomed by Internet users and engineers,[15] was unacceptable to the international community; even the EU withdrew its support from the US (though characteristically it would not say which solution it favoured). A UN World Summit on the Information Society in November 2005 brokered a short-term compromise, with the creation of an Internet Governance Forum in 2006 comprising representatives of governments, industry and civil society groups.[16] It remains to be seen how effective the Forum is, or whether it will descend into a waffly talk-shop allowing the US to kick the issue into the long grass.

2:⟩
What's Around the Corner?

Technologies

So we have a new virtual space which allows action, interaction and, crucially, exchange of resources to take place. Despite the many differences between this new space and the traditional arena of political action, they both share these crucial features. One of the consequences of this is that the Internet, like the real world of politics, gives rise to circumstances where questions of justice (and morality more generally) can be raised. Where a limited supply of resources exists (such that we cannot all have everything that we want) and human self-interest operates, then we have an instance of what Scottish philosopher David Hume termed the 'circumstances of justice'.[1] To decide between competing claims to these limited resources we need guiding principles – principles of justice. Where competing claims exist with regard to the benefits and burdens of the new technologies, it is very likely that principles will be needed for dispute-resolution there too.

Justice is a philosophico-legal concept. Its explication and application to the new space will require analyses both philosophical and anthropological. The philosopher is required to delineate the general characteristics of justice. The sociologist, anthropologist, political scientist or lawyer is required to understand how the general concept of justice is implemented in a complex society, controlled by imperfect institutions and understood by a large population with little legal training.

All well and good. But, without an understanding of how technological developments can change and structure a society, wondering about justice and technology is an exercise in science fiction at best. For our discussion of justice to be relevant we need to know what to expect from our technology in the future. We need to know roughly where current research is going, in order to make intelligent guesses at its possible destinations. This will be the subject matter of justice; the goods upon which the concept operates. Of course, there is no way of predicting what will occur – all sorts of new ideas, entrepreneurial ventures and changes of social and economic context will happen over the next few years, and each of these unpredictable events will have a deep impact on technological development. We must guard against our assumptions about the future being just wild guesswork – often, in political books about technology, we are treated to wild utopian or dystopian fantasy, according to taste, which may be fun to write and fun to read, but from which we ultimately learn nothing. We have instead to understand technology, and its relation to society and to a capitalist economy.[2] Only on this basis is it possible to talk about justice, or what justice requires, in any meaningful or helpful sense.

We know our guesses are bound to be wrong, but informed guesses coupled with a lively sense of our own ignorance are the best that can be managed. We must not confuse the new possibilities created by technology with massive new possibilities for our lives generally; technology is transformative, but equally it supports a relatively small part of our lives. As information scientist Charles Jonscher puts it:

> I have gleaned two lessons from the history ... of electronic technology ... The first is to regard almost any prediction of the future power of the technology itself as understated. The second is to regard almost any prediction of what it will do to our everyday lives as overstated.[3]

In this chapter we will briefly review some aspects of current ICT research to try to get a sense of where we might end up. This is not to say (as some do) that technology will take us over, or that robots will be keeping us all as pets in 2020. It is to say merely that, if some of the current hunches pay off, technology will be able to do a lot more for us in ten or twenty years – if we want it to, and if we run society to enable it to.

To begin with, let us look at some of the general trends that ICT has created, and which have been christened Moore's Law, Metcalfe's Law and Coase's Law. These are not laws in the same sense as the laws of physics or as the laws of the land – but they are remarkably robust nonetheless.

Moore's Law

Gordon Moore is an electrical engineer, famous (and doubtless rich) for having founded the Intel company, the world's biggest computer chip maker. In the 1960s, Moore observed the ability of engineers to decrease the size of computer chips at each design cycle; each time a new chip was designed, engineers managed to reduce its size dramatically while keeping costs, and more importantly the complexity of the circuitry, stable. As the chips get smaller, computers get more powerful (because more circuits can be crammed into the same space) and quicker (because communicating circuits are closer together). And though there are physical limits to the amount of miniaturisation that can be performed (the bizarre statistics and paradoxes of quantum physics come into play at small enough sizes), Moore could see that those limits were a long way away.

So, in 1965, he proposed the law that bears his name:

Every eighteen months, processing power will double while cost remains constant.

This implies increasing usefulness and speed for computers. Given these implications, it is not surprising that computers have spread to almost every sector of society in the intervening forty years.

Moore's Law is an observation – it is certainly not a law of nature. There is nothing necessary about it. But, incredibly, it has remained true for the last forty years. Every eighteen months or so, computers *do* double in power. This doubling, over time, builds up exponentially to produce a massive increase, almost too large to comprehend. In the forty years since Moore stated his law there have been twenty-seven or so doublings. Which means, if we give the initial level of power the arbitrary value 1, that the amount of power available now compared with 1965 is $1 \times 2 \times 2 \times ... \times 2$ (27 times), i.e. 2^{27} (= 134,217,728). The 4004 chip in 1970 contained a couple of thousand transistors, whereas the Pentium 4 Processor in the year 2000 contained something in the order of a hundred million.

Moore's Law doubtless won't always remain operative. Indeed, within fifteen or twenty years it will be pushing up against the limits of quantum physics.[4] But even if the growth of computing power slows down slightly, it will still be formidable.

What does this actually mean for us? In the first place, it means that doing a bit of mindless computing is very simple and cheap. When computers first started in the 1950s, they were set on relatively straightforward problems, such as multiplying large numbers together. These were problems that humans could do just as easily by hand; in fact, it actually took the computer scientists longer to program the sums into the computer than it would had they sat down with a pencil and paper and done them themselves. Of course, they were aware of that – but they knew they were pioneering an important technology.

Nowadays, things are different. Storage of data is trivial and cheap. No one need ever bother to throw away data again. iPods, for example, carry colossal quantities of information; early models carried five gigabytes, later models can hold up to sixty gigabytes. How much is that? Well, the average American consumer over a standard lifespan generates about 100 gigabytes of data in the form of financial, health and educational records and so on. So your iPod, the size of a deck of cards, could carry half your life about on it. And come the next generation, it could take all your life and more.

We also need no longer be sparing with computation. We can illustrate this with the example of computer chess. Chess is an interesting game in computing terms, because it is very well specified. There are precise limits to what you can do, and to what your opponent can do in response. The environment plays no part in the game. So, in theory, you could calculate how to win exactly by extrapolating far enough ahead. The beauty of chess is that, even though there are so few moves at each stage, if you look even a few moves ahead there are millions of possible combinations. For instance, at an early stage of a chess match say there are roughly twenty possibilities for each move. If you look only six moves ahead (three moves each, not very far), there are 20^6 possible games – or 64,000,000. Over the course of an entire match (up to, say, a hundred moves, or fifty each) the number of possible games is astronomical. Because of this, chess players learn to recognise interesting positions, productive strategies and so on; they only need look at a small number of move combinations, because they have the knowledge of chess to tell moves with potential from silly ones. That is, a chess player will intuitively be able to identify 'candidate moves' and immediately dismiss other moves as non-starters. In the early days man could always beat machine, because the machine had no idea which moves were likely to be more productive – it had no grasp of candidate moves – and could not look far enough ahead to counter the chess player's skill.

The first chess program was written by Alan Turing in 1950, and the first article about computer chess was written by Claude Shannon in the same year – both (independently) legendary figures in computing and the information sciences. The first victory of a computer over a human was by NSS in 1958, which beat a secretary who had been taught chess an hour earlier. In 1966, MacHACK VI became the first machine to enter a tournament against human players (one draw, four defeats). By the end of 1967, MacHACK VI had managed three wins over human players and was made an honorary member of the US Chess Federation. In 1977, the first grandmaster lost to a chess player – although under blitz conditions.[5] In 1985, grandmaster Garry Kasparov beat the top fifteen chess computers 32–0. By 1989, the IBM computer DEEP THOUGHT could analyse two million positions per second, and was beating grandmasters regularly in tournament play.

In 1996, Kasparov became the first world champion grandmaster to lose to a computer under tournament conditions, though he eventually beat IBM's DEEP BLUE 4–2. In three minutes, DEEP BLUE analysed fifty billion positions; Kasparov analysed ten. By the next year, DEEP BLUE was analysing two hundred million positions per second, and gained revenge over Kasparov, beating him over six matches.[6]

Machines now play better chess than all but the finest human players; the best machines are about as good as the best humans. But the machines aren't more intelligent; they are purely and simply capable of looking so far ahead, mechanically, that they can counter all but the subtlest strategies. In the progress of the chess computer, we don't see the progress of artificial intelligence (which is what the pioneers of computer chess thought we would see). If the new generation of chess computers were based on progression in the field of artificial intelligence then, like human players, they would be demonstrating such things as positional understanding. Instead, what we see is Moore's Law in action. It is a victory over intelligence by brute force.

Metcalfe's Law

The second law is about computer users, not computers themselves. Robert Metcalfe is the creator of the Ethernet protocol which helps computers communicate with each other in a network. We have already seen in chapter 1 how networks can be useful. Metcalfe formulated a law to do with the amount of communication that becomes possible in a network.

The utility of a network is equal to the square of the number of users.

The increase in usefulness of a network increases much more rapidly than the number of users. Square numbers increase very quickly: 1^2 is 1, 2^2 is 4, 5^2 is 25, 10^2 is 100. 100^2 is 10,000. $1,000^2$ is 1,000,000. So a small network of a few members has relatively small utility; a well-populated network is proportionally much more useful.

A prime example is the telephone service. When Alexander Graham Bell patented the first telephone the system itself was pretty well useless – because no one else had a telephone. Once others got them, the amount of cross-communication possible was much greater. Then, once the utility of the network was proven, it became attractive to non-users, who began to flock in. The result is that nowadays virtually everyone has a telephone, and it is almost impossible to imagine life without one. Indeed, the telephone has changed our understanding and assumptions about the world: in literature no longer is it possible to have a plot hinging on someone's ignorance of the outcome of remote events. Similar, but even faster, growth has happened with mobile telephony and email; what were once small, niche markets have grown out of all proportion as more and more users have joined the network.

Computer systems, nowadays often built on the network model (recall the Internet itself from chapter 1), also comply with Metcalfe's Law. The utility that can be gained from multiple opportunities to communicate gets larger and larger. The giant networks that are being built from computers, linking both human users and artificial pieces of software, have a great deal of potential, and we will see the importance of network effects again and again.

Coase's Law

Coase's Law concerns the development of ideas about firms, organisations and markets, and was initially put forward by Nobel-prize-winning economist Ronald Coase in 1937.[7] One mystery of economics is why we have firms at all. Why can't a free market organise individuals, using contracts, in the same way? Traditional economics, Coase realised, couldn't explain why firms arose.

For the worker, there should, in theory, be no difference between working for a firm or being self-employed to do the same task; in each case a contract would govern what the worker would do. He or she would enter into the contract freely, and be prepared to take or leave the market rate for the job. But firms and markets are very different beasts.

Markets are highly distributed, they are not located in a single spot, and contain many buyers and sellers who have little connection with each other. No one in a market can affect anyone else in that market, except by offering incentives to perform some action. Similarly, no one in a market need know anything about anything else other than his or her own needs and preferences, and the prices of the goods or services he or she wishes to buy. The only question that someone in a market need ask is: do I wish to exchange these resources of mine for those currently owned by the seller? This is one reason why markets work so well: no one needs to interact very much with others, and no one need know anything about others. It is a very economical way of doing business.

Firms have the opposite set of characteristics. They are not distributed, they are very hierarchical, everyone in the firm will probably be physically located in one of a small number of offices, factories or other premises, and they are connected by links of authority. A large number of workers are (typically) managed by a smaller layer of middle managers, who defer to a small number of senior managers and directors, who are the servants of the owners (shareholders). No one in the firm (qua worker) acts in his or her own interests; they act in the interests of the shareholders. But neither do they guess what the interests of shareholders are. Managers interpret the interests of shareholders and translate them into actions. Managers further down the hierarchy decompose those actions into more specific actions, until at the bottom level of the hierarchy the worker actually does something productive.

The net result is that, unlike in a market, firms demand a lot of knowledge of people, especially further up the hierarchy; managers need to know everything that is happening in the firm below them, and also need to have a decent grasp of the issues concerning those above them. To work in a firm, workers forego some of their rights of decision-making; they agree to let certain people determine what they do during certain times of the day, and within agreed limits (e.g. workers should not be obliged to break the law or endanger their own health). In return for this surrender of independence, workers are paid a salary out of the firm's revenues.

If markets were efficient distributors of resources (a basic assumption of much of economics), reasoned Coase, then there would be no need for an inefficient monster such as a firm. Consumers' needs would be met much more cheaply without firms. Hence markets cannot be as efficient as is often thought. Alternatively, if the hierarchical command-and-control systems that firms typically use were suitable, then why are there markets? Why isn't there just one firm, or one hierarchical structure, governing every-thing, as in the Soviet Union? His early investigations into this problem led to a slow revolution in the understanding of the impor-tance of organisational structure.

Basically, Coase's insight was that the actions and transactions that people need to perform during any economic activity are not cost-free; they impose *transaction costs*. So, for example, one has to find customers, and one has to find other people who are willing to sell one the raw materials necessary for the job. Finding out who the relevant suppliers and consumers are is time-consuming and expensive. Bargaining for the best price is expensive – it takes time and plenty of phone calls. Enforcing lots of ad hoc contracts can be expensive. In short, individual transactions impose costs.

But a firm can absorb many of these transaction costs by standardising its interactions with other economic agents, and by exploiting economies of scale. In other words, one firm doing the same thing a hundred times is much cheaper than one hundred individuals each doing the same thing once. So there is a general payoff if people arrange themselves in a firm.

Why, then, isn't there a single firm? For the opposite reason. Firms impose costs; the hierarchical structure means that information passes very slowly from shop floor to boardroom, so the firm may not act as nimbly as it might to meet market demand. (How often have we seen big industrial giants, like IBM, toppled by bumptious startups, like Microsoft used to be, because the latter could move quickly to anticipate market demand?) As the size of a firm increases, so the cost of organising transactions increases, until it is the same as the transaction costs; at this point, the firm is at its optimum size.

These thoughts lead to Coase's Law.

The organisational structure evolves to deal most efficiently with the cost of economic transactions.

In particular, those transactions that are uncertain in outcome, recur frequently and require substantial investments (of money, time or energy) are more likely to take place within a firm, and those that are straightforward, non-repetitive and require little investment are more likely to take place across firms in a market.[8]

This is a very simplified picture, and indeed a controversial one, but it gives some indication of why firms are the size they are. It also implies that as market conditions change, so will the optimal size of the firm. In particular, if the costs of transactions fall, then the optimal size of a firm will fall.

Coase's predictions, long ignored in economics, have been seen to be very relevant, because the net result of the development of the Internet and the WWW is to reduce transaction costs. Sending a series of emails is cheaper than making phone calls. Finding information is nowadays trivial; finding the cheapest supplier of something is infinitely easier using an Internet search rather than a foot-slogging wander up the High Street, or an afternoon with the Yellow Pages, or the use of an agent (such as a travel agent). Indeed, there is a lot of computing research devoted to the development of ultra-cheap software agents which can whizz around the WWW looking for cheap offers. And also note that the WWW is worldwide – a manual search for information tends to be restricted to one's immediate locality, or at best one's home country, which means potentially missed opportunities.

So what we would expect, as ICT becomes more widespread, is that transaction costs in business fall, and so the size of businesses falls. And this is exactly what we have seen. We see many more small businesses, much more use of consultants in industry, and the phenomenon of *downsizing*, where big firms get rid of whole layers of middle managers – exactly the people who used to be competitive as they coordinated information around large corporations. Once the coordination of information was simplified and made cheaper by computers, those middle managers became redundant.

The human cost of downsizing is neither small nor trivial. But the development of ICT made it inevitable. Indeed, the joint lesson of the three laws we have looked at is very straightforward: computers are having, and will continue to have, an immense effect on our lives. They will enable us to store much more data – our collective memory, if we might loosely call it that, will be dramatically enhanced (Moore's

Law); more and more of us will be sucked into the wired world as it grows (Metcalfe's Law); and, as this happens, the conditions of work, and our potential independence from managers and bosses, will alter dramatically (Coase's Law).

We do not want to paint an overoptimistic picture, but we do think that the picture is generally upbeat. We also think that the integration of ICT into our daily lives, during work, rest and play, will continue to increase, and that this is, by and large, a good thing. But many patterns of behaviour, ways of life, will be disrupted. Often we will see change for change's sake. Often, changes that benefit many cause misery for a few. Less often, changes that benefit a few cause misery for many. We are not cheerleaders for technology, but neither are we technophobes.

In the remainder of this chapter, we will sketch some likely directions of computer development. These are educated guesses based on the cutting edge of current research. But the trajectory of technological research is not entirely predictable, so don't hold us to these.

Liberation of the computer

So what technological advances can we expect in the future? The first is one that science fiction writers have explored for years: the liberation of the computer. Computers have not been fixtures in our homes for very long; for many, no longer than fifteen years or so. But in that time they have blossomed; by 2000 more than half the homes in the United States contained a computer. In the United Kingdom, the 50% mark was passed in 2002.

Traditionally, the computer was a number of big white boxy things that sat in the spare room. It was often quite grubby and covered with youthful fingerprints; the screen was covered with a layer of dust and edged with an assortment of Post-It notes. Popular uses for home computers would include: banking, contacting friends via email, working from home, schoolwork, marketing efforts for small-scale businesses or events, reading the news, writing and archiving correspondence, and entertainment, including downloading music and playing online games. For all of these activities, the user would have to sit in the spare room with the computer.

As Moore's Law enabled smaller computers to gain more power, the laptop was invented. The computer came out of the spare room, and could be used on the train, or between work and home. Wireless technology (WiFi) has allowed the Internet to be accessed away from fixed telephone lines. In accordance with Metcalfe's Law, WiFi is becoming much more popular and usable as the network of users spreads; for instance, there are now WiFi 'hotspots' – such as airport lounges and coffee shops – where owners of suitably equipped laptops can surf the Internet.

Currently, WiFi can only cover a few tens of yards in each direction. A new standard, WiMax, is under development; this should be able to cover tens of miles, and would therefore be useful, for example, in rural environments. However, it is expensive and may well not catch on, but the day is likely to come when entire countries are blanketed with wireless access paid for through taxes; Internet access could be available to all. Such an approach could certainly be of interest in the developing world, where fixed telephone land lines are unreliable, sometimes because of poor maintenance, sometimes because of violence, theft, warfare or terrorism. Access to the Internet, say for educational purposes (particularly where there are shortages of teachers) or for spreading simple public health messages, could be very important in the developing world. The Internet could provide access to large quantities of useful information in oppressive states. No one expects the Internet to solve all the problems of the developing world, but equally there is no doubt that it could do some good. When we look for ways of rendering access to the wired world more equitable, such technologies will be potentially useful media.

The individual blossoms

A second development we can expect, as computing power increases and computing devices get smaller, is increasing customisation. Most of our access to information is currently given through public, general media. Television channels cater for all tastes, newspapers report news from everywhere about everything.

However, it is now possible to look for news or information about the subjects you are interested in, and indeed written from the point of view with which you agree. Even traditionally rich public information spaces are being impoverished. When there was a small number of TV channels, having to cater for a wide variety of tastes, then one was always liable to be presented with a programme which one would not have chosen to watch (for example, the programme that followed the one you *did* want to watch). One television would usually serve the whole family (by the mid-1960s, there were about five people per television licence in England[9]), so one would be exposed to all sorts of stuff. The BBC's lofty ideals, which produced such marvellous and informative programmes as *Civilisation*, *Life on Earth* or the long-running series *Play for Today*, meant that the programmes upon which one stumbled accidentally might be of a very high quality indeed. And in pre-remote control days, the distance from settee to television was just far enough to deter the couch potato from turning off.

But the digital revolution has removed this model of television-watching. In 1999, there were thirty-nine million TV sets in the United Kingdom, or about 1.5 per household; many families had individual sets for individual members of the family. Remote controls have removed the cost in time and effort of changing channels (the common practice of channel-hopping might take one to unfamiliar territory, although only for a fraction of a second). Ideals have been displaced by ratings, which has led to decreasing diversity in schedules, particularly in peak time. The existence of hundreds of digital TV channels has fragmented audiences, which has removed an element of common experience for people, as well as enabling channels that only cater for single tastes to emerge, such as science fiction, old 'classic' TV drama, pornography, sport, news or the arts. The old 'broadcasting' model is being replaced by 'narrowcasting'.

One can use technology to structure one's own experiences. Video was the first step here, and now clever DVD devices allow you to watch or record programmes and even filter out the adverts – in effect, creating your own channel. Eventually, you should be able to download programmes to watch whenever you like from a central menu; the stations will cease to take any responsibility for scheduling, but will instead charge a fee to download entertainment onto the hard disk of your TV or DVD player.

It will become increasingly possible for information-aware individuals to cocoon themselves away from inconvenient or offensive views, and to feed themselves only the information they want to know. Furthermore, as the computer becomes liberated, this faculty will spread; armed with mobile phones, wireless Internet and clever, small devices, people will be able to travel around, talking only to their friends, hearing only the things they want to hear. Personal space will be increasingly mediated through technology.

Sometimes this will be harmless; some people may not be interested in politics and will only want the sport – indeed, they may only want the news about the Miami Dolphins. Their favourite music, be it Mozart, Elton John or Ghostface Killah, will pound into their head the whole time. They will talk to their friends and conduct their business while ignoring, or even being unaware of, the people in their actual physical locality.

We see people heading this way even now. The trend is bound to increase, as a generation which has only known such peripatetic selectivity reaches adulthood. Is this a good thing or bad? Or just a matter of taste? The question needs further discussion, which we will provide in chapter 6.

Integration

Customisation is just one symptom of a major effect of the digital revolution. Digitising information dramatically affects the way that information can be handled and accessed. In particular, many devices can use the same information in a standardised form – or information can be displayed, and sometimes interacted with, in a number of ways by one device.

What until recently have been firm dividing lines have melted away. The distinctions between your TV, your computer, your personal stereo, your games console, your camera and your mobile phone are being chipped away (pun intended). That is not to say that you will, in future, just need to go out and buy one device for all these purposes. Technology evolves to fit into the warp and weft of social and private life, and it is not easy to predict exactly what will work – otherwise it would be simple to become a millionaire.

Many technological developments have been touted, only to die off. Using one's TV as a computer seemed like a really cool idea, so the men in suits at some technology firms thought. Teenagers who didn't want their entire family reading their emails, and mums and dads who had only just mastered being able to program the video, begged to differ, and that kind of system seems to have died a death. On the other hand, the development of the mobile phone from an intrusive piece of business equipment to a must-have fashion item was not spotted for a while by the major corporations – and the first movers in the market, Nokia, became one of the world's most successful companies on the back of their perceptiveness. Similarly, text messaging was initially dismissed by mobile phone companies as a minor add-on to phone packages.

But there is no doubt that there will be changes, however unpredictable, to the ways in which we access information. Aspects of life will alter. Parents may, or may not, find it more difficult to prevent their children gaining access to unsuitable material. Entertainment may, or may not, become more interactive. And industry is likely to have to restructure; the clear distinctions between products such as cameras, televisions, audio systems and computer chips rationalised a particular set of distinct industries. But now they are being brought together. Computer makers might start to get into the telephony business; mobile companies might start to provide their own entertainment customised to the small screens of their products. In fact, a number of firms, including O_2, Nokia and Toshiba, are piloting TV services for mobiles, and in the world's largest mobile phone market, China, the author Qian Fuzhang has written the first novel designed to be read, in chunks of 4200 characters, by subscribers on their mobiles.

But this integration is not guaranteed to happen. One of the most catastrophic industrial mergers in business history was between the entertainment giant Time Warner and the Internet service provider AOL (America Online). At the height of the hi-tech share boom at the end of the last century, Time Warner became convinced that it should have a greater Internet presence. Time Warner handed over 55% of its shares to AOL, a much smaller company, to create AOL Time Warner. It was a disaster. The corporate culture at Time Warner failed to attract, or assimilate, the geeks of AOL, and the optimism of the boom years faded in the new millennium, as advertising revenue plunged and hopes of a strong synergy between the two companies faded. Shareholders sued, claiming that AOL's value had been fraudulently overstated. Eventually, the merged giant was split back into its constituent parts, which now carry some $25bn of debt.

We, the consumers, may sometimes feel we have little power against the mega-corporations, but actually, collectively we have quite a lot.[10] There is no doubt that digital convergence – the integration of devices – will take place, though no one can guess how it will happen. Conversely, it is doubtful whether all the big changes in our absorption of media have yet been predicted. We are always capable of upsetting the cosy worldview of the suits in the boardroom.

Memories for life

The digitisation of information, combined with the effects of Moore's Law and the rapid spread of computer ownership, has led to a new phenomenon: the democratisation of content. Nowadays, almost certainly for the first time, we have a society with more writers than readers. All sorts of documents get written, principally but not exclusively at work, and published, either by being printed and being distributed by hand or by being posted on the web. Eighty-five per cent of the information recorded in print media every year is in office documents.[11] Doubtless many of these documents are never read; others are read by no more than a handful of people. Nevertheless, such documents have a very high potential readership. It was only a couple of decades ago that the barriers to entry in publishing were so high, and the technologies for writing and copying so time-consuming, that documents were rare and were often saved, consciously, for posterity. Nowadays, everything gets saved routinely, but unconsciously. Perversely, conscious effort is now required to get rid of information.

This is not only a private matter. In the days when TV programmes were stored on videotape, which was bulky and expensive, programmes were often junked after a few years and the tapes reused for new projects. Many classic or fondly remembered programmes have thus been lost. For example, the BBC's broadcasts of the Apollo moon landings in 1969, incredibly, seem no longer to exist. However, in the age of digitisation, everything can be stored; the most inane drivel spouted by the most irritating grinning ninny on children's TV will be stored for an astonished posterity.

Back in the world of the consumer, the digital camera (which is overtaking the film camera in sales terms) has made possible the creation of digital photographs that are much easier to create and store; no more posting the negatives off to a chemist for processing. The fact that you can delete or enhance poor photographs makes photography less nerve-racking, and the fact that there is no intermediary between you and your pictures means that you can take sensitive or private shots with more confidence. Although maybe we should record that the intermediary sometimes plays an important role; the abuse of Iraqi prisoners by British soldiers of the 1st Battalion the Royal Regiment of Fusiliers was exposed when the hapless photographer took the film to be developed at a shop in Tamworth.[12]

The net result is that the human race produces about five exabytes of digital information, in print, on film, or on magnetic or optical media, annually; that is about thirty-seven thousand times the total amount of information contained in the Library of Congress. Or, put another way, it is equivalent to the total of every word ever spoken by human beings in the entire history of humanity. This equates to about 800 megabytes of information per person per year, which is approximately the same as every man, woman and child on the planet writing two full-length books every single day (this book probably contains about one megabyte of information). And that is only stored media; a further eighteen exabytes is transmitted via information channels, i.e. television, radio, the Internet and the telephone (98% of this is phone calls).[13]

Moore's Law has rendered the storage of this information (relatively) trivial, with the result that each of us is now capable of storing much more personal, private stuff. In the days before writing, the storage of information was via oral means, storytelling, legend, ritual and so on. Writing allowed memory to be outsourced, but even with the invention of paper, storage was hard. Only the most worthy information got stored in libraries. Now, any information can be stored digitally, so the content in information repositories has been democratised; time was that only portraits of rich or famous people were kept, but now your three hundred images of Auntie Nelly can go down in history alongside all the pictures of Prince Charles, Michael Jackson or Nelson Mandela.

In other words, we are reaching the state where it is possible to talk about memories for life. We are increasingly able to record much of our lives, and to preserve those records for longer periods. This will be a revolution in the history of the lives of ordinary individuals. It is almost impossible to guess how much this democratisation of information will affect society, but we might surmise that it will go far beyond being able to prove that you wore that purple V-necked sweater at your twenty-first birthday party three decades ago. Socrates spoke, and Plato wrote, about the dramatic effects as society became literate.[14] The invention of movable type created a second wave of change.[15] The digitisation and democratisation of information may well create a third wave.

Managing information

The upshot of all this is that new ways will have to be developed for managing information. Saving information is, presumably, no bad thing in the abstract. If knowledge is power, then more knowledge means more power. However, large repositories of information bring with them their own problems.

It is not just the quantity of information, or even the quality, that counts, but also its accessibility. You have to be able to navigate through the stores of information to get to the bit you need. To see this, consider the traditional-style telephone directory, which lists people's names in alphabetical order alongside their phone number. It's a very usable way of getting from someone's name to their telephone number, which is what most people want to do with their directory most of the time. Sometimes, though, people want something else. Some people, such as the police or suspicious spouses, may have a telephone number and want to see whose it is. In that case the phone book is no good – short of looking through all the entries one by one, there is no way of achieving that goal. Sometimes, what you want to know is the name of a good Chinese restaurant in the vicinity; again, the phone book is useless for that, which is why the Yellow Pages came into being. The usefulness of a directory depends on what you want to use it for, not only the information it contains.

Indeed, consider the phone book rewritten in a random order, or in numerical order, rather than alphabetised. It would contain exactly the same information as the normal phone book. You could say that you would be certain of finding the information you need; if you were after someone's phone number, all you would have to do would be to go through the book systematically, looking at each name until you spotted the one you needed, and then check the phone number next to it. The flaw in the scheme, though, is that, assuming you could concentrate that long, it would take seemingly forever. In practical terms, it would be quite impossible. If such a phone book was to be useful, it would be for some other task: if in numerical order, it would allow the police to trace people from their phone numbers; if in random order, it could be used for generating random numbers, or for allowing random samples of the population to be telephoned (say, for a public opinion survey). It is the organisation of the information that is all-important.

At the close of the film *Raiders of the Lost Ark*, the Ark of the Covenant, a source of incredible power, is located and recovered by Indiana Jones. This caused a problem for the film-makers: as the movie was set in the years prior to World War II, then why, viewers might ask, would the Americans not use the powers of the Ark to destroy the Nazis a long time before 1945? The answer in the film was ingenious. The Ark is packaged in a crate and sent to a government warehouse. A forklift truck puts the crate down next to some other crates. The camera pans back. More crates are seen. Back goes the camera further. More crates. And as the camera recedes further from the crate containing the Ark, it becomes clear that the Ark is surrounded by an unfeasibly large number of similar crates, and the inference is that the Ark has remained, with other art treasures, crated up in a warehouse somewhere, unseen and undiscovered for years. Crated up and stored, even in their own possession, it has become as lost to the Americans as it was lost to the Jews thousands of years previously.

Information can be like that. Bureaucracies generate information; they crave it and feed on it. And then they store it. In the days of paper, the loss of information was simple to achieve. Papers were filed, usually by a small group of people who often had idiosyncratic filing systems. When that group was dispersed, be it through promotion or retirement, the papers would become near-impossible to find.

It was thought that the computer would change all that. But, while the ability to search for information improved (and the ability to file documents under multiple headings improved the filing problem), the increased storage capacity meant that bureaucracies actually ended up collecting much more information that once again outstripped their ability to wade through it.

The danger, then, of the collection of the vast quantities of information that we are collecting, thanks to Moore's Law, is that we drown in it. We have so much information that we cannot use it properly; such a predicament is called *information overload*. For very many people, getting the information they need when they need it is getting harder and harder as more and more information is collected. The result is that *information* or *knowledge management* is becoming more important. Given vast quantities of information, methods are needed to navigate through that information so that people can find what they need. These methods fall essentially into three types.

First, the increase in computing power (Moore's Law again) means that searches can be quicker. However, even though computing power seems to double every eighteen months, the quantity of information we are producing is increasing even faster, so we can't simply rely on brute force.

The second method is to structure the information in clever ways. We saw the difference in usefulness between the alphabetically structured phone book and the randomly structured one. All information is like this: it can be structured to make things easier to find. Even our own brains store information in such a way as to facilitate its timely recollection. We keep a small quantity of information in our short-term memory that is easy to access; this information is what we need for the task in hand. Once that information ceases to be immediately useful, it gets shifted into the long-term memory, where it is harder to recall.

In the computer, there are many equivalent organisational tricks. For instance, in the Microsoft Windows environment, files are kept in *folders* that have a hierarchical structure (i.e. there can be folders within folders). The hierarchy means that we can intelligibly cut down our search space. For instance, suppose someone needs a copy of the slides for a talk he gave last year (he wants to give the talk again to a different audience). If he had to search through all the thousands of files on his machine, they would be practically impossible to find, especially as he may have no idea what the slides are called. But the hierarchical folder structure enables him to locate them easily. He looks first in the folder called My Documents, which contains, er, his documents. This contains a few documents and more folders; the list doesn't take long to search. One of the folders is called Talks – which looks promising. He opens this folder and can see that it contains another folder, called Politics Talks. Contained in this folder are only a few files, and the search is simple. He can see a file called Bournemouth-seminar-2004; as the talk he wants to reproduce is the one he gave at Bournemouth University, this is probably the file. The search, thanks to the hierarchical structure, is simple from start to finish.

For a giant corporation, there may well be more to it than that. But the main message is that information can be stored and indexed to make it easier to find.

The third method is to have cleverer searching methods. Even given our clever storage and indexing systems, the amount of information appearing – and the smaller margins available in competitive businesses – means that we will still have more work to do to find specific data. We need to look not just harder, but smarter. What do we mean by that? Well, consider the Web: a massive, unstructured dollop of information. Searching used to be by fairly simple methods, but the Web soon outgrew them. The Web would have been useful as a store of information, but would hardly have outgrown its geeky roots if the situation had stayed like that. Then in 1998 along came Google.

Google is a very clever search system that ranks web pages on a rough-and-ready measure of importance. The result is that typing a few key words into Google helps you find the information you want. It is not foolproof, of course. If you type 'Bush' into the system, it has no idea whether you mean George W. Bush, George Bush Sr, Kate Bush, a shrub, the rock group that produced *Sixteen Stone* and *Golden State*, or even the metal lining of an axle hole. So it will return every web page that it can find that contains the word 'bush', irrespective of meaning (a mere 86,700,000 of them at the time of writing). Its PageRank system clearly privileges the second president of that name, as the top site of those millions is www.whitehouse.gov. This ranking of pages helps users to search more effectively, and one measure of that effectiveness is that 30% of Web users use Google at least once a week. Another is that it has changed the language: 'to Google' has become a verb. And a third measure is that the developers of Google were able to spin off their company for a cool

$23 billion (a figure that, unbelievably, was felt by financial commentators to be disappointing!).

Better methods for searching will mean more information recovered quicker. That, one hopes, will generally be a good thing. But not necessarily. Intelligent searching may – may! – improve the ability to find things out. We are getting better and better at extracting weak signals from noisy data. This means that we, as individuals, will be less able to exploit the government's inability to use its own information. For instance, you give certain information to the taxman, and other information to other bodies about what you spend (credit card firms, for example). If anyone was able to amalgamate those various sources of information and extract knowledge from them (admittedly, a very difficult task at the moment), much more intrusive surveillance of one's personal affairs would be possible. Is this a world we are prepared for?

Furthermore, the computing power that would be required is available to the private sector. It has traditionally been the case that democracy has managed to restrain invasions of our privacy, because our representatives can legislate against the government 1) using its spies, both human and technological, too freely; and 2) devoting too much effort to sifting through the information it has got. And this has been sufficient, because only governments have been able to afford the large expense of both mass surveillance and large-scale information processing. However, improved computing techniques and technological development have now put surveillance and processing within the purview of many other organisations, both benign and malign.

We will discuss, in chapter 8, how the effects of enabling governments, corporations or individuals to establish relationships between facts which would ordinarily be buried under a mass of irrelevant information could well be equivocal. The extraction of signals from noise, a product of human ingenuity, is likely to cut both ways.

The Semantic Web: intelligence online

As we argued in chapter 1, the WWW is perhaps the most important technological development within our scope. The Web is now of colossal size. According to the heroic research of Lyman *et al.* at the University of Berkeley, California, the web contains 167 terabytes of fixed content (i.e. web pages that appear as written by authors). Not a small amount: a terabyte is a thousand billion bytes, or a million megabytes – or fifty thousand trees turned into paper and printed on. A typical academic research library is about two terabytes.

But the fixed content of the web is only a very small part of the Internet. Much of the web is generated on the fly from information held in databases. So for example, when you call up the home page of your Internet bank, the page is created for you, with your account details, latest transactions and balance as it stands that very minute. You will never see that page again unless you save it as a separate file. The information held in databases such as these (the so-called 'deep web') amount to some 91,850 terabytes of data.[16]

The Web is getting very large, and is getting increasingly difficult to navigate through, despite the brilliant technology of Google and others. As a result, researchers are working on how to make web computing more intelligent. The aim is to provide computers with more understanding of what they are presenting to the user. (The term 'understanding' should be taken metaphorically here; we will lapse, for convenience, into psychological language when talking about computers and the information they store, but this should not be taken to mean that we take a particular stand on the fraught question of whether machines can think.)

Foremost among these developments is the Semantic Web (SW), developed under the guidance of the main architect of the Web itself, Sir Tim Berners-Lee.[17] The SW extends the Web by providing more expressive computer languages for the Web to be written in, and by changing the focus from documents to data. Whereas the WWW asks people to expose their documents to public view, and to link those documents to other relevant documents, the SW asks people to expose their data, and to link them to other relevant data.

The main language of the WWW is Hypertext Markup Language (HTML); this tells the computer how to arrange a web page on your computer screen. The SW tells the computer much more. First, it provides Extensible Markup Language (XML), which allows you to tell the computer what things on the page are. Take, for instance, Oneworld's homepage, http://www.oneworld-publications.com/. On that page is a mention of *The Politics of Apocalypse* by Dan Cohn-Sherbok, and a photograph of the front cover. XML would allow the author of the page to tell the computer that 'Dan Cohn-Sherbok' is an 'author', 'The Politics of Apocalypse' is a 'book', and the book cover picture is a 'book cover'.

Nothing very earth-shatteringly complex there. So the SW adds a second language, the Resource Description Framework (RDF), which allows you to say how the objects are related. So RDF enables you to tell the computer that 'Dan Cohn-Sherbok' is the 'author-of' 'The Politics of Apocalypse'. The file containing the book cover photo is the 'cover-of' 'The Politics of Apocalypse' and so on.

The third layer of the SW is based on yet another language called OWL, which allows you to create so-called *ontologies* – that is, speci-fications of concepts. It is the ontology layer that is the key to the real power of the SW, because it enables your computer to make some relatively clever inferences about what it is displaying. So, for instance, an ontology of people's jobs would tell you that an 'author' is a 'person'. 'Persons' have, among other things, 'phone-numbers', 'addresses', 'email-addresses', 'pictures', 'positions', 'salaries', 'homepages', 'hobbies', 'criminal-convictions', 'publications', 'spouses', 'siblings' and so on.

These layers allow the computer to do some quite nifty, if routine, things. If you liked *The Wine of Wisdom* you might want to tell the computer that you would like to send an email congratulating the author. On the current WWW, that task might take up a tedious half-hour, maybe even longer. But the computer, knowing that 'The Politics of Apocalypse' is a 'book' (first layer, XML) and knowing that 'books' have 'authors' (third layer, OWL), can try to find out who is the 'author-of' 'The Politics of Apocalypse' (second layer, RDF) and discover that it is 'Dan Cohn-Sherbok'. First layer information tells it that 'Dan Cohn-Sherbok' is an 'author' and third layer information tells it that 'authors' are 'people'.[18] 'People' have 'email-addresses' (third layer), so the computer can have a good search around the SW to try and locate the email address of 'Dan Cohn-Sherbok' and, if it can, it can set up an email from your email account, ready for you to fill in the text.

In other words, the SW holds out the possibility that searching for, retrieving and publishing information could be much more intelligent and targeted than the current version of the WWW allows. The inference described above is hardly conceptually very difficult, but it is exactly the sort of relatively routine information-processing task that it would be very useful to be able to automate. The SW is growing all the time, though currently tiny compared with the WWW as a whole, and has yet to break out of the academic/nerdy ghetto; it has yet to achieve sufficient size to benefit from the network effects predicted by Metcalfe's Law. But, given enough content on the Web written in XML, RDF and OWL, thereby creating the value of large networks that Metcalfe's Law predicts, much routine office work could be given to computers. Even if the SW does not take off, there is no doubt that some method for processing information intelligently and automatically is needed, and will arrive in due course.

Computing on tap

The Web also allows another important innovation – outsourcing one's computing needs – on the lines of *grid computing* and *web services*. Grid computing is based on a simple idea: computers can be linked together. In particular, pulling together computing power from geographically distributed computers to work together on the same problem can be just as effective as applying a single supercomputer to the task. Furthermore, if enough very powerful computers are linked, then the resulting 'computer' might actually be more powerful than any individual supercomputer around. In a world where computational power could be created in such a way, computation might be available much like electricity down a wire – you draw down what you need when you need it, and don't worry about where it comes from. Hence the term 'grid computing', by analogy to the electricity grid.

The technique of harnessing distributed computing power has been most famously exploited by the SETI@home project. SETI (Search for Extraterrestrial Intelligence) looks for extraterrestrial life by sifting through large quantities of data drawn from radio telescope readings around the world; it looks for regular patterns in the noisy radio signals. As we have seen, finding weak signals in noisy data is one of the most difficult information-processing problems there is. So the SETI project made available a screensaver which anyone could download. What the screensaver does is to make your computer join in the processing effort; any spare computing power not currently in use is devoted to the search (so far fruitless) for little green men. Over four million computers are currently linked to SETI@home, making it the largest 'computer' in the world.[19]

These developments are having a strong effect on science in general. In recent years, scientific research has become much more focused on the generation and analysis of giant quantities of data. Research into grid computing has largely been driven by the need to process this data (the new data-heavy scientific paradigm is often called e-science). So, for example, the Large Hadron Collider is a big particle accelerator designed to find evidence of the occurrence of very rare subatomic events; it will generate terabytes of data every year. To process that information, a grid of eighty-seven different computer centres has been created.

There are currently EU and US initiatives to create common standards for grid computing; the end result of all this effort may well be a global grid, a data-processing version of the Web where computing power becomes part of the infrastructure, not something you provide for yourself.

Another method of providing computing power on tap is that of web services, the idea of distributing not computing power per se, but expertise, over the Web. A web service is a computer program (or software agent) whose services you can invoke for specific tasks over the Web. So, for example, you might be setting off on a holiday. The Web has made it possible for individuals to search for relevant information about flights, hotels, prices etc., thereby allowing them to usurp the traditional role of travel agents (and thereby save middleman fees, as predicted by Coase's Law). But the collation, comparison and presentation of all that information is just the sort of routine clerical task that today's more powerful computers gobble up with relish. So, rather than you doing an automatic search of the web and a manual examination of the results, computers can do the whole lot for you.

This is all well and good, but you would need a quite complex piece of software to do that, and that software might have to be updated every year or two to keep up with technical standards and changes in computer formats. So your complex piece of software might only be used once or twice before it gets junked with your old laptop. How much better, then, to have an external company to offer the web service; it can change its software as often as it likes, but you would still just ask the company for the service (in the same way as in the offline world you might ask a company for the same service over and over, unaware of – and not caring about – any changes in its internal management structures that were needed to respond to changing business circumstances). The travel agent returns, but in virtual form, with all the cost savings that this implies.

For small, specialist tasks, we may find ourselves relying less on our own resources, instead buying them in from outside.

Sharing

As Coase's Law predicts, computers have broken and will continue to break down barriers between all sorts of domains. The common-sense distinction between 'me in here' and 'the world out there' gets increasingly stretched as our technologies improve. That is not to say that technology will lead ultimately to a Buddhist negation of self, but that more and more functions will be outsourced to external agents.

Economically, this is hard to explain. For example, the open source software movement goes against all economic thinking. Open source software is a way of writing programs that relies on individual unpaid and voluntary contributions by thousands of programmers. No one owns the programs, and they are free to use. This is in contrast to proprietary programs, where the code is copyrighted by an organisation and jealously guarded as a piece of intellectual property. Microsoft's Windows operating system is an example of the latter, the rival Linux operating system an example of the former (initially developed by Linus Torvald, who waived the copyright).

Why would people share scarce resources (specifically, programmers' time and skill)? In the case of open source software, writing good code for all to see increases a programmer's prestige among his or her peer group. Quite often the explanation is even simpler: geeks enjoy doing it.

Information (including software) is a good that is very amenable to sharing. Different people can use it simultaneously (it is a 'non-rival good', in economic jargon). Metcalfe's Law predicts the increasing value of information as more people use it; hence sharing software can increase its value more efficiently than making people pay for it (Tim Berners-Lee gave away the underlying ideas for the WWW, contributing directly to the speed of its spread). Further, the Web means that distributing information is very cheap, and coordinating the programming effort is straightforward because it is easy to locate people who are interested in helping out.

It has recently been argued that technological advances mean that sharing will increasingly feature in the economy of the future, based on the model of the open source movement, even for physical goods – and even for rival goods.[20] We are following this path, as we have moved from sharing information to sharing other aspects of computing technology, such as computing power, as described above (the participants in the SETI@home project receive no rewards). Computing power is a rival good, yet is being shared nonetheless. Similarly, peer-to-peer sharing systems involve people sharing the memories of their computers to store, say, digital copies of pop songs; computer memories are rival goods as well. But advances in technology have meant that when one buys a computer, one has plenty of spare memory and power (thanks to Moore's Law) which one can share if one wishes. The gains from selfishness are smaller in the Internet age.

Intelligence everywhere

Computing will become increasingly ubiquitous. Moore's Law not only makes it possible to squeeze more computing power onto a chip of a given size, it allows the same power to be provided by smaller and smaller chips. Computers are getting tinier and more readily disposable. As wireless technology improves, and the coverage of at least the advanced Western democracies with the wireless network spreads, it will become feasible to connect objects of any sort to the Internet. For example, if a tiny computer was inserted in your central heating system, then it could interact with the on-board computers in your car to turn the central heating on when you were, say, within five miles of home. Computer chips can be made so small and flexible that they can be inserted into pen and paper – imagine filling in a purchase form and the information being transferred immediately to the vendor. Or a newspaper whose advertisements change depending on where you are standing. Or a discarded Coke can that could tell the authorities whose credit card was used to purchase it.

If computing power can enhance the function of anything, then it will get that power; Moore's Law makes it extremely cheap to provide. This notion of *ubiquitous* or *pervasive computing* looks likely to become a reality. Soon computers will be in everything, and they will be harder to avoid. Furthermore, they will be talking to each other more and more commonly. Metcalfe's Law tells us that networks become more useful as they grow. Actually, they become more powerful. And as computers become more ubiquitous or pervasive, and their networks grow, they could start to exhibit very intelligent behaviour.

For example, in your house, your alarm clock could send a message to your central heating system just before it went off; the central heating system could tell the toilet seat to warm up; the toilet seat could tell the coffee pot to start to boil; the coffee pot could put the toaster on; the toaster could tell the car ignition to warm the car engine; the car seatbelt could tell the garage doors to open; the garage doors could open the gate; and the gate could turn the central heating down once its sensors detected that you had passed through it.

None of the individual computers in that chain of messaging events is doing anything very clever, but the result is actually emerging intelligence: relatively intelligent behaviour by the system as a whole that is flexible, and can adapt easily to your needs and your changing routine (such as on weekends). It would not be possible for a human to program the house, car and household goods to behave that way whilst retaining flexibility and adaptability; indeed, for many years the sub-discipline of artificial intelligence tried unsuccessfully to find ways to do just that. Nevertheless, the network of relatively stupid computers and messaging systems manages to achieve a global level of intelligence that would, in this case, save the householder time while cutting down on the consumption of resources and thereby also being good for the environment.

OK, perhaps this example is silly – no doubt fine-tuning the details of such a system would be more trouble than it would be worth. But the point is that we should not underestimate the cleverness and adaptability of several computers strapped together; there is not just an increase in power, as with grid computing, but also an increase in the complexity of problems which the computers together can tackle.

Our wired world

In a celebrated essay on the new electronic media, Marshall McLuhan wrote:

> Our private senses are not closed systems but are endlessly translated into each other in that experience which we call consciousness. Our extended senses, tools, technologies, through the ages, have been closed systems incapable of interplay or collective awareness. Now, in the electric age, the very instantaneous nature of co-existence among our techno-logical instruments has created a crisis quite new in human history. Our extended faculties and senses now constitute a single field of experience which demands that they become collectively conscious. Our technologies, like our private senses, now demand an interplay and ratio that makes rational co-existence possible. As long as our technologies were as slow as the wheel or the alphabet or money, the fact that they were separate, closed systems was socially and psychically supportable. This is not true now when sight and sound and movement are simultaneous and global in extent.[21]

McLuhan was ahead of his time (the piece was written in 1962); the interplay he anticipated did not happen with the advent of computing. But Moore's Law, Metcalfe's Law and Coase's Law have meant that the costs of interplay between computing systems are decreasing all the time, and the seamlessness that McLuhan expected is beginning to emerge.

In this chapter we have not tried to predict the future, only to pick out a number of prominent trends in development and directions in research. We certainly do not claim, as will become clear below, that all the developments we canvas will be benign. Many of their effects could be exploited by very unsavoury customers indeed. Neither, as we made clear at the beginning of the chapter, do we believe that these technological changes, even if they came about exactly as we have suggested, would radically change the nature of human existence (*pace* commentators such as Kevin Warwick, Donna Haraway or Susan Greenfield[22]). Living through technological development does change your view of it; but *it* does not change *you*.

How super-futuristic the sliding doors on *Star Trek* seemed in 1969; how incredible the communicators. But now even the most cut-price supermarket has automatic doors, and mobile phones are everywhere. Does any of that make us feel super-futuristic? Absolutely not. Life goes on, abetted – sometimes hindered – by technology. The shape of things to come will be determined partly by scientific developments, partly by commercial pressures, partly by military pressures and partly by consumer demand.

But technology does change our effectiveness in action, our control over the world, and our political and economic relationships with each other. And not always for the better.

3:⟩
What's So Special About Information Technology?

Talking 'bout a revolution?

So technologies there are aplenty, and their effects will be widespread. But hold on there. Although our outline of technological development so far has been relatively upbeat, we shouldn't forget the down side. Half the people on the planet have never made a telephone call. A mere 12% of the world's population is linked to the Internet (of which the US alone contributes one-third). There are more phone lines in Tokyo than in the whole of sub-Saharan Africa. Internet access in Uganda costs more than a month's income for the average Ugandan. US citizens with a college degree are sixteen times more likely to have access to the Internet and eight times more likely to have a PC at home than those with only an elementary school education. The disabled are three times less likely to have access to the Internet than the able-bodied. By 2004, 49% of all households in the UK were online, but this included only 3% of the poorest households.

Any casual bit of Googling – assuming you happen to be amongst the privileged 12% – is likely to unearth similarly sobering figures about the low level of ICT proliferation. Given such statistics, we might be forgiven for wondering what all the fuss over a supposed ICT revolution has been about. What such statistics do indicate is the unfolding pattern of control over ICT resources and technological developments. As the social impacts of the recent wave of techno-logical innovation become more visible, it appears very much as though the new technologies are being laid over more traditional patterns of inequality. If there is a revolution underway, then it is controlled by a small minority of well-placed people, even if it affects us all. Initial hopes that the invention of the PC or the Internet would lead to a more equal or democratised society quickly faded. The new technology and its distribution were co-opted rapidly by big business.[1]

Evidence of this pattern was first discovered in the early 1990s as commentators noted a gap opening up between those who have access to ICT – the so-called 'information-haves' – and those who do not – the 'information-have-nots'. This gap was termed the *digital divide*, and the label, for good or ill, stuck. There are many possible such divides, e.g. between information-rich people and the information-poor, information-rich regions and the information-poor, and information-rich countries and the information-poor. The arguments and solutions about these divides are themselves very disparate.

The apparent existence of a digital divide raises the question of what, if anything, we should do about it. Why should we find it especially troubling? After all, inequalities are commonplace in our world. Vast inequalities are tolerated – even celebrated – in many spheres of human life, so why should inequalities in access to ICT be any different? The existence of a Mercedes-Benz divide (to borrow a worn example) gives politicians and policy makers little cause for any real concern. Nevertheless, governments around the world have often treated ICTs as if they are very different types of goods to commodities such as cars. ICTs have been treated as though they are resources whose distribution should not be dictated purely by the operation of the economic market.

Tony Blair's 'New Labour' government in the United Kingdom is a case in point. Since its election in 1997 it has spent billions of pounds of public money trying to plug the perceived info-gap. This included an election pledge struck on the back of a deal with British Telecom

(BT) to install Internet connections in every one of the 30,000 schools in the UK by 2002 (in return for the lifting of 'asymmetry' rules that prohibited BT from using its network to provide home entertainment). This is typical of governments around the world. The proposal to give all schoolchildren in the US their own laptop computer received relatively little critical condemnation. One wonders what sort of public outcry there might have been if the proposal had been to distribute cars, air-conditioning units or mobile phones in a similar manner. Yet all of those, surely, are essential to certain ways of life in Western democracies.

There is obviously some kind of distinction implicit in this asymmetric political treatment, with ICT on one side and goods like phones and cars on the other. Can we bring the basis for this distinction out?

There are certain types of good – perhaps health care or education are the least controversial examples – that are special. It is widely (though not universally) thought that it is not appropriate to determine their distribution by the ability to pay, or via bargaining and exchanges in markets. There are certainly arguments about this; many refuse to accept that the distinction of a special type of good exists, in a meaningful sense, at all. Neo-liberals, for example, insist that free markets are the fairest and most efficient way of distributing all goods. On the other hand, anti-capitalists reckon that every good should be considered 'special' in this way, and that everything should be doled out on the basis of some other principle, such as need.

In most Western democracies, it is generally accepted that all goods need to be rationed, and that rationing by price is, by and large, the best trade-off between fairness, liberty and simplicity. However, all a market controls is the process of distribution, not the outcome, and sometimes the outcome of a distribution of a good is (or seems to be) important. In such circumstances – which can vary from country to country – a consensus often develops that the said outcome cannot be left up to the anarchism of a free market. For example, a free market in education, though it would be a fair way of *distributing* education, does not produce a fair *outcome*, in that richer parents can secure a better education for their own children by paying more for it; so an unfair distribution system, whereby rich parents and even the childless subsidise poor parents to some extent, is chosen in most countries.

Once we treat some goods as special, we endow them, wittingly or not, with a certain ethical import. But are ICTs really like health care and education? On the face of it, this seems improbable. Yet public policy initiatives in this area have largely treated ICT as so obviously important that combating the digital divide requires little by way of reasoned justification. Is there a suspicion, as argued recently by former Blair advisor Peter Hyman, that we are in one of our periods of pointless modernisation-worship?[2]

It is time that we subjected such assumptions about the ethical significance of ICTs to scrutiny: an important, though much-neglected task. We may well find that there are good reasons to treat ICTs as special, and that governments are correct to do so. But this raises a further very important question: on what basis should ICT be distributed? Here the waters are even murkier. These are questions of social justice, because they raise issues at a very high level – the level of the design of social and political institutions. Current notions of universal access to ICT, or equal opportunities for access to ICTs, that appear to motivate public policy initiatives are especially underspecified. We aim to scrutinise these ideas, thus laying the foundations for our enquiries in the rest of the book. Stating this more formally, our investigation will cover a number of interrelated aspects:

- What kind of social good is ICT? What are its functions and do these make it different from other commodities?

- Are there societal obligations to provide access to certain ICT resources and training?
- What inequalities in the distribution of ICTs are morally permissible?
- What limits do provider autonomy and the individual liberties and rights of citizens and producers place on the just distribution of access to, and use of, ICTs?

This chapter will offer tentative answers to the first two questions. We will look briefly at the third question in the next chapter, but this and the final question form a framework of enquiry for much of the rest of the book. This is because many of the subsequent issues about ICT – from security and privacy to democracy and trust – are affected in important ways by what the social status of ICTs is determined to be, and what levels of access individuals have to those resources. Until we know more about the facts of the matter, thinking about questions of distribution, justice and politics would be going off half-cocked. Alas, as we shall see, this often appears to be exactly what has happened in the case of many government initiatives.

Is ICT special? Ethics, needs and preferences

To infer from the existence of an inequality in the distribution of a certain good that this distribution is automatically an inequity is to fall prey to a fallacy in reasoning that Scottish philosopher David Hume called the 'is/ought' problem. To move, without explanation, from a statement about how the world *is*, to a statement about how the world *ought* to be is to commit a grave logical error. It illegitimately jumps the divide between a fact and a value, turning an empirical observation into an ethical claim. If an inequality in ICTs is an ethical matter (one that ought to be corrected on grounds of justice) but an inequality in expensive cars is not, then the reasons why this is so must be explained.

To provide such an explanation we should try to determine what properties a good or resource would have to possess in order to make its distribution an ethical matter. These properties, which would not be possessed by ordinary goods such as electric tooth-brushes, would render the goods that possessed them a 'special' class of goods, and would legitimate their unusual treatment. If it is possible to identify such a property or range of properties that certain goods share which makes them special, then we can easily examine whether ICTs also share that property. If they do, then they too would be subject to ethical requirements in terms of the level and pattern of their distribution across individuals.

How might such a view of special goods be fleshed out? Here we need to get a bit more philosophical. What is at work in the notion of an inequality in certain goods having ethical significance is the distinction between a need and a preference. Understanding this can help illuminate why some inequalities are ethical issues and some are not.

We all have preferences. You might prefer tea to coffee, soaps to documentaries, or pushpin to Pushkin. But we also have some preferences that are so important that they are in a league of their own. These preferences are for goods or resources that we need, regardless of whatever else in life we may want. Food, shelter, clothing, basic health care and rights over our own body are all examples of what many people believe to be basic human needs. Without adequate levels of these, an individual is unable to pursue other ends in life. A society that fails to provide for such basic needs does its citizens a serious injustice. A society that fails to satisfy citizens' preferences for caviar and expensive champagne, however, does not necessarily fail in its duty of justice in the same way. Not all preferences are created equal.

Claiming that certain preferences have such weight that they sanction special treatment is not, of course, entirely uncontroversial. Describing human needs is often a tricky business, and some philosophers and politicians that have tried to render the concept of needs coherent have despaired of ever finding an adequate description. These are important concerns that we must keep in mind as we proceed, but they do not deflect us from the fact that we do treat certain things as needs even if there is debate at the margins about the content of those needs. There are some goods that are commonly viewed as inappropriate for distribution through market exchanges between those who are economically unequal. This keeps the conceptual distinction between needs and preferences open. Political philosopher John Rawls calls the resources that satisfy these basic needs *primary social goods* because of their fundamental social importance. Rawls's view is a particularly well-worked-out position and for this reason is instructive for our enquiry. Primary social goods are:

> things which it is supposed a rational man wants whatever else he wants. Regardless of what an individual's rational plans are in detail, it is assumed that there are various things which he would prefer more of rather than less. With more of these goods men can generally be assured of greater success in carrying out their intentions and in advancing their ends, whatever these ends may be.[3]

As Rawls recognises, by designating some preferences as being endowed with special moral weight or value in this way it is possible to overcome a particularly sticky problem that besets alternative approaches to demarcating needs and preferences. This problem concerns the measurement and comparison of individuals' happiness, and is what economists and philosophers call the problem of interpersonal comparisons of well-being.

To see this problem and how the proposed view of a class of special goods overcomes it, we need to imagine a system without the needs–preferences distinction and how it would attempt to distribute goods. Crude versions of the philosophical position of utilitarianism attempt just this. According to utilitarianism, the aim of mechanisms such as public policy is to maximise people's happiness. In terms of distributing goods, this could mean attempting to satisfy the preferences of individuals to the greatest extent possible. But, as we have seen, people have diverse preferences. The satisfaction you gain from a good claret may be completely different to the level of satisfaction that someone else gets from drinking the same beverage. Similarly, how do we compare these levels of satisfaction not only across individuals, but also across goods? Is your satisfaction from drinking the claret greater than the jazz enthusiast's satisfaction from listening to Miles Davis's *Kind of Blue*?

In the absence of any distinction between classes of preference, the choice is either to avoid distributing any goods at all – in effect, throwing one's hands up in despair at the thought of ever achieving anything – or to try and balance things like individual levels of satisfaction. The latter is often subject to the complaint that it would mean pouring massive resources into the meeting of preferences that might be extremely expensive (and even deliberately cultivated) but only return a moderate amount of satisfaction, such as the taste for expensive champagne.

The money economy gives us a rough-and-ready way of doing this, using money as a store of value, a sort of economic 'battery'. The measure of how much satisfaction someone expects to get from a good or service is the amount of money he or she is prepared to pay for it. But this cannot achieve interpersonal comparison of satisfaction, because we do not all start off with the same amount of money, sad to say. Money gives us the accuracy that utilitarianism demands, but at the expense of any method of correlation between people. The need to correlate is vital, as Rawls points out.

> Some method of correlating the scales of different persons is presupposed if we are to say that the gains of some are to outweigh the losses of others. It is unreasonable to demand great precision, yet these estimates cannot be left to our

unguided intuition. For judgments of a greater balance of interests leave too much room for conflicting claims. Moreover, these judgments may be based on ethical and other notions, not to mention bias and self-interest, which puts their validity in question. Simply because we do in fact make what we call interpersonal comparisons of well-being does not mean that we understand the basis of these comparisons or that we should accept them as sound. To settle these matters we need to give an account of these judgments, to set out the criteria that underlie them. For questions of social justice we should try to find some objective grounds for these comparisons, ones that men can recognize and agree to. At the present time, there appears to be no satisfactory answer to these difficulties from a utilitarian point of view. Therefore it seems that, for the time being at least, the principle of utility makes such heavy demands on our ability to estimate the balance of advantages that it defines at best an ambiguous court of appeal for questions of justice.[4]

Rawls's solution to the problem is to suggest a truncated set of preferences that can act as an objective measure for comparing the claims that individuals make on resources. These preferences, enshrined in the set of Rawls's primary social goods, reflect the fact that, in our everyday discourse, we make regular interpersonal comparisons, and that we do so normally over a small range of goods.

For instance, we might find it more than a little odd if someone with a broken leg asked the medical consultant for the cash equivalent of the operation to reset the limb so that she could go on an African safari holiday. Even if the patient would prefer the cash to the relief from the pain and the return of mobility – even if it was a dream holiday – this request clearly is at odds with the importance that most people attribute to mainstream medical treatments. Basic medical care is a far weightier good than foreign holidays. Paying for

INEQUALITY.COM

the latter from the public purse is likely to strike most people as perverse in a way that curing a straightforward debilitating medical condition is not (hence the regular public outcries that trail stories of young criminals being packed off on expensive holidays at the taxpayer's expense).

The fact that we do use such a metric in our daily political discourse, and that such a distinction is philosophically coherent and defensible, does not, of course, mean that we ought to use it. How can we be sure that our intuitions are reliable in this respect?

To address this concern we only need look at the role of primary social goods *in absentia*. As Rawls notes, primary social goods are those 'things' that every person requires regardless of whatever else they require or what their plans of life are. They are the goods or resources that enable us to pursue our other ends in life, or what philosophers like to term *conceptions of the good life*. So, without an adequate level of one of these goods, an individual would be frustrated to some extent in their pursuit of what they consider to be their conception of the good life – they would not be able to function at a level that is 'normal' for their society. A lack of a primary social good, then, impairs our normal social functioning. We can see the idea behind this through such obvious examples as health care. Failing health can cause us to fall short of the normal level of functioning for humans. In turn, this can cause the pursuit of our own ends to be impaired (by making them more difficult to achieve, and so forth). The purpose of health care is to restore normal levels of functioning and, for this reason, is often adjudged to constitute a primary social good.

Note here that changing factors, such as the level of technological development, can play a crucial role in determining what counts as normal levels of social functioning. Taking health care once more as the example, we can see that only in the past 100 years or so has health care had such a central role in maintaining the normal level of functioning of individuals. This is because the advance in medical science in the last century has been enormous. Previously, visiting a doctor when you were ill had been fairly pointless. Similarly, in the economy of the nineteenth century, or the agricultural economies of the early twentieth century, the value of an education was at best equivocal; you could earn a decent and reasonable wage, certainly enough to function normally, with just your brawn. But this is much less true in the twenty-first century; the economy demands much more from us than mere muscle. A reasonable education is essential now in a way that it was not 150 years ago. So, the resources or goods that we might be said to need will change over time.

Reductions to functioning need not always be immediately physical or economic in the way implied by these examples. Functioning can be impaired through other factors, such as lack of opportunity, discrimination, or restrictions to movement, speech and thought. Such restrictions undercut the ability of individuals to function at a normal level. In turn, this narrows the opportunities for individuals to pursue and revise their conception of the good. So, we have a chain of influence that runs from needs and their impairment, through the available opportunities, to the pursuit of our chosen ends. The distinction between needs and preferences can be understood, on Rawls's account, as a distinction between their relative positions on this chain.

The 40:30:30 society

Rawls makes the case for a number of resources falling within the category of primary social goods, including certain political and social liberties, specific levels of economic income and wealth, and various opportunities for economic, educational and political participation. Our concern is more specific, namely, whether ICTs fall under this heading, either because they themselves are primary social goods or because they are prerequisite for others. If ICT is to have this role, then it is likely to be because of its massive social, economic and political transformative effects – in other words, how it affects things like employment and educational opportunities, work and leisure, levels of income and wealth, the opportunities for political participation and so forth.

The greatest impact of ICT has been at work: the realm of production and exchange. Here the emphasis has started to shift away from physical goods produced in factories and workshops towards information and information processing. ICT has ceased to be a smart extra that you might use to add value to your production processes; it is now, like electricity, part of the infrastructure, and is being explicitly included as such in official policy-making efforts, such as the UK Office of Science and Technology's Intelligent Infrastructure Foresight programme.[5] The ICT industry itself is dwarfed by the network of e-services ('e-' signifying that they are digital services) that have become available: electronic publishing, financial services, trading and brokering, e-commerce, entertainment of all possible kinds, security, surveillance, earth resources information, environmental monitoring, digital imaging, and data mining and processing.[6] The patterns of technology, as described in chapter 2, have altered to meet these new demands.

This shift in the emphasis of production to an information economy has ushered in a transformation in work and employment (as predicted by Coase's Law). Despite widespread fears that unemployment accompanies technological development, in reality a shortage of employment has not been one of the problems faced in the last two decades within Western societies. In the US – the world's most technologically advanced country – some twenty-seven million jobs were created during the period of most rapid uptake of ICT between 1979 and 1994 (60% of which were in technical and professional occupations, meaning an upgrading of the skill profile of the occupational structure), and from 1992 to 1996 over ten million new jobs came into existence. Moreover, unemployment remained at approximately 5.5% throughout the 1990s, despite the incorporation of women into the workforce around this period.[7]

What has changed – with alarming rapidity – is the educational entry level for many jobs. Now you need a university degree to get a job that your parents could have obtained upon leaving school at sixteen years of age. Sociologist Steve Fuller has argued that the degree is needed to get the job, not to do it; once you are safely behind the desk, you need never use all that painstakingly acquired knowledge again.[8] The need for qualifications reveals two hidden costs of the knowledge economy. First, we have academic rent-seeking; by making qualifications the key to getting jobs, a role for academics in society is ensured, even if that role is not particularly consistent with the traditional values of higher education. Secondly, as more and more people chase more and more qualifications, the signals that those qualifications send are drowned in more and more noise. This reduction of signalling power is another way of saying that there is grade inflation.

Inflation has occurred right across the board. Perceived changes in the patterns of employment reflect, on the one hand, a decline in real wages for full-time male workers (and a stagnation in women's wages) and, on the other hand, the increasing job insecurity that arises as the full-time career-type employment pattern fades away. As sociologist Manuel Castells states:

> Job instability and lowering of real wages are linked to major structural changes made possible by information technology: globalization of the economy and decentralization of manu-facturing and services and transformation of firms' operations through networking and subcontracting. Under such condi-tions management has a number of options vis-à-vis labor: automate, relocate production, outsource part of the produc-tion, downsize, and network.[9]

The result is a move away from the once standard full-time contract towards temporary employment, part-time work, self-employment, subcontracting and consultancy. This shift in labour occurs at all levels, but is especially significant at the lower end of the income scale, where unskilled and semi-skilled workers end up in a burger-flipping cycle of low wages and job insecurity.[10] At the other end of the scale, however, the workforce has become increasingly well qualified and highly specialised:

> As a result, a major polarization occurs between a core labor force, with high skills, and a mass of disposable labor that can be used or replaced or employed under different statuses, depending on the needs and requirements of the market. Each discontinuity in the work's trajectory could send into oblivion some workers who, by falling in one of the 'black holes' of the new socioeconomic structure, will find it difficult to reinstate themselves in the pool of the fully employable. Thus, even though mass unemployment does not exist, there are growing segments of semi-employed, in and out of the labor market, creating a potential danger for some individuals, particularly among minority youth, to join the ranks of the criminal economy. Decreasing cultural skills forbid entry into the informational labor market that increasingly requires the ability of 'symbol processing,' in Reich's expression.[11]

Forecasting the rise of a multitude of differing levels of access to new technologies, and the skills necessary to utilise them, Will Hutton speaks of the 40:30:30 society in which only the top 40% represent the secure and well-paid information processors.[12] The middle group forms an information proletariat, often employed on a casual basis and increasingly fearful of unemployment due to competition from other countries where lower overheads exist. Think here, for instance, of recent outcries in the UK about outsourcing call centres to India. The bottom 30% of citizens either exist on casual unskilled labour or are dependent upon the welfare state and have little or no access to, or experience of, the technology that drives the economy and their society. Indeed, looking back to our survey in chapter 2, what we will inevitably see is that cleverer and cleverer information processing will be automated, and the security and good pay of the top 40% will also come under threat from automation and outsourcing.

The international dimension

Snapshot measurements of Internet access from around the world indicate that some form of exclusion from ICT exists in most countries, though the gap has decreased in recent years. Internet penetration rates are still showing such a divide. Some representative countries will serve as examples (see table 1).

Even in the more developed countries exposure to ICT is still only moderate, and is restricted predominantly to those who already work in areas that are ICT oriented. Without ICT experience many are being denied the opportunity for gaining employment within the information-handling industries. As geographer Peter Hall observes, this is a significant instance of socio-economic exclusion:

> The informational–digital revolution has transformed urban economies: the brawn jobs that existed in plenty thirty years ago have vanished and will not return; the only jobs that offer any kind of lifetime prospects are in information handling, and they require ever more sophisticated educational qualifications. But substantial numbers of young people, perhaps as many as 40 percent in western countries are leaving school without these qualifications and are effectively going onto the streets.[13]

Recent figures seem to bear out Hall's prediction. A 2004 International Labour Organisation survey found that total youth

Table 1: Internet and ICT penetration[1]

Country	% urban[2]	Number of Internet users/1000 persons[3]	PCs/1000 persons[4]	Mobile phone subscriptions/1000 persons[5]
Australia	89.3 (1996)	372	514	574
Cameroon	38.3 (1987)	3	3.8	20
China	36.1 (2000)	26	20	114
Greece	58.9 (1991)	128	78	725
India	27.8 (2001)	7	5.8	5.5
Ireland	57.0 (1996)	234	387	722
Israel	92.9[6]	240[7]	256	842
Japan	78.1 (1995)	456	349	573
Lebanon	60.1 (1970)	84[8]	55	205[9]
Libya	85.3[10]	4	NA	9.5
Mexico	71.3 (2000)	35	69	202
Morocco	51.7[11] (1994)	14	14	13
Portugal	48.2 (1991)[12]	349	117	769
Saudi Arabia	77.3[13]	13	62	111
South Africa	53.7 (1996)	70	68	208
Tajikistan	32.6 (1989)	0.5	NA	0.3
Tonga	32.1 (1996)[14]	10[15]	NA	1[16]
UK	89.1[17]	400	367	784
USA	75.2 (1990)[18]	499	625	446
West Bank[19]	NA	26	NA	14[20]

unemployment worldwide had reached eighty-eight million, nearly half of all jobless persons (while the young accounted for only a quarter of the working population as a whole). The young also contribute 130 million to the 550 million working poor who remain below the poverty line, generally calculated as an income of $1 per day. Halving youth unemployment would add about 4% to global GDP, or about $2.2 trillion.[14]

Coupled with the reorientation in production and exchange is a change in the urban setting. The traditional role of the city as the hub of commerce is being broken down as the digital revolution conquers the limits of space and time in such a way that individuals do not have to be located together in order to do business. One can work

Table 1: footnotes

[1]Data from various Britannia Books of the Year.

[2]Most recent census (year of census in brackets).

[3]2001.

[4]2001.

[5]2001.

[6]1995 estimate of *de jure* population.

[7]Figure approximate, as a result of differences in counting the Israeli population.

[8]2000.

[9]2000.

[10]1995 estimate of *de jure* population.

[11]Includes Western Sahara.

[12]Not the most recent census (2001), but the latest with these published figures.

[13]1990 estimate.

[14]Data for *de jure* population.

[15]1999.

[16]1999.

[17]1990 estimate of de jure population.

[18]Not the most recent census (2000), but the latest with these published figures.

[19]Excludes East Jerusalem.

[20]1997.

just as effectively from home in the suburbs as one could from a city-centre office. The symbolic analysts no longer need to spend time commuting, or renting expensive office space, when they can work from outlying areas. In vacating their traditional residential areas in city centres, however, the top 40% of society have left behind an increasingly impoverished underclass of citizens in the inner-city housing estates.[15] The balance that once existed in the city centres between the city workers and the traditional working class population is disappearing. 'Increasingly, the central economy is fed from the elite corridors and the exurbs; the ancillary workers are found in parts of the intervening areas, while other areas become in effect separate islands, no longer functionally connected with the city.'[16]

Functioning normally

Even in the last decade or so, we have seen opportunities for work and employment being affected and transformed by developments in technology. When we consider all the other areas of social existence – education, politics, entertainment, leisure activities, consumption, communication – then the impact of these technological develop-ments is likely to be even greater, and is likely to affect the ability of individuals to function normally to a much greater extent, as whole swathes of civil society move online. This concern is summed up neatly by Pippa Norris:

> The chief concern about the digital divide is that the underclass of info-poor may become further marginalized in societies where basic computer skills are becoming essential for economic success and personal advancement, entry to good career and educational opportunities, full access to social networks, and opportunities for civic engagement.[17]

Work and employment opportunities form merely one dimension

where differential levels of access to ICTs may affect normal social functioning. But, as Norris indicates, the impact of ICT goes far beyond just economic exclusion. 'Normal social functioning' may well also include:

- *Consumption*: being able to consume certain goods, at least up to some reasonable minimum level for their society. This corresponds broadly with the better-known idea of economic inequality and poverty.

- *Savings*: accumulating savings, entitlements to pensions or the ownership of property. This may be increasingly important as societies age and become less able to generate sufficient surpluses of wealth to support their pensioners.

- *Production*: engaging in an economically or socially valued activity, such as paid work, education or training, retirement, or family rearing or caring.

- *Political*: engaging in the collective enterprise of improving or protecting the immediate or wider social or physical environment. This includes things such as voting, joining political parties, campaigning, running for public office and calling officials to account.

- *Social*: engaging in social interaction with family and friends, and identifying with a larger social group or groups. This includes the availability of personal support and the opportunity to feel part of a wider community.[18]

Failure to achieve any or all of these is a hallmark of what is now called *social exclusion*. Although the concept of social exclusion is not without its critics, it does illustrate that ICT, being integral to all or most of these dimensions, has the potential to contribute to the exclusion of individuals from their society.

Given this list of factors in 'normal social functioning', it is quite clear that, as ICT becomes ever more ubiquitous, an understanding of and familiarity with ICT will become more important merely to achieve normality. This is a change to which we are having to adjust. As a rough rule of thumb, the generation of people born after, say, 1980 should be completely at home in a technologically driven world. Those of us who are older will have to learn skills that the younger people picked up at their mother's knee (or, rather, at the foot of the television set). It has been remarked that older people are 'digital immigrants', whose mastery of the techniques and tools required for ICT literacy is second hand, slightly forced and has to be learned. Younger people are 'digital natives', cool and comfortable with the technology. Of course, younger people will still need to keep pace with changes – ICT, though etched onto silicon, is not cast in stone – but doing so is generally easier for them, given that they do not have the start-up costs of learning about an entirely alien environment. So the exclusion problem, if exacerbated by ICT, may be transient; time may heal the problem. As older people die off, then their computer illiteracy will become less of an issue.

This, however, is a complacent attitude. It may well be that, as lifetimes lengthen, there will still be large numbers of digital immigrants well past the mid-point of this century. But, more to the point, recall that the digital divide is not just an age thing; it is related to income both between societies and within them. Hutton's 40:30:30 ratio may or may not accurately reflect the numbers of people within each category, but it is reasonable to imply that none of the three groups has any kind of numerical advantage over the others. In particular, the voice of the disadvantaged is quite heavily outweighed (by something like 70:30).

To create a just society in which everyone is able to work, consume, save, produce, take part in politics and socialise to whatever extent they desire, it is surely essential that everyone has sufficient access to ICT, and the skills involved in leveraging that access. This may only have become true recently, but in the developed world, ICT is now undoubtedly part of the vital mix that enables everyone in a society to pursue their own idea of the good life. Furthermore, it will become a greater part of that mix as time goes on and it becomes central to more and more of society's functions. It will also be increasingly important in the developing world.

However, distributional questions are not as simple as all that. Even relatively straightforward examples of areas where people need access to services to function in a society can raise awkward questions. For instance, health care is one such area; it is incumbent on the government of a just society to ensure access to health care for all its citizens. All well and good. But what of the people who can pay more for better services? What if the demand for health care outstrips the money available for supplying it? What of the borderline treatments, such as cosmetic treatments, some of which are clearly frivolous but others of which are necessary for psychological well-being? What of the effects on the markets for drugs, which need to generate large enough profits to compensate the pharmaceutical companies' expensive research and development methods? There is more to the distributional question than meets the eye.

If that is true of health care, it is even more the case with ICT, an industry which is developing all the time – indeed, its entire history is a mere half century or so. It is all very well to call for a just distribution of ICT and cyberspace. It is rather trickier to define what a just distribution actually consists in. We don't claim we know all the answers. But in the next chapter, we will examine some of the theoretical problems with the claim, before moving on to more practical concerns in the second half of the book.

4:>
All Things Being Equal ...

Not just what, but why (and how)

Our investigation began with the idea of the Internet as a space for political action. The trajectory of our discussion so far has taken us through an identification of the various political issues raised by the new technologies to a narrower focus on just one of those issues, namely the question about the distribution of access to ICT. In the previous chapter we began to make the case for thinking about ICT as a resource whose distribution should not be allowed to vary entirely in line with the unfettered market, but one that it is in some sense a 'special' good.

The case for viewing ICT in this light is far from complete. We have only looked at one dimension – the impact of ICT on the world of production and exchange – out of the many that we identified. We must reintroduce some of the other dimensions or issues, in order to complete our case that ICT raises issues of justice. We must also look at other political issues raised by the new technologies, but which fall outside the purview of justice. In the following chapters we will cover a number of further variables in order to fill in these gaps – the dimensions of democratic decision making, security, trust, privacy and so on. Inevitably, more variables mean a more complicated picture. They introduce more noise, rendering it more difficult to pick out any clear or certain path through the issues to an acceptable resolution.

Before we set off in a myriad of directions, we need a vehicle and some road markers to help us get to our destination. That is, we need some idea of the underlying aims that drive possible responses to these types of political issues. If the distribution or the use of ICTs is to be fairer or more ethical, then we need some understanding of what this might actually mean – what solutions, positions or ideas are available. Once this understanding is in place, we will also need a framework for assessing and deciding which of the various possibilities should be followed up in order to arrive at an acceptable solution. This chapter will stick with the subject of the digital divide and how it impacts on the world of work – particularly the idea of opportunities to enter that world. We will develop a number of principles that could guide solutions for combating the digital divide, and we will suggest how they may be thought about rationally to decide which is the most acceptable. Keeping this narrow focus will allow us to put this framework in place for the further investigations to come. Once in place, we can use the framework to navigate through the complicated terrain of the other issues.

Nailing things down

Continuing the theme of the digital divide and exclusion from productive activity, let us look at the types of ideas that tend to underpin policies and programmes (actual and potential) aimed at ameliorating these problems. As we noted in the last chapter, whether or not ICTs are actually special goods, they are treated, if only implicitly, by many governments around the world as though they are. From the most technologically advanced right down to the least, many states operate on the assumption that the digital divide raises some ethical concerns. Consequently, the idea that access to ICT should be organised in a fairer, more just manner is a view that is common not only to governments, but also to commentators. As W.J. Mitchell, one of the latter, writes:

> When access to jobs and services is delivered electronically, those who have good network connections will have an

advantage, whereas those with poor service or no service will be disadvantaged and marginalized. So common justice clearly demands that we should strive for equitable access – and, in particular, to ensure that members of low-income communities are not further disadvantaged by exclusion from the digital world.[1]

Similarly, the International Telecommunications Union (the ITU) included the following statement in its Draft Declaration of Principles, issued in 2003:

> Connectivity is a central enabling agent in building the Information Society. Universal, ubiquitous, equitable and affordable access to ICT infrastructure and services constitutes one of the challenges of the Information Society and should be an objective of all stakeholders involved in building it.[2]

Of these four criteria from the ITU, perhaps the most prominent, and the one singled out by Mitchell, is 'equitable access'. This is clearly important – and indeed accords with our discussion in chapter 3. But, given that there is agreement on the centrality of equity, does that tell us what 'equity' means in the particular context of ICT? What qualifies as 'equitable' access? Our argument so far leads us to agree with its importance, but it does not tell us exactly how things should be arranged. Agreeing that a certain state of affairs is unfair does not magically produce a picture of what a perfectly fair state of affairs would look like.

And what about the other criteria from the ITU? 'Universality' is the buzzword of the day. In order for the distribution of ICT to be fair, access has to be universal. But in order for this to be helpful to public policy makers, further clarification is required. The problem is that, beyond the obvious meaning of 'universal', the notion lacks specific directive content.

Universality tells us nothing about what level of access individuals should have. Saying that universal access to water has been achieved is fully compatible with a world where, at one end of the scale, some drink water containing the residue of human remains, excrement, pesticides and other pollutants, whilst others drink the purest water from defrosted Arctic icebergs. When charities such as Oxfam campaign for donations to improve water supplies in famine-struck areas of the world, we all understand that they have further criteria to meet than just access to any old water, however filthy.

Admittedly the analogy between ICT and drinking water is not perfect (only one is vital to sustain human life, for example), but it does illustrate the point about 'universal access' being rather too general or vague to be of much use. Do we really mean by universal access to ICT that just any old access will do? More importantly, is this what governments mean by universal access? Sometimes, unfortunately, it seems as though it is. In the UK the criterion of universal access is satisfied by the creation of local IT centres, computing facilities at local libraries, the distribution of reconditioned computers and the provision of computing facilities in schools. Imagine that you do not have a computer of your own. Your local library has several that you can use. All it takes is two bus journeys to reach it. Do you have access to ICT? Quite probably. Is it the same kind of access as the university academic with the latest powerful computer gadgetry sat on his desk? Definitely not. It differs in terms of both quality and (personal) cost. The access does not compare in terms of effectiveness. What about the child whose school has several computers donated by local firms when they replace their employees' machines? Do these compare with the state-of-the-art IT suite stacked full of the latest models and Pentium processors at the private school just up the road? Unlikely. Does it satisfy universal access? Definitely. Even within schools this can be problematic. Some children have computers at home, some do not. But if the school has IT facilities then all have access. Homework that would benefit from such things as Internet searches for information disproportionately disadvantages those who do not have a computer at home, despite access being 'universal'.

Unlike water, the effective use of ICT is determined by certain preconditions whose satisfaction is independent of the simple provision of the infrastructure. So, for example, use of ICT requires a certain level of training on the part of the user. You can't just sit at a terminal and start using it – there is a learning curve to ascend. It also requires certain linguistic skills. The Internet is conducted in an increasingly international and homogenised version of English, and support for other languages online is terribly variable. Indeed, many minority communities with idiosyncratic alphabets can end up being forced to interact online in an unfamiliar idiom. It may be desirable to help preserve some languages or cultures, such as the Welsh language; ·but, given that almost all Welsh speakers are also speakers of English, what need is there to provide materials or content for computers in Welsh? It doesn't affect access. Age is also a factor. It is well known that uptake of the Internet is greater among younger people than older ones; what is perhaps less remarked upon is the way that the content available on the Internet is skewed towards the young (or at least towards the new). Googling 'Justin Timberlake' gets you 1,290,000 hits, whereas 'George Formby' gets you 45,900. Well, maybe the iniquity there isn't too glaring. But the language and rhetoric used online, and the attitudes conveyed by much of the content, are more geared towards the MTV generation.

So merely talking of universality is not enough; there is a need to flesh out the type of access that is justified. The remaining criteria from the ITU – affordable and ubiquitous – sound less problematic than 'equitable' and 'universal'. Are they?

'Affordable' certainly seems more straightforward, but actually it is not. The idea of affordability, presumably, is that people do not have to pay more than is feasible. But here we immediately come up against the needs/preferences distinction mentioned in chapter 3. The cost of access to ICT may be relatively low, or may be artificially held below market prices, or whatever. But if people spend their money on other things that they find more attractive, then ICT will not be affordable to them. Actually, the cost of a computer and broadband access in most of the developed world is affordable by the vast majority of the population, but nevertheless the price might be quite steep if you are not terribly interested in that sort of thing.

Finally, 'ubiquitous'. Again, this could mean one of a number of things. What about a remote region of a country? Should that really have the same degree of access, however that is defined, as the capital city? Maybe the inhabitants have accepted that their region will be relatively deprived of resources; that might even be half the fun of living there.

There is some evidence of an awareness of the need for, or use of, more finely tuned criteria in determining the appropriate level of ICT access. Consider the following statement from Policy Action Team 15 of the UK's Social Exclusion Unit.

> The rapid spread of ICTs is changing many aspects of modern life ... [The ICT revolution] is seen as a turning point, a major leap for society equivalent to the industrial revolution. Much of the UK is well placed to take advantage of it. At the same time, however, Britain faces the problem of a society divided socially and economically. The gap between the worst off and the rest of the country has increased over the last two decades. In some of the poorest neighbourhoods people face severe deprivation. Access to the benefits of the 'information revolution' is often the most difficult because of the lack of awareness, skills or opportunities. People living in deprived neighbourhoods *should have the same opportunity* to benefit from the rapid spread of ICTs rather than being further excluded by them.[3]

This statement provides more of an idea about what might be behind current drives to make the benefits of the information society accessible to all. The Social Exclusion Unit is expressing the notion that, just because someone hails from an economically or socially deprived background, this does not mean they should be further excluded from the benefits that accompany the ability to utilise the developing technologies. All should have the same opportunities, regardless of factors such as class, familial background, sex, race and cultural backdrop. This is simply another way of expressing the thought that opportunities to access ICT should be equal.

This, then, is one way of conceiving of how the notion of universal access might be fleshed out. We have seen in earlier chapters how the proliferation of recent technological developments has come to affect all areas of human existence and interaction, often in the most profound manner. Access to jobs and careers can be significantly influenced by the degree to which individuals have ICT capabilities. Thus, things like equality of opportunity, more broadly (as well as political equality), can depend, in part, on the existence of differential levels of access to ICT. Talk of universal access is intended to help realise this broader equality of opportunity with regard to things such as jobs and educational opportunities. If everyone has access, then equality of opportunity is easier to secure. The problem is, as we have seen, that not all access is equal. The question then becomes one of what level of access is required in order to facilitate equality of opportunity more broadly? The obvious answer here is *equal* access to ICT. In short, equal opportunities for access to effective ICT resources and training is required in order for equality of opportunity (broadly conceived) to obtain.

But, whilst we may defend the principle of equality of opportunity in relation to jobs, educational places and the like, it is not immediately obvious that this logically requires equal opportunities for access to ICT. To make some of these ideas clearer, it is necessary to look at equality – as a distributive principle – more closely.

Meritocracy

Let us try to abstract a little from the details of the arguments over public policies that are aimed at ameliorating some of the problems raised throughout this book. Instead, let us think of what should drive – at the level of norms or principles – public policies. We will start with the idea, noted above, that universal access to ICT – as a remedy for the digital divide, and as part of the solution for social exclusion more generally – means equality of opportunity for access to ICT.

Equality of opportunity is also a useful point of departure for this investigation because it is a widely known and generally accepted principle. Political philosophy, unlike the real world of politics, usually takes equality as a baseline or starting point for further investigation. For thinkers such as those we have encountered so far – such as political theorist John Rawls – treating individuals as anything other than equal requires significant justification. For many non-philosophers the assumption of equality as the norm is strikingly incongruous with everyday assumptions and intuitions. Although we will see reasons in support of assumptions of equality in due course, it is important to note that one area where equality is accepted by a large majority of individuals in the real world is in terms of opportunity. Equality of opportunity generates a consensus the likes of which few other political principles share. Even those on the libertarian right of the political spectrum – such as the neo-liberal governments of Margaret Thatcher and Ronald Reagan – endorse some version of equality of opportunity. For such libertarians the idea that some individuals would be in their jobs because they were white, or male, or born to a privileged family background is heinous, because it undermines the efficiency of the free market. Those who are there in virtue of, say, their privileged background may well be keeping more talented persons from occupying those roles.[4] Those talented individuals would, *ipso facto*, be more productive. Similarly, gender-biased societies exclude significant potential talent.

Equality of opportunity – at least in the guise of 'meritocracy' – is, therefore, even attractive to those who usually reject the ideal of equality per se. This is now deeply embedded in the Western psyche regarding the appropriate criteria for employing people, at least within certain fields. Imagine, for instance, the type of reception that would be given to a proposal to sell commissions in the armed services. For most of us the criteria for achieving officer status in the army should include such things as aptitude for soldiering and leadership, not the ability to pay. In fact, it is only in recent years that most armies in the Western world have operated a system of merit as the basis for selecting officers. Nevertheless, the efficiency and fairness of such a system is now widely accepted as being correct.[5]

Needless to say, not everyone accepts equality of opportunity. There are still those who view certain people as inferior, or less deserving than others. This can be based on features such as sex, race or religion. Yet, despite the existence of these views, there remains a remarkable level of consensus on the ideal of equality of opportunity. We need, then, to develop this notion a little more, and to see how it might translate into the world of access to ICT.

The literature on equal opportunities – both theoretical and empirical – is vast. It is useful, at the level of norms, to break the concept down into some basic types. The first, which we have already encountered, is that of simple equality of opportunity, or what has become widely known as 'meritocracy'. Under this simple version individuals are formally equal to pursue their preferred career, job or the like. That is, there are no legal barriers to entry into positions other than attributes directly relevant to the role. For example, a society that legislated directly to prevent non-whites from entering the legal profession, or to allow only Oxbridge graduates to become physicians, would violate this simple version of equality of opportunity. If an individual has the appropriate qualifications and other requisites, then they should have the same opportunity to pursue their chosen path as any and everybody else who meets those same criteria.

What lies beneath the surface here are two motivating ideas. One (a pragmatic point) is that to do otherwise would be an inefficient use of talent. The second (an ethical point) is that to do otherwise would limit people's opportunities on the basis of features of themselves over which they have no control, such as their sex, race or social background. Where we hail from, the colour of our skin and our gender are things determined outside our control. Because we bear no fault or responsibility for these things, it would be unfair for our life chances to be determined by them. They are arbitrary characteristics, morally speaking. Removal of legal barriers to employment helps to achieve a meritocratic system – one where individuals are appointed to positions on merit, rather than genetic or social chance. Because the pragmatic and the ethical coincide, we get a pleasant convergence of ideas which improve both the system and the opportunities for the individual.

One of the problems with meritocracy is that it does not follow its line of reasoning through to its logical conclusion. If efficiency and non-responsibility are the motivating factors, then there must be more to the story than merely removing legal barriers to employment. Meritocracy makes individuals formally equal to pursue certain careers, but it leaves unmitigated the effects of where one actually starts in the race for those careers. Meritocracy, that is, only operates at the point of entry to employment and education opportunities; it remains silent with regard to the story that precedes that point. Yet social class, family background, race and gender can all have an enormous impact on things prior to employment opportunities, such as quality of schooling and levels of educational attainment. For example, two individuals with equal talent for becoming a physician will have remarkably different chances of actually fulfilling that ambition (or, indeed, of even discovering that ambition) depending upon the familial and social backgrounds they hail from. Children of wealthy parentage are more likely to realise their ambition to become doctors than children of poorer parents.[6]

If equality of opportunity is to fulfil its intentions of efficiency and fairness by bringing those with the requisite talent to the relevant qualifications and jobs, then it must seek to correct arbitrariness at an earlier point in the story. As James Fishkin writes of the principle of equality of opportunity:

> According to this principle, I should not be able to enter a hospital ward of newborn infants and predict which strata they will eventually reach merely on the basis of their arbitrary natural characteristics such as their race, sex, ethnic origin, or family background. To the extent that I can reliably make such predictions about a society, it is subject to a serious level of inequality of opportunity.[7]

John Rawls terms this view *fair* equality of opportunity in order to distinguish it from the simple version, and describes it thus.

> The thought here is that positions are to be not only open in a formal sense, but that all should have a fair chance to attain them. Offhand it is not clear what is meant, but we might say that those with similar abilities and skills should have similar life chances. More specifically, assuming that there is a distribution of natural assets, those who are at the same level of talent and ability, and have the same willingness to use them, should have the same prospects of success regardless of their initial place in the social system, that is, irrespective of the income class into which they are born. In all sectors of society there should be roughly equal prospects of culture and achievement for everyone similarly motivated and endowed. The expectations of those with the same abilities and aspirations should not be affected by their social class.[8]

On this view, advantages such as being born into a privileged background are considered as an undeserved benefit because they hinder individuals from competing on a level playing field. In this, they are as arbitrary as, say, skin colour. Fair equality of opportunity advocates compensating individuals for their undeserved disadvantages in the distribution of goods in order to ensure that those with similar talents and abilities (and who are prepared to make the same level of effort) should receive the same level of socio-economic advantage. For example, this might translate into offering better quality education to those from poorer backgrounds. The same is true of the opportunity to influence the democratic process. Whilst our current system often allows the use of greater resources to obtain greater influence, fair equality of opportunity, in respect to political equality, would hold that factors such as wealth, social background, sex and ethnic origin ought not to endow individuals with greater levels of influence than others.

Let us briefly re-enter the world of ICT and outline what this means for the digital divide and levels of access. Given that those who currently have effective access to ICT – at both the domestic and global levels – are advantageously placed in socio-economic and political terms, the solution is to distribute, via various mechanisms, resources in such a way that a situation is engineered where the opportunity for access to ICT is roughly equal. Thus, not only should opportunities to enter the ICT-based labour market be made formally equal, but so too should opportunities for obtaining ICT access and education via institutions such as schools be equalised. That is, these opportunities should not favour those whose social background places them within easy reach of the education for hi-tech employment.

So what policies might promote equality? One obvious type of policy includes licensing and rationing. Such a policy looks at patterns of demand within a market and then tries to adjust that market, making it more expensive to kit oneself out with top-of-the-range stuff while ensuring that the less well off have adequate equipment. So, for certain types of ICT, one might require licences, which will reduce demand (either by increasing prices or by disallowing the purchase of particular items), as well as distributing basic equipment for free (at least to some).

One example of this approach is the French government's online Videotex service (a two-way communications network transferring text to be read on television screens), Minitel, which was rolled out in 1982. It had a lot of points in common with the later Internet, and was intended to be used for online purchases, accessing information (such as stock prices or telephone numbers) and also for informal chat. However, it was a highly centralised service. Terminals were given free to telephone subscribers, with the result that Minitel was seen in a very large number of French households. Other countries that experimented with Videotex, such as Ireland (Minitel) and Canada (AlexTel), tried a less centralised and egalitarian distribution method, relying on the demand side rather than the supply side, with the result that the system never took off in either country.

A second example of such an approach would be a national ICT curriculum, which might also be extended to adult learners. But if all children were taught a demanding curriculum, then that might mitigate, at least to some extent, the effects of inequalities of access to ICT at home. Many of the children who have access to computers at home will of course benefit from routine familiarity with the technology; on the other hand, beyond a certain level they may not actually use it in a very educational way.

A third example is perhaps the most obvious – a government could take over the cable or wireless network and ensure that it is evenly distributed to all its citizens.

It should be noted that the ideal of equality (whether it is applied to opportunities or to any other good) is a comparative ideal. Those who endorse egalitarianism seek to eliminate the gap between individuals (or groups of individuals) along some specified dimension. In this sense, what is at issue is the relative level of advantage that exists between people. The greater the size of the gap, the worse it is, according to egalitarianism. It is simply a bad thing if some people get more than others.

Egalitarians do not always care about equality to the exclusion of everything else. Other considerations might enter the picture, such as the number of beneficiaries of a particular act of distribution, or the size of the benefit. But, for egalitarians in the strictest sense, these are largely secondary considerations. It may, under certain circumstances be permissible to trade equality off with other considerations, but doing so defeats, to a lesser or greater extent, the primary objective of achieving equality. What matters, rather, is narrowing the gap between individuals as much as possible. In terms of equality of opportunity, for example, it might be good that there are more opportunities to be had rather than fewer, but the main aim is that everyone has the same level of opportunities.

In principle, this often looks attractive, but such stark egalitarianism often runs into perverse practical implications. For instance, imagine that the only way of achieving equality of opportunity for access to ICT is to bring everyone's access down to the lowest level. Those who are best off will have their access reduced to the level of the worst off.[9] This does indeed seem perverse. It is what is often termed the *levelling down objection* to equality by economists.

Yet, if we are committed to such a view of equality, then we are committed to saying that, in one way at least, this must be a good thing. An analogy might help us to appreciate fully the perversity of such a position. Imagine that half of a population is born blind whilst the other half is born sighted. Then the principle of equality says that putting out the eyes of the sighted so as to make everyone equal (albeit blind) would, in one way, be a change for the better. The reason for this counterintuitive result is that the ideal of equality is, as we have seen, a relational ideal: what is objected to is the gap between persons, not the level that certain persons are at. Hence, if we can make people equal by putting out the eyes of the sighted, or if an Act of God reduces the better off to the level of the worst off, then this is something that would be welcomed, on at least one level, by egalitarians.

> A man walks into a bar, orders a beer, and on tasting it cries, 'This is awful!'
>
> 'What do you mean?' asks the bartender. 'This beer is made with very shiny, very quiet equipment. It's brewed in a beautiful part of the Black Forest in Germany. The workers are very happy while they make it, and very well dressed I might add. The aroma during brewing is exquisite. What's not to like?'
>
> 'But it tastes terrible,' says the man. 'Don't you care about your customers?'
>
> 'Of course I do,' the bartender replies, 'but they all like different beers, and this is the only one that pleases them all equally, and we wanted to be fair.'
>
> 'You mean people actually like this swill?' says the man.
>
> 'No,' says the bartender, proudly. 'Nobody likes it at all, and so no one likes it more than anyone else.'
>
> Finishing his beer, the man is impressed. 'In that case,' he says excitedly, 'pour me another!'[10]

The obvious reaction here is to object on the grounds that, in claiming that equality matters, we are not claiming that equality is the only thing that matters. Equality is not the only value in our moral armoury. Such moral pluralism might, for example, claim that utility also matters (the size of the benefit and the number of people who will benefit), so that we should aim not only for equal distribution, but for equal distribution at the highest possible level. Thus, putting out the eyes of the sighted might in one way be better, but can be rejected because of the existence of some other value (e.g. the invio-lability of a person).

There is, however, a significant problem with this type of moral pluralism. Such a claim amounts to saying that blinding the sighted would be acceptable if it were not for the fact that another moral principle happened to be sufficiently weighty to intervene. It just happens to be the case in this situation that another principle clashes with equality. This is not only an odd way of looking at the moral world – that moral values can sometimes lead to obnoxious outcomes if other values do not, fortunately, conflict with them to stop them happening – it also does not remove the initial objection.[11] Egali-tarians would still say that levelling down is in one way (at least) better. But we believe that blinding the sighted, or Acts of God that reduce the better off to the level of the worst off, are in no way good news. There is absolutely nothing good in levelling down.

Lest this is thought to be purely an academic objection to equality, it is worth noting that the idea of levelling down resources in the real world is not that far-fetched. It is easy to see how policy directives could operate on this assumption. For instance, the development of new, useful but extremely expensive technology which might, for example, give those who could afford it a much greater opportunity to exploit other resources could be made unavailable to the general public out of a desire to maintain equality of opportunity. This would, in effect, hold everyone at a lower level of opportunity, even in the face of a distribution that would make some better off in terms of opportunities whilst rendering no one worse off. As economists have noted, this is an extremely inefficient way of proceeding.[12]

Sufficiency

A different view of what 'universal' access to ICT might mean is ensuring that everyone exceeds a certain minimum level of access.

The point of public policies, in this sense, is to make sure that everyone is on the right side of that threshold. It doesn't matter where they are on the right side, just so long as they are on it. So, there can be disparities (even large disparities) in levels of access, but this is neither unjust nor unfair so long as everyone has a sufficient level of access to be able to achieve the ends we have attributed to ICT access and use. Social inclusion is satisfied by providing sufficient resources.[13]

In such a system, a government should not ordinarily assume responsibility for achieving sufficient access if such access would occur anyway. For example, it should not merely replace with a centralised system the decisions that most (if not all) citizens would have made in a free market situation anyway. So, for instance, it might be decided in some hypothetical future that access to mobile phones was essential for citizens (or some specific group of citizens) to play their proper part in the life of the community and the nation. There might be a number of reasons for this: they are important means of security, making calls for help possible in certain situations; they might be used to vote in elections or referendums; they might be used by parents to track the whereabouts of their children; they might be used by the government to track the whereabouts of everyone; important governmental edicts might be circulated by texting; and so on. So it might be deemed important by policy makers that everyone should have a mobile phone. On the other hand, the operation of the mobile telephony market has itself created a pattern of very widespread distribution that we might imagine would only increase by the time of this hypothetical future. So that future government might decide that it need take no action because the distributional problem was solved easily by 'natural' economic processes.

Other goods might well *not* arise from an unfettered market. An obvious example is training. Most governments provide ICT equipment in their publicly run schools that enables youngsters to get used to ICT, although the market, again, seems to be providing them with the actual equipment (for instance, a recent survey in Canada showed that only 6% of students between Grades 6 and 10 claimed not to have a computer in their house[14]). However, their home usage of computers might be driven by desires that may or may not have educational side-effects, such as playing games, joining chatrooms or buying things. A government training programme might well include rather more educationally relevant matters, such as being able to discover information online about arbitrary topics or being able to distinguish between information that is reliable and that which is not. But the government here, as opposed to the egalitarian position discussed earlier, would only be concerned with providing the basic training that it estimates everyone should have; it would not be concerned with correcting imbalances where certain children, through the luck of having wealthy parents, are more able computer users than their poorer fellows.

Another potential way that the government could try to influence the distribution of cyberspace is to improve the ability of the population to join it. So, for instance, it could try to improve the roll-out of broadband connections, perhaps by cajoling telecommunications firms to provide the hardware for free, by providing tax breaks or low-interest loans for firms who invest in the market, or by using similar measures to try to blanket a country with WiFi connections. Alternatively, it may try to even up connections across the country. In general, there will be richer pickings for telecommunications firms in cities whose economies are service-based, as opposed to centres of manufacturing or rural and remote regions, so a government might focus on improving connections in such relatively deprived regions. It could do this by, say, bundling licences to run broadband connections, so that a licence to serve a lucrative city carried with it responsibilities to connect with rural areas too.

These methods for providing ICT support differ from the egalitarian methods discussed above in that they try to increase access only for those whose level of access is below some determined level; they do not try to even things up any more than that. There is, for many people, an intuitive feeling that this is a better way of going about things than the simple egalitarian principle.

However, numerous problems beset the sufficiency principle. First, specifying accurately what would count as a sufficient level is often a difficult task. Moreover, it would be subject to constant fluctuation and change, depending upon such things as new technological developments, prices and proliferation. At an epistemic level this would be a Herculean task. Even if it could be done, other problems remain. Setting sufficient access at a low level would imply that inequalities above that threshold have no moral significance whatsoever. This is an intuitively rather strange, if not perverse, idea, especially for those with egalitarian leanings who are looking for a more defensible principle than equality.

By contrast, setting the threshold high can also have odd consequences. For instance, one possible outcome is that resources will be directed to raise those closest to the threshold as a priority. All things being equal, it is easier to move those across the threshold who are only just below it than to invest more resources to help those who have further to go to travel across the sufficiency line. A numerical illustration helps here. Imagine that 30% of people in a given society are deemed to fall below what is accepted as a sufficient level of some imaginary resource. A budget of $30 million is allocated by the government to alleviate this problem. Policy designers come up with two possible policies. Policy A will target the very poorest members of the community and move them across the threshold. But policy A is very expensive per person, so $30million will only reduce the level that falls below the threshold to 25%. Policy B, by contrast, targets those who are very close to the sufficiency threshold. Because the target group is so close to the threshold, Policy B is less expensive per person to implement – which in turn means that more people can be helped. Policy B will therefore reduce the number of people who fall below the sufficiency line to 15%. Clearly Policy B shifts more people to a satisfactory level, and this is one important consideration. There is clearly something odd about ignoring those who need the resources most, but nothing of this concern enters the sufficiency view. Again, this seems to go against common sense. The whole point of stipulating a minimum sufficient level is to raise those who are worst off to an acceptable position, not to relegate their position down the list of immediate concerns.

Furthermore, the ICT industry is driven by entrepreneurial innovation. It used to be that government scientists were in charge of computer research, and the main innovations were in algorithms and programming languages. Computers – as commonly portrayed in 1960s films and TV series – were the size of wardrobes, and would line the walls of laboratories. Then large corporations, such as IBM, got involved and eventually took over, and computers became easier to use, thanks to better languages and interfaces, but there was still a big hierarchical model whereby a single computer doled out time to a number of terminals connected to it. That central computer could only be afforded, and maintained, by large firms. But the rise of Microsoft and Apple unleashed a fiercely competitive industry where computers are now tiny and powerful, embedded in all sorts of devices, and quite stylish; the response to market forces has been unarguably beneficial to the individual user. By insisting on certain distributions of software, hardware or know-how, though, governments can distort the market for them, and cause resources to be diverted from where there is genuine demand to where some people think they ought to go. This is inevitable in any industry in which a government intervenes to ensure just distribution, and it is of course a political question as to how the balance is to be struck. But it is worth pointing out here that the risks of stifling market-driven innovation are fairly high, in ICT and other technological industries.[5] We will return to this point in the final chapter.

Prioritarianism

The ideals of equality and sufficiency are, it seems, beset by a number of difficulties. Nevertheless, they both capture at least some of the concerns that usually motivate attempts at social engineering. But an alternative principle needs to be developed to overcome the counterintuitive results of the levelling down objection faced by equality, and to incorporate the concern for the fate of those worst off.

When objecting to inequalities, individuals often give the reason that there is something wrong when some have greater (undeserved) benefits than others. Yet such reasoning is often a response not to the inequality itself, but rather to the fact that some people have too few of these benefits.[16] When we consider those who are substantially worse off than ourselves, it is the circumstances of their situation that cause our moral distress. What underlies this distress is not a quantitative difference (as though what matters is that they have less than us), but a qualitative condition.

It is vital to keep this distinction between the relative levels of inequality and the conditional quality separate. Unlike equality, we need a non-comparative principle. The gap between the better off and the worst off is not, in itself, the important factor in questions of distribution; the worst off receive priority regardless of their relative position. We can call this the *principle of priority*.[17] A concern for benefiting the worst off is seen as part of egalitarianism, yet prioritarianism and benefiting people equally are quite distinct ideals. Often prioritarian claims might be made in terms of comparisons between groups or people (which accounts for the common conflation of equality and priority), but this does not render priority synonymous with equality. As philosopher Derek Parfit writes:

> People at higher altitudes find it harder to breathe. Is this because they are higher up than other people? In one sense, yes. But they would find it just as hard to breathe even if there

were no other people who were lower down. In the same way, on the Priority View, benefits to the worst off matter more, but that is only because these people are at a lower *absolute* level. It is irrelevant that these people are worse off *than others*. Benefits to them would matter just as much even if there were no others who were better off.[18]

Thus, despite any terminological slippage, the distinction between the idea of giving priority to the worst off because they do not have sufficient and the idea of aiding some because they stand in an inferior position with regard to others should not be conflated. In short, in prioritarianism the gap between the better off and the worst off is not morally salient as it is for egalitarianism. This does not mean that the reduction of inequality cannot have instrumental value for the prioritarian. Indeed, one method of prioritising the need of the worst off is to redistribute to them from the better off – in many cases equality and priority will coincide – but in so doing we do not view equality as intrinsically valuable. Similarly, if benefiting the worst off meant increasing the gap between the two groups, then this too would be a legitimate prioritarian move.

Note that this might well be key to any successful application of a principle of justice to ICT. If it could be shown that market forces will drive the innovations and the reductions in price that will ultimately benefit everyone in society – as free-market advocates claim – then that is consistent with prioritarianism. But equally, the prioritarian may get impatient if the claimed benefits of markets do not emerge swiftly enough.

Priority does not, therefore, fall prey to the charge of inefficiency or levelling down that besets egalitarianism. Because prioritarianism does not hold inequality as bad in itself, it is not forced to admit that reducing the better off to the level of the worst off would in any way be better. If the worst off are in their position through no fault of their own, then they may well have a legitimate claim to be raised up. Here equality and priority are likely to coincide. But what the worst off do not have is a claim to reduce those above them to their level.

Distributing cyberspace fairly

We have seen how ICT comes in myriad forms, and how it is essential for several different areas of life and endeavour (chapter 2); this is why we think that some sort of fair or just distribution of ICT is essential (as we argued in chapter 3). This chapter has characterised our understanding of 'fairness' in a little more detail. A prioritarian method of distributing cyberspace seems to be a more appropriate principle than those connected to ideas of equality. But such an 'intu-ition' is hardly solid ground upon which to recommend a course of action with regard to ICT policy. Prioritarianism may seem more appro-priate than equality as a guiding principle for addressing the digital divide, but is it?

There are at least two issues that need addressing in order to arrive at a firm answer to this question. The first is how we actually decide – and not just intuit – on the superiority of one course of action, programme or principle over another. In other words, how we determine what is, in actual fact, fair? The second is that any such suggested solution will, at this stage, be woefully incomplete. Because of the many ways in which ICT affects us and the several different ways in which we use it, questions of how to distribute it or how to use it fairly will depend on what technologies are around to distribute, how one can increase access to them and what access means in that particular context. Context is all important here. Providing suggestions for the myriad of problems raised by ICT – and not just the digital divide – will depend upon how these potential solutions handle the different contexts in which they are expected to operate. Clearly, then, the two issues are interrelated. The second will be the focus of the rest of the book. In the final section of this chapter we want to say something about the first.

When faced with competing claims to social resources, or when thinking about possible social responsibilities to provide those resources, how are we to assess the merits and drawbacks of different proposals? Our intuitions and our personal circumstances may not be a reliable guide to making such a choice. If we are talented, have a good education and the potential to earn vast swathes of cash in the unfettered market, then we are likely to prefer a social system or set of rules and policies that allow us to profit from our talents and background. Similarly, if we hail from a less affluent background, have a poor education and little marketable talent, then we might well think that equality in all its forms is what suits us best.

But here's the problem – when thinking in this way we are literally thinking about what suits *us* best. We are selecting principles on the basis of our own interests; we are being partial. As we noted in the Introduction, however, the political space – indeed, the very point of maintaining a functional political sphere or set of institutions – goes far beyond our mere self-interest, and necessarily so. If we are to perpetuate our political space, then selecting its organising principles according to self-interest will not get us very far. Maintaining a public sphere requires cooperative action, and if we only view things in terms of naked self-interest we will be unlikely to achieve this.

Does this mean that when we think about these sorts of questions we need to reason in a perfectly impartial manner, as though our personal attachments and concerns are irrelevant? Fortunately, not. To do so would be extremely demanding of individuals, as well as unrealistic. It would create a complete disjuncture between our private and our public (political) interests. The worth of any 'solutions' or principles that came out of such a process would be minimal. Partiality is not necessarily a bad thing, though it can be. Who, for instance, could reasonably object to the partiality that parents show in loving their own children more than they love the children of other parents? Indeed, how could the activity of parents reading bedtime stories to their own children (but not to the children of other parents) be thought, from any reasonable view, to be illegitimate even though such action gives their children a head start on children that do not receive bedtime stories?[19] Yet the parent who murders her child's competitor for a place on the school cheerleading team goes, without doubt, beyond the limits of legitimate partiality. There are just some things you cannot do for your children. Judging the rules by thinking about whether they suit you is to apply the wrong test, it is the wrong kind of partiality.

The question, then, is one of how much partiality or self-interest should be deemed legitimate when deciding on political matters. What we require is an unbiased method for thinking about how biased we should be allowed to be when deliberating and deciding about the rules. We have already put much of this method of deliberation in place in this chapter, albeit in a non-explicit form. We now need to spell out this framework of deliberation in more detail.

Recall that, earlier in the discussion of meritocracy and equality of opportunity, we noted that one of the motivating factors acceptable to nearly all parties – even those less inclined to social engineering – was that allocating social goods on the basis of arbitrary features of individuals, such as their sex, place in the social order or skin colour, was morally dubious. These features of individuals are entirely irrelevant when it comes to such questions and they are things over which individuals can be said to possess no responsibility. Allocating resources (jobs, educational opportunities) on the basis of things for which someone is not responsible is unfair.

Once we accept this very minimal and reasonable premise, we are able to build a more rigorous framework for thinking about wider ethical and political questions. This framework should, by extension, be one where the rules for distributing and utilising goods should be justifiable without reference to these morally arbitrary features. It should, in other words, be impersonal. So, imagine that you don't know certain things about yourself, such as your position in the social hierarchy, the level of education that you have or the affluence of your familial background. Imagine you don't even know things like your gender, race or religion. If you exclude these things then you are less likely to make a decision about the political rules of your society on the basis of your own interests. If someone asks you what the rules should be – how, given what we know about the social and economic impacts of the new technologies, access to ICT resources should be distributed, who should pay for them and who should control them – you are able to ignore any factors influencing your judgement that derive from thinking about how those rules would apply to you. Instead, you think about these questions impersonally.

The usefulness of this approach is manifold.[20] The test for judging a set of rules fair is that people who are ignorant of how they would be affected by them personally would choose them. It may turn out that a set of rules does indeed benefit you as an individual, but this is not why you chose them; indeed, you would have endorsed the rules even if they turned out not to be beneficial to you personally.

An analogy should make this clear. Academic exams are typically anonymised before marking. This is done for a reason: to ensure fairness. On a personal level, university lecturers no doubt like many of their students and hope that they do well (and dislike some too). But if they were to know whose exam paper they were marking this might, even if they intended to be as fair-minded as possible, have some influence over the grade they awarded. Non-anonymised exam scripts introduce the possibility of the wrong kind of partiality. That someone displays characteristics that you dislike – such as aggressiveness or extreme self-interest – is irrelevant to a judgement about their academic ability (though it might be relevant in other situations, such as interviews for jobs in the care industries). Making judgements about exam grades impersonal ensures fairness and impartiality by removing information that is irrelevant to the situation.

So we have a basic test or framework for thinking through political issues. It is one that formalises the basic idea that arbitrary personal characteristics or details should not form the basis for choosing a set of public rules that affect everyone in our society. Those who care not just about their own well-being, but also about living under rules that treat others fairly, should endorse rules that can be justified from this impersonal standpoint.

What does this tell us about such things as equality, sufficiency and priority? Does this framework lend support to our intuitive defence of one over the others? Much of the detail is yet to be worked out, but we can see that this method of reasoning does lend some support to prioritarianism. If we are thinking about the distribution of some resource in the absence of information about our social position, natural talents, familial background and so forth, then we are likely to be risk-averse. If we stand a chance of being badly off, then we will want to make sure that as few people as possible are badly off, in order to minimise that chance. Does this mean we would choose equality? No, not really. We need not be that risk averse. We might accept that people should be allowed to benefit from their disproportionate natural talents but still think that those who do not have such talents should not suffer because of it (just in case we are numbered amongst the latter). Or we might think that it would be irrational to hold everyone back for the sake of equality if an unequal position made the worst off better off (again, because it might be us benefiting from it).

All this is fairly abstract, though. Our positions might change when we start to consider other factors, such as the existence of a whole set of other people outside our own societies who are even worse off in terms of ICT resources than ourselves. At least, however, we would have the impersonal framework to help us steer through this complex terrain. To make these ideas more concrete, in the next four chapters we look at some more focused aspects of ICT use, in order to demonstrate that the ways in which ICT can help people's lives vary widely according to the context. We will look at four areas. We will begin by looking at the international dimension, and consider the disparities and injustices between nations as the world globalises (chapter 5). Then we will focus on the politics of an individual nation, looking at the general principles governing a democracy (chapter 6), and the ways in which technology can aid government and governance (chapter 7). Finally, we shall focus on the ways in which ICT can threaten an individual's privacy (chapter 8). Of course ICT has big social effects in more contexts than this, but these are four important and significant areas where it is arguable that the political issues have yet to receive the major public airing they perhaps deserve. Only when we have seen ICT in political action can we come to reconsider the distributional questions that we have been addressing here (chapter 9).

5:⟩
Globalisation, Poverty, Priorities

Small world

Having established a framework for analysis, we now begin a more detailed look at the opportunities presented and problems caused by ICT. These opportunities and problems are visible from many different perspectives; we will begin at the international level.

The rise of the term 'globalisation' to a central position in public consciousness over the last decade has been nothing short of meteoric. It is near impossible to read a daily paper without finding some mention of the phenomenon. Government policy documents, academic writings, electronic media – all are replete with references to globalisation.[1] That the world has become significantly closer, smaller or more unified in all manner of ways is a thought that looms large in the background of contemporary conceptions of our existence. Globalisation is enlisted to explain various features of the changing world, and is employed as a description of the turbulent times in which we live. Critical to the process of globalisation is ICT. Indeed, ICT forms a necessary component of the onward march of globalisation. Without the technological developments of recent decades the much-trumpeted closer union of national economies, politics and cultures would be impossible. In short, technology makes globalisation possible. It may even make it inevitable.

Yet, as we noted earlier, the global ICT picture is an uneven one. ICT is scattered across the globe, not spread evenly. The concentration of ICT resources and know-how in some geographical locations, and its virtual absence in others, has given rise to the concept of a global digital divide, which has knock-on consequences in terms of economic and social exclusion. Technology and wealth are closely related. Unsurprisingly there is a close relationship between poverty and access to ICT. The purpose of this chapter is to examine the concepts of globalisation, technology and the global digital divide, and to track the relationships between them, probing and questioning these ideas – are they too simple, too glib? – whilst building a picture of the social impacts of technology as well as the shape of things to come.

What is globalisation?

Surprisingly, the actual meaning of the word 'globalisation' is relatively unclear. There is a general feeling that the world is getting smaller, but how can we cash that metaphor? Is there an increase of interdependence – that is, are people more affected by decisions taken elsewhere? Or is there a decline in cultural diversity? Some people scent American imperialism, others an ideological mono-culture – capitalism running riot. Still others look to the decline of the traditional nation state: at the top level, many nations are pooling sovereignty, most notably countries of the European Union; at the lowest, many states have failed, such as Somalia, Liberia and Afghan-istan. There is a sizeable constituency of people who are just against it, whatever *it* may be. Indeed, for the more hysterical critics, *it* is everything they don't like.

For instance, in one terrible incident in 2004, nineteen illegal Chinese immigrants to the United Kingdom, picking cockles from a beach, were drowned by the sudden flow of the tide. They were working for wages that were tiny and exploitative, from the point of view of the rich West. The provision of health and safety measures seems to have been minimal. The workers were unable to read warning signs. And, as a final horrific irony, some of them seem to have hidden from the rescue teams whom they believed would deport them.

This dreadful event was oddly taken up as evidence of the evils of globalisation.

> The sordid underbelly of free-market globalisation is on display at that sandbank in Morecambe Bay. Working people are being uprooted from their communities across the world by the unchecked movement of capital and brought to Britain in order to provide cheap labour.[2]

So here, the evidence of globalisation is merely that workers from one country are working in another. Hmmm. The author seems to ignore the fact that the workers were illegal. The system tried, unsuccessfully, to prevent the import of these workers. Had they, and their gangmasters, obeyed the law, they would still be alive. Isn't the point about globalisation that divisions between nations and communities shrink? In which case, evidence for globalisation would be that it was possible for Chinese workers to move to Britain legally, and work there for as long as they liked, before returning home – or moving on to another country. What actually happens is that governments the world over attempt to prevent people moving freely from A to B. Genuine globalisation would remove the social interstices in which people-smugglers thrive.

So the author of the anti-globalisation article is completely incorrect. Were there true globalisation, the cockle pickers would have been working legally. They would not have had to pay giant premiums to people-smugglers to get them to Britain. They would not have felt obliged to flee from their rescuers. If we are to understand globalisation, we had better be able to think more rationally about what phenomena are involved.

Anti-globaliser George Monbiot is not opposed to globalisation per se. But he does see capitalism at its worst, and most undemocratic, at work.

Corporate and financial globalization, designed and executed by a minority seeking to enhance its wealth and power, is compelling the people it oppresses to acknowledge their commonality. Globalization is establishing a single, planetary class interest, as the same forces and the same institutions threaten the welfare of the people of all nations. It is ripping down the cultural and linguistic barriers which have divided us. By breaking the social bonds which sustained local communities, it destroys our geographical loyalties. Already, it has forced states to begin to relinquish nationhood, by building economic units – trading blocs – at the level of the continent or hemisphere.[3]

This account sees globalisation as separable – economic globalisation, in his account, leads to cultural and linguistic globalisation. This is surely right; we can imagine integration between peoples happening in different spheres and sectors. On the other side of the argument, free trade theorist Jagdish Bhagwati concurs.

What *is* the globalization that is in contention? Globalization can mean many things ... Economic globalization constitutes integration of national economies into the international economy through trade, direct foreign investment (by corporations and multinationals), short-term capital flows, international flows of workers and humanity generally, and flows of technology ...

Economic globalization is the favored target of many of the critics of globalization. It is distinct from other aspects of globalization, such as cultural globalization (which is affected ... by economic globalization) and communications (which is among the factors that cause the deepening of economic globalization).[4]

Each of these theorists, one anti-, one pro-, seems to see an implicit three-layer model. At the top, there is cultural and political integration – the increasing lack of distinctiveness in our lives, as indexed by geographical, religious or linguistic space.[5] This tends to be seen as increased Americanisation – McDonald's and Starbucks take the flak in Britain. So anti-globalisers who focus on this aspect of it tend to merge into more traditional anti-Americanism.

But it is important to keep these things separate. Sometimes anti-globalisation is a by-product of a deeper anti-Americanism. French Gaullists resist the march of globalisation and global economic integration; they promote *la Francophonie*, subsidise French movies and shun Hollywood. But what we have seen for the last couple of centuries, not least in the person of current French president Jacques Chirac, is rather a jealousy of American power, and the desire to replace it with equivalent European power (steered from Paris, of course).[6] So the anti-globalisation implicit in Gaullism is dependent on the Americans being those with most global reach; the establishment of the EU as a counterweight to American hegemony – Chirac's explicit foreign policy – would legitimise global integration once more. A world of people sipping fine Burgundies and savouring foie gras would look a lot better, from this point of view, than the current one where slurping Coke and scoffing Big Macs is more common.

We also need to distinguish between different methods of achieving global integration. If we focus on the policies of the most controversial politician of our generation, President George W. Bush, we see a sympathy towards neo-conservative ideas of spreading democracy through benighted areas. Bush, and the thinkers behind him, believe that the terrible problems of discontent in the Middle East, for example, are caused by oppressive governments frustrating the will of the people, who are radicalised by the frustration. Anti-Americanism will follow, on this account, from the US's sponsorship of many of these governments, most notably Saudi Arabia and Egypt. So Bush does wish to spread American power to facilitate the democratisation of the Middle East, but he is certainly not in favour of integration. His trade policies have been positively protectionist, and have been largely responsible for undermining the World Trade Organisation's Doha Round. Furthermore, he refuses to surrender US sovereignty in a number of areas, ignoring substantial international consensus on the Kyoto climate change treaty or the International Criminal Court, for example. Bush may or may not be an imperialist, but he is not a globaliser in this sense.

Thirdly, it is not only America which has global reach. For example, sociologist Olivier Roy has written of globalised Islam. One Muslim in three now lives as a minority in a non-Muslim country. Globalisation has created a new religiosity which, for many, supersedes established versions of Islam that have developed within individual cultures, with all the compromise and flexibility that such embedded development entails. The spread of Islam across the globe has blurred traditional connections between religion, society and territory.[7] Globalisation does not just mean the advance of America.

The second layer of globalisation is economic globalisation, the convergence of the world's economies. Both Monbiot and Bhagwati, from their different perspectives, believe that economic integration will tend to cause cultural integration. Furthermore, economic integration seems to imply the spread of capitalism; capitalism, it is assumed, will drive out alternative methods of running the economy.

The links between economic and cultural globalisation are no doubt not that simple, as political scientist Amy Chua reminds us.[8] She points out that, in many societies, those who do best from the spread of free markets are often ethnic minorities; free markets can lead to increasing inequality and violent backlashes from impoverished indigenous populations against immigrant traders who are seen, however unfairly, as 'doing well' out of the disruption. Economic integration can provoke cultural and political counter-reactions.

The third layer is an infrastructural substrate – the influence of technology, specifically ICT. It is this that drives much of the economic convergence. As our understanding of money has become ever-more theoretical, we now use computers to store it; money becomes 1s and 0s in a computer's memory. It is information. And ICT can transfer information around the globe in the twinkling of an eye. Transport costs of more tangible goods have declined rapidly. Communications are now trivial, with satellites replacing cables.

So improvements in technology drive convergence of economic factors, which helps remove barriers – geographical and psychological – between cultures and peoples. We can argue as to whether this is an increase in democracy or oppression. It is undeniably an increase in liberty – we can certainly do more things. Anti-globalisers in this sense wish to restrict the liberty of others to communicate and trade. They would argue that such liberty impinges upon the lives of others in unacceptable ways, arguments that are traditionally found on the left wing, but which also surface on the right, for instance in the speeches of Pat Buchanan and Enoch Powell.[9]

Although integration at the cultural and political levels causes both concern and joy, it is economic integration that is taken by most of its advocates and critics as the most important indicator of globalisation. As one of the leading academic observers on the network society writes:

> If globalisation is widely acknowledged as a fundamental feature of our time, it is essentially because of the emergence of global financial markets. Indeed, to say that capital is globalised (or, more accurately, globally interconnected) in real time is not an incidental remark in a capitalist economy. While the process of financial globalisation has long historical roots and has gradually expanded over the past quarter of a century, its acceleration can be traced back to the late 1980s. To select, rather arbitrarily, a symbolic event, I would suggest the beginning of this new era was signalled by the City of London's 'Big Bang' on 27 October 1987, when the

deregulation of capital and securities markets occurred. This is to emphasise that deregulation and liberalisation of financial trading were the crucial factors in spurring globalisation, allowing capital mobility between different segments of the financial industry and around the world, with fewer restrictions and a global view of investment opportunities.[10]

Economic globalisation is the stuff of debate. The technological developments that underpin it tend not to be so controversial. The net benefits of the transport revolution are the most disputed, as the environmental effects of, for instance, increased air travel are being felt more widely. But the ICT revolution that has occurred has been less discussed.

It was thought, during the boom of the final years of the twentieth century, that computers would change the economy forever. Yeah, right. The new millennium celebrations were followed by an almighty hangover as the stock market crashed and the productivity gains from the new knowledge industries were put in rather more sober perspective. Ironically, it was the mechanisms of capitalism that exposed the pretensions of the Internet entrepreneurs.

We should also try to avoid sliding into a glib determinism, assuming that technology will march on willy-nilly. The deployment of technology does not suddenly open borders. Even the anarchic Internet is very closely regulated by oppressive regimes such as China (which in effect runs its own giant Intranet) and Saudi Arabia (where Internet users report about 500 sites per day to the censors[11]). Technology certainly lowers the costs of transactions. It also increases access to other cultures. It will therefore tend to integrate peoples and aid globalisation. But it can also be used to reverse the process. China's regulation of the Internet is aided by state-of-the-art firewall technology designed to increase computer security. And Islamic neo-fundamentalism spreads virulently in the often-febrile online space, as we will discuss in more detail in the next chapter.

The links between technology, economic globalisation and cultural globalisation are not as clear cut as many would have it.

ICT and globalisation

Although the exact causal link between ICT and the different types of globalisation is not entirely clear, ICT is what we might term the mechanism or medium through which economic interdependence and integration operate. Without recent technological advances the liberalisation of markets and the rapid growth of international trade and investment would have been impossible. This link between economic, social and political upheaval on the one hand and technological innovation and development on the other, as portrayed by ICT and globalisation, is nothing new. Karl Marx, the original commentator on social structure and revolution, observed the intrinsic link between technology and economics nigh on two hundred years ago. Marx's insights are particularly striking given that the capitalist period he was commenting on was still in embryonic form.[12]

According to Marx, the level of technological development in a society dictates its economic form (what he termed the 'economic base' of a society), and this, in turn, determines the shape or type of its social and political structure. The very great differences between the old feudal system and the emerging capitalist system – in terms of which classes were dominant and subordinate, what freedoms, opportunities and so forth existed – were to be explained in terms of the different levels of technology (and who owned or controlled those technologies) in these two societies. Marx famously remarked that the capitalist system would have been impossible without the Spinning Jenny. Before the invention of the Spinning Jenny – that is, before the mechanised production of cloth – the process of spinning and weaving cotton into cloth was performed on the basis of a relatively small-scale cottage industry. Moreover, spinning and weaving were skilled jobs. This meant that the quantity of cloth produced was low and its price correspondingly high. The poor were priced out of the market, unable to afford the clothes they made.

The mechanisation of textile production changed all of this. Unskilled or low-skilled machine operatives replaced craftsmen and craftswomen, pushing down the relatively high wages that their expertise commanded, and increasing profits. The new processes were astoundingly faster. Vast quantities of cloth could be produced. This had the effect of driving down prices. So, although those who lost out through the introduction of technology shouted very loudly (understandably), in fact many more people benefited: the unskilled workers, for whom there were plenty of new jobs; the poor generally, who could now afford the mechanically produced clothes; and the new rising class of entrepreneurs. This effect of technology – making routine what was previously the preserve of expertise – is often unsettling yet generally socially beneficial over the medium to long term. New technologies have been responsible for virtually all the growth in the Western world in the last two hundred years.[13]

Technology also meant that surplus goods were produced which could be exported overseas to exotic destinations such as India and beyond, where massively prosperous markets were just waiting to be tapped. On top of this invention, then, rose a whole system of international trade and employment, and a corresponding social and political edifice (one that was created by and perpetuated this state of affairs).

Incidentally, this also provides the beginnings of an answer to our earlier question of whether recent developments in ICT really constitute a revolution. For Marx, revolution occurs at many different strata and substrata. The most visible, quick and often bloody manifestation is political revolution – the changing of the system of political power and control. But political revolution is carried on the back of a broader social and economic revolution, and, in turn, technological developments that provide new ways of meeting human needs and preferences. These latter manifestations of revolution often occur over a protracted period of time, which may make them less obvious to the casual observer. If a revolution in ICT is truly underway, then it will drive significant changes at the social and political level. So, on this Marxist reading of recent history, the three-layer model of globalisation, from technology to economic structures to cultural and political structures, does look potentially revolutionary.

Much of Marx's view about these matters is now discredited. This is largely because he held a particularly stringent, unidirectional view of how technology determines economic and social structures. The balance of academic opinion on this matter is now strongly tilted against this type of strict technological determinism and in favour of a more balanced, reciprocal model of influence between social structures, and economic and technological fundamentals.[14] However, even if we reject Marx's extreme deterministic view, the kernel of truth in his insight remains undamaged: technological innovation and economic (and political) change are closely interwoven. The direction of causality may not be as clear cut as Marx had opined – it may be bi-directional in that they are mutually reinforcing – but their interdependence is beyond question.

ICT as a mechanism for globalisation is crucial. As Castells writes:

[The] extraordinary growth of tradable financial value is possible only because of the use of advanced mathematical models, made operational by powerful computer systems, fed with and constantly adjusted by information transmitted electronically from all over the world. Domestic deregulation, liberalisation of trans-border transactions, financial wizardry and new information technology have succeeded in mobilising potential sources for investment from everywhere to everywhere, and from whatever to whenever.[15]

Or, as Simon Jeffery explains:

So how does the globalised market work? It is modern communications that make it possible; for the British service sector to deal with its customers through a call centre in India, or for a sportswear manufacturer to design its products in Europe, make them in south-east Asia and sell them in North America.[16]

The effects of technological innovation on globalisation are fourfold. First, there are improvements in transport and financial instruments. Secondly, there is the improvement of communications. Thirdly, we see productivity increases in information processing. And fourthly, we have also seen the technologising of finance.

Improvements in transport – specifically the lowering of the costs of getting goods from A to B – have been very influential, though they are beyond the scope of this book. But, in passing, we should note that cheap air travel, the development of the container industry and other innovations such as refrigeration mean that even highly perishable goods can be dug up out of African soil and served on European dinner tables before they are ruined. Thanks to intermodal containers (i.e. containers that can be transported by lorry, ship or rail), goods that used to have to be unloaded from lorries, warehoused on the docks, then loaded into ships – and the process reversed at the other end – now go straight from ship to lorry (this innovation also helped smash the power of longshoreman unions, and cut the opportunities for theft[17]). Much is made of the advantages in low labour costs that India or China, say, have over the European Union or the United States, but if the costs of getting the goods to the EU or US markets are too high, such advantages are cancelled out.

Furthermore, the commercial world has changed. A hundred years ago, most international trade was in raw materials, foodstuffs or processed commodities such as steel – heavy, bulky and costly to transport. But now finished manufactures dominate trade – and their value is unrelated to their size or weight. So transport costs as a proportion of the cost of bringing goods to market have plummeted.

On the financial side, new instruments such as mercantile insurance and futures or derivatives markets take much of the risk out of trade in goods over long distances. Reduction of risk of course means reduction of profit, but equally potential losses are much smaller, which matters a lot more if we want capitalism to spread wealth around, rather than concentrating it in small, privileged sectors.

ICT is important for these secondary industries too. For instance, derivatives markets can get fiendishly complex. Suppose you are selling a good (potatoes, say). You plant a field of potatoes now, while the market price is at some level $X. But when you harvest and sell the potatoes some months later, the price will be at a different level, $Y. If $X < Y$, then all is well – you make more money than you may have anticipated. But if $X > Y$, then you lose. The uncertainty of the future increases the risks of growing and selling potatoes. So what you can do, to hedge the risk and reduce the uncertainty, is to sell the field of potatoes when you plant it for a guaranteed price. This is called a 'futures' market; you are not selling potatoes, but potato futures. If the price of potatoes falls while they are growing, then you gain; if it rises, then whoever you sold the futures to benefits. Futures markets are so-called 'derivatives', in that the market is not in any actual consumable good or service, but is derived from such a market.

All well and good; any commodity that takes time to make or grow can determine a futures market. But futures themselves are also marketable. Potato futures, bought at sowing time, can also be traded until harvesting – their prices can go up or down too. Which means that they can also be hedged – if there are enough buyers, you can, in effect, trade in potato futures futures. A derivative is an agreement to buy an asset at a fixed time in the future at a fixed price; a derivative is itself such an asset, and so you can go into agreements to buy derivatives themselves at a fixed time and at a fixed price. And so on and so on. Each derivative, because it is tradable, can lead to another derivative market, and this can go on indefinitely, which is where the fiendish complexity comes from. And big number-crunching computers can be used to spot minute fluctuations in markets – fluctuations or irregularities that may be very small, but which can be significant if the investment is very large. A difference of 0.01% does not sound much, but if you have invested $10,000,000, that is still $1000, which is better than a poke in the eye. As each tiny buying and selling opportunity presents itself, computing power enables investors to 1) identify the opportunity through the murk of large quantities of financial data; and 2) do it quickly enough to take advantage of it.

But derivatives can lead to problems; Freddie Mac, the US's government-chartered mortgage firm, got itself into trouble in 2003 after misusing derivatives. Nick Leeson famously bankrupted an entire bank by chasing losses on derivatives markets, which remains a pretty impressive feat. Investment guru Warren Buffett has called them 'financial weapons of mass destruction'. Be that as it may, the market in over-the-counter derivatives contracts increased from $3 trillion in June 2001 to $8 trillion in June 2003.[18] As perceptions of our living in a 'risk society'[19] increase – perceptions strongly linked to perceptions of globalisation – it is inevitable that risk management measures will continue to spread.

The improvement in communications has also been a central driver of globalisation. The cost of a three-minute telephone call from New York to London has fallen from $300 in 1930 (at today's prices) to under $1 now. The instantaneity of communications, and the immediate transfer of pretty well unlimited quantities of information via the Internet, in many different media including video and text as well as voice, means that one can now communicate with the outside world just as comprehensively sitting in a coffee bar, an airport or even an area of wilderness – as long as it fell under a wireless network of some sort – as in one's office. Decisions now need not be delayed until the right amount of information is amassed, because this can happen instantaneously; nor do they need to be based quite so often on inadequate knowledge; or delayed whilst a decision-making team is assembled in one geographical location. Furthermore, distance is no object; it is a trivial matter to read the day's newspapers from Brazil, or India, or Australia, even if one is based in Philadelphia. All of this removes aspects of the risks of economic activity overseas, and therefore makes it more tempting to more people.

Advanced communications have also led to a more recognisably global politics. While it is true that most politicians, in democratic countries at least, focus on the constituency that actually elects them – foreigners don't have votes – this is not always the case. There are some politicians so certain of their home country's votes that they feel liberated to solve the problems of the planet as well (Tony Blair, Gordon Brown), some who understand the value of a well-timed anti-American stance for domestic consumption (Gerhard Schröder), some who feel that their domestic position will be boosted by their rubbing shoulders with international statesmen (Silvio Berlusconi) and some who feel that, as their preferred ideology is universally valid, their duty to mankind and to their own voters happily coincides (George Bush, Jacques Chirac).

But the main difference between the politics of the twenty-first and twentieth centuries is the role of the television news. During the appeasement crisis leading up to World War II, British Prime Minister Neville Chamberlain was able to dismiss the Eastern Europeans then falling under the Nazi yoke as 'people of whom we know nothing', and implicitly, therefore, not the sort of people worth shedding good British blood for. If the implication was not necessarily true, the premise certainly was. Nowadays, the situation is different. There are many peoples about whom we know nothing engaged in savage wars – but despite our ignorance of them, we are able to see, thanks to the ubiquitous television news cameramen, the suffering of 'ordinary' people, yanked out of political context. Voters, when presented with pictures of the appalling agonies of the innocent victims of war, now tend to demand of their governments that they 'do something'.[20] Think here of the unique pressure brought to bear on individuals by the screening of pictures of starving children during the original Live Aid concert in 1985. As a direct result, Western democracies are now much more interventionist than they would have been before the screening. Failures to act, as in Rwanda or Darfur, now tend to be accompanied by hand-wringing, rather than the shoulder-shrugging of the cold war era. It is no longer the case that the Western democracies' politics can be entirely introspective.

Communications themselves are of course important aspects of many firms' competences. ICT enables two dramatic shifts in provision of information. In the first place, information can be provided by firms anywhere in the world – call centres are increasingly being situated in countries such as India in order to take advantage of low labour costs (and serviceable English language skills).

Secondly, it is the customer who now does a lot of the work in finding the answers to problems, via more-or-less irritating innovations such as FAQs (Frequently Asked Questions) and the endless pressing of buttons on telephones, which may well solve the problem before you even get to a real person on the other end of the line. In the United Kingdom, the National Health Service now offers a telephone service called NHS Direct, with an online version at http://www.nhsdirect.nhs.uk/, which allows patients to diagnose themselves or be diagnosed by nurses twenty-four hours a day; smart expert system technology guides neophytes and novices through the thickets of medical theory that, until recently, were the preserve of expensively trained doctors. About half the callers are advised how to take care of themselves without the intervention of a general practitioner, leading to great savings in costs for the NHS itself.[21]

We should also not forget that 'information' is not just verbally communicated; software is information. So effective communications mean that even the writing of computer code can be outsourced to countries where the labour is cheaper than in Silicon Valley. Bangalore, India, is now home to a burgeoning industry of software developers and other business processing professionals that will, it has been forecast by India's IT industry lobbyist NASSCOM, employ four million Indians by 2008 and generate $80 billion of sales.[22]

This is related to the third important effect of ICT, the increase in productivity. As noted above, a common effect of technology is to make routine some task that previously required expertise for its performance. Traditionally, the tasks that have been made routine have been physical – manufacturing, agricultural or services requiring physical presence. Woodcarvers, labourers, weavers, security guards – these are the sorts of people who have tended to lose their jobs because of technology. However, nowadays, ICT is doing the same for all sorts of white-collar jobs. Payment of wages or expenses, provision of after-sales service, international legal services, processing of payments, human-resources services and general information processing are all automatable or semi-automatable, and therefore exportable. There is no need for each firm to do all of these things at its head office. Business services can easily be bought from specialist providers. As with the unfortunate Luddites, many white-collar workers find themselves unable to compete, but the gains for the many will often (if not always) outweigh the losses of the few.

The fourth way in which technology pushes globalisation is in the digitisation of finance itself. Money has functioned in a two-level way throughout its history. First of all, there is some commodity that is used as a store of value (generally, though not always, a precious metal). Secondly, tokens are also issued that entitle one (it is one of the jobs of a government to enforce such entitlements, at least in theory) to some share of that value store ('I promise to pay the bearer, on demand, the sum of one pound').[23] The nominal quantity of tokens available might exceed the value store by some margin, but that is no problem as long as confidence is retained in the system. If confidence ebbs, the results, as in Weimar Germany, can be catastrophic. More recent serious failures to retain confidence in major traded currencies are the United Kingdom's ejection from the European Exchange Rate Mechanism in 1992, which destroyed its Conservative government, and the collapse in 2001 of the Argentinean currency board system that pegged the peso to the dollar (during the crisis Argentina went through three presidents in a week).

In the twentieth century, economists began to argue that actually it was only the tokens of exchange that were important. There need be no link to an underlying store of value. In effect, a country would produce goods to a value of so much and print money to the value of so much, and the value of the money would of necessity be determined by the value of the goods and services produced. Produce more goods and the money would be worth more; print (or lend) too much money and its value would decline. Government might not always be trustworthy, which is why the last century saw inflation rates that were historically very high as the gold standard withered away. Even now, the dollar – which currently acts as the world's *de facto* store of value – is falling in value as Americans go on an unprecedented borrowing spree.

As far as technology is concerned, the interesting development is that bank accounts themselves now act as value stores. But bank accounts are virtual – once cash has been deposited, all the owner has is a statement saying how much money he or she possesses. And the accounts of banks have gradually shifted online; the 'real' store of the value of your banked money is a set of 1s and 0s in a computer somewhere. Money has become information – and so can be transferred and traded easily. I can send my cash to any part of the world instantaneously. The fact that transfers often take a few days is thanks only to connections with older and slower clearing institutions; there is no reason in principle why, when I pay a bill online, that money should not appear in the other party's bank account immediately.

These four types of technological development have helped push the world's economy towards greater integration – globalisation, in short. None of this implies that such integration is inevitable, nor that, once it has happened, it will be irreversible. History provides many lessons to show that barriers that have been removed can reappear just as quickly.

Is globalisation a myth?

The rapid technological development of the late twentieth century has many historical parallels, not least the nineteenth-century industrial revolution, which also included many technologies that aided the integration of the world's economies (perhaps most notably the telegraph). Indeed, the world's economies did converge as a result, at least up to the First World War. But technology, as we have repeatedly emphasised, is only part of the story. If globalisation is to occur, then governments have to regulate accordingly to remove barriers to trade. As trade economist Jagdish Bhagwati puts it:

> [T]oday's most dramatic change is in the degree to which governments have intervened to reduce obstacles to the flow of trade and investments worldwide. The story of globalization today must be written in two inks: one colored by technical change and the other by state action … [This leads to] a disturbing observation: governments that can accelerate globalization can also reverse it. Herein lies a vulnerability that cannot be dismissed complacently. The earlier globalization, in the end, was interrupted for almost half a century with rising trade barriers epitomized by the infamous 1930 Smoot–Hawley Tariff of the United States and declining trade

flows and investments after World War I through to the Great Crash of 1929 and World War II.[24]

Globalisation, in a complex, dynamic world, will always be two steps forward and one step back – or one step forward and two steps back. Elections in democracies tend to promote insularity – in the United States in 2004, the two candidates, George Bush and John Kerry, fell over themselves to criticise the offshoring of jobs to countries such as India, despite the complete lack of evidence that this trend was doing the American economy any harm. Nationalism, in both democratic and non-democratic countries, usually trumps good sense. Rich countries try to open up the economies of poor countries, on the (correct) ground that more trade will help them – but it never occurs to George Bush to cut the giant subsidies to American cotton farmers, or to Junichiro Koizumi to stop featherbedding Japanese rice farmers, or to Jacques Chirac to put an end to the EU's Common Agricultural Policy, which absurdly uses European taxpayers' money to impoverish farmers in the developing world (although Prince Charles does rather well out of it, so it can't be all bad). On the other hand, poor countries seem more than willing to cut off their noses to spite their faces. Barred from rich world markets by unfair tariffs and subsidies, they impose even higher tariffs on each other.

So we should not be surprised that the evidence for globalisation is equivocal. For example, export and import levels of countries, taken as a percentage of gross national product (GNP), have not risen dramatically in comparison with previous decades. In fact, the level of international trade in 1973 was actually lower than the levels of international trade in 1913. Even by 1994, some countries had not recovered to their pre-World War I levels of import and export.

Similarly, globalisation should mean that import and export levels (as indicators of international trade) would increase on a worldwide basis, and not become concentrated within particular trade blocs, such as the European Union. Nevertheless, the reverse seems to be the case. From the 1960s to the present, trade between member states of the EU has increased whilst export from EU members to non-EU members has decreased.

At a theoretical level things become even murkier. For example, if globalisation is breaking down barriers, this implies that there must have been a pre-globalisation world made up of politically and economically autonomous units (nation-states) which spawned those barriers. As Justin Rosenberg points out in his *The Follies of Globalisation Theory*, this means that those who tout globalisation theory – with all the radically transformative consequences this view has – actually end up buying into a rather conservative, inaccurate and much-challenged model of how international politics actually works.[25]

This 'Westphalian' model upon which the globalisation view is founded is largely mythical. The Peace of Westphalia of 1648 has given rise to a view of global politics based upon the interaction of autonomous and economically self-sufficient political units (i.e. states) that are internally homogeneous and which assert absolute jurisdiction over bordered territorial spaces. As a reflection of historical reality, this is dubious. Even within the period when the Westphalian system is said to have been at its strongest (from the mid-seventeenth century to the mid-twentieth), the rise of industrial capitalism in England at the end of the eighteenth century created an entire network or web of significant relations above and beyond the nation-state, and fundamentally transformed politics (such that supra-territorial relations expanded without contradicting territorial sovereignty).[26]

The territorial view at the heart of the Westphalian model is seriously undermined, for instance, by the rise of the cotton industry that lay at the centre of English industrial development. Cultivation of the raw material took place in the American south by a labour force that was transported there from Africa. The production of cotton goods occurred in the Lancashire factories that inspired the hymn *Jerusalem*, and which drew upon an army of wage-labourers from the surrounding countryside. The final products were sold on the markets of Europe, and in India and beyond. Cotton cannot be located in one single place, nor does it resolve matters to allow that it existed in a number of such spaces, for each site depended upon the others for its own existence in the cotton chain. As Rosenberg writes:

> [T]he reality of the early nineteenth-century cotton industry cannot be described without identifying the way it related all these distant places to each other organically in a single division of labour. Its real (and in fact its only) existence lay in the social and ecological relations by which millions of human lives were inter-connected both within these different places and across the vast distances which (territorially) separated them. There is no way of representing those relations as places on a map.[27]

Such examples should make us wary of assuming that technology will produce globalisation *simpliciter*. Even the terms of the debate are complex. For the sociologist Anthony Giddens, the past couple of decades – the decades of globalisation – represent a distinct and radical break with the modern period. A decoupling of time and space is what differentiates the last twenty years or so. With instantaneous communications, knowledge and culture can be shared around the globe simultaneously – in other words, for Giddens, this conceptual decoupling is to a large extent technologically driven. But the example of King Cotton undermines the prior claim that the concepts were ever as tightly coupled as has been assumed. In that case, the so-called period of globalisation is but a continuation of already existing social and economic forces. Globalisation, in other words, is simply another stage of modernity, not a break with it. Contemporary events and changes are continuities of previous developments, and parallels can be found throughout history, as Will Hutton argues, in conversation with Giddens:

> Inequality and power imbalances exist just as they have always done. There has been technological change since the

Industrial Revolution. Both Churchill and Bismarck insisted in their time that their countries lived through unparalleled transformations. What do we believe is so different about this era of change we're going through that allows us to redefine our political ideas and beliefs? How did we arrive at the conclusion that something so fundamental is going on with economic and social structures that the old distinction between left and right is outmoded? It is much deeper than just talking about information technology, satellite communication and financial markets. The argument has to be that the changes are of such degree that there has been a fundamental challenge to the operation and our understanding of capitalism.[28]

So, the jury is still out. Even if we were sure of the 'facts' about globalisation, we have still not discussed whether globalisation is a good or a bad thing – a surprising omission, some might think, as this seems to be *the* political issue of our day. But this is not an issue we need to resolve, though we certainly need to understand the background to it as laid out here. The development of certain technologies, notably ICTs, is tending to bring nations together. They can decide to stay apart if they can – but if they try to conduct their economic affairs without trade, aid or political interaction with other nations, the result will be impoverishment and, at worst, famine and oppression, as in North Korea or Zimbabwe.

Uneven technological development

Marx thought that capital would create a world in its own image.[29] In this prediction he seems remarkably astute. What he neglected to mention, however, was that this development would be a combined but uneven one. The development of countries would be tied together on the same path, but their rates of progress would be markedly

INEQUALITY.COM

divergent. Nowhere is this truer than in the case of digital technology. If there were reason enough to be concerned about the inequalities in access to ICT within countries, then the differential levels of access between countries is truly staggering – recall table 1 of chapter 3.

Admittedly, we should approach such statistics with a certain degree of caution. Data on global ICT diffusion can be a bit iffy, and many data sets about global patterns are created from the aggregation of country-level empirical studies that often differ in their methods of collection and focus. Such global statistics can, therefore, be a collection of data from very different types of surveys, and as such, they may not represent an entirely accurate picture of actual distribution. Data collection has, however, improved in the last few years, so we shouldn't overstate the worry. At the very least, there is a strong indication of the existence of a global digital divide. This raises several questions, notably 'why?' and 'so what?'

How do we explain the existence of a global digital divide? The most obvious reason might be to do with economic development. The diffusion of the new technologies might vary directly with the level of a country's economic development. There is considerable empirical evidence to suggest that this is indeed the case. The most highly developed countries – in terms of GNP – such as the US, the UK, Israel and New Zealand, tend to display much higher take-up rates on things like personal computer ownership and Internet access. Similarly, the more under-developed countries of the world (such as Myanmar, Rwanda and Sudan) are the ones that have least access to ICTs.

The link between patterns of ICT diffusion and economic development are pretty clear, and not entirely unexpected. But levels of economic development do not explain the full picture, for there are some interesting cases that do not fit neatly into this model. There are some less-developed countries (such as Taiwan, South Korea, Poland and Slovakia) that display higher than expected levels of Internet access, and, conversely, there are some well-developed

142

countries (most notably Saudi Arabia) where access is pitiful. What explains this set of anomalies? Primary here are the factors of human capital and level of democratic development within a country.

Human (sometimes social) capital refers to those properties that allow individuals to live and work productively together in an atmosphere of respect and mutual trust. Those countries that invest more heavily in the areas that lead to higher levels of human capital seem to be more likely to have higher levels of Internet access and personal computer ownership than those countries that do not invest so heavily. Education is the most visible, and probably the strongest, route for increasing levels of human capital. Similarly, if (excluding the English-speaking nations) English language skills are a core component of investment in education, then a country is likely to have a higher incidence of Internet access (because the vast majority – almost 90% – of Internet sites are in English). This would help explain why those more developed countries that invest resources into improving English language skills (such as the Scandinavian nations) outstrip equally well-developed countries that don't (such as the southern European nations) in terms of Internet access.

Political development – in terms of levels of democratic proce-dures – may also help to explain why some richer nations having a less than expected level of Internet access. Saudi Arabia and China (as rapidly developing countries) are well documented for their attempts to control computer ownership and Internet content. Both countries have invested massive sums of money in developing firewall technology to prevent their citizens from accessing websites from outside their borders and to censor content. In effect, as we noted earlier, China and Saudi Arabia have created their own Intranets. The same is true of other countries that score low in terms of democratisation levels.

On the other hand, we must beware of taking Internet access as a proxy for access to ICT more generally. The Internet is undoubtedly the most important and interesting part of the ICT revolution, but it is not the only one – a point to which we will return later in this chapter. Countries such as China that have low levels of Internet diffusion may well have higher levels of access to other new technologies. The nationalistic turn that Chinese communism has taken from Deng Xiaoping's premiership has focused on cementing the Communist Party in place at the head of a relatively conservative society, but within that (to Western eyes) rigid hierarchy, technology has been deployed for the benefits it confers. Such benefits absolutely do not include democracy and free speech; in these respects, China follows the 'Asian values' thinkers in valuing social stability rather more highly than free speech.[30] This example should remind us that different cultures react to the benefits and costs of technologies in different ways – and that they may draw the line between benefits and costs differently.

ICT, global poverty and global inequality

Whatever the explanation for the existence of a global digital divide, one thing is abundantly clear: inequality in access to ICT is closely tied to economic inequality. Those countries that suffer poverty are most likely to be the ones that have the lowest levels of the new technologies. Once again, Southeast Asia is a case in point. Some of the countries in this region, where some of the richest and poorest nations in the world rub shoulders, are world leaders in the development of digital technology, whilst others are amongst the most ICT-deprived in the world. Not surprisingly, empirical evidence suggests a strong correlation between levels of wealth and levels of ICT diffusion. Look back once again to table 1 from chapter 3.

OK, some may say, so what? Even if there is a connection of some sort between technological development, globalisation and poverty, there are some who say it should not be a cause for concern. Technology take-up rates have always followed the same pattern. It is unrealistic to expect instant equal diffusion of technology. However, over time, diffusion rates do increase at a predictable rate to the point where near-saturation levels exist. Evidence for this optimism does exist, especially for developed countries such as the US. Take-up rates of the older media, such as radios, TVs and micro-waves, followed an S-shaped curve, with a slow beginning followed by rapid growth, and slow development again once the technology had matured. Things like Internet diffusion appear to be taking the same path, though it is still a little early to predict with any reliability.

This seems too sanguine. Whilst this might be true of developed countries, it is unclear whether the same pattern will occur across the globe, and if it does, whether it will occur at a sufficient pace. Countries such as Indonesia, the Philippines, Vietnam and Cambodia still have a very low level of (fixed-line) telephone and TV access, despite these technologies having been available for well over half a century. Many African nations are even worse placed.

Furthermore, these relatively simple measures of the digital divide, based on the availability of the physical technology, may actually understate the case. The concept of access should really be expanded to mean *effective access* (see chapter 9). Effective access requires rather more than mere access. For instance, are users suffi-ciently literate? Can they read text interfaces? If they can read, can they write (on a standard keyboard a complex South Asian script requires several keystrokes per letter)? Does the Internet contain the content they really need or are interested in, in a form which is meaningful to them? And is the interaction sustainable – that is, can people pay for the services they access over the long term?[31]

There are reasons, then, to be sceptical of any suggestions that impoverished nations will catch up naturally, in a sufficiently short time, with the more developed countries. Current markets in technology appear to exclude such people.

OK, fair enough. But is it possible to do anything about it? It may be unfortunate, but perhaps it is merely the way things are. The digital divide is simply a manifestation of the process of technological advancement. Lack of technological development is an unfortunate fact about the world. But this does not give us reason, the sceptic continues, to think that it is somehow anyone's fault, or that there is a responsibility to change this.

Why should we think the global digital divide is a moral matter? Merely pointing out that a global digital divide exists does not give us reason to think that it ought to be closed. How responsible for the developing world is the developed world? Is it helpful, or paternalistic, for developed countries to try to close the digital divide? Maybe there are greater priorities for aid – clean water, curbing the trade in small arms, cheap retroviral drugs, debt relief, educational programmes. Indeed, when we look at what those in the developing world spend their own money on – and remittances from legal and illegal immigrants to the developed world from the developing world dwarf the total amount of government aid – we don't see any strong desire to invest in ICT.

There is undoubtedly some truth here. As a matter of urgency, preventing starvation and premature death via the provision of food supplies and medicine is clearly a priority. To deliver shiny desktop PCs to starving citizens in refugee camps outside Darfur would be ridiculous, if not perverse. On the other hand, the notion of bridging or closing the digital divide is not totally absurd. For example, better working conditions, education and wages are of importance in the medium to long term. Of course, relief for an immediate and present problem or danger is important, but it does not provide a great deal of scope for preventing problems reoccurring in the future. If we are genuinely to make poverty history, as a current campaign exhorts, then we have to provide measures to raise standards in the future – in short, we have to invest, not consume.

Technological infrastructure is central to a country's economic development, in particular the productivity of its workers. Any long-term solutions must include this feature. If our concern is to help poverty-stricken nations stand on their own two feet and provide for themselves, then the assistance of the more developed nations is necessary. And this assistance must come not only in the form of immediate aid, such as famine relief, but also in the form of assistance to struggling populations to provide for themselves once the famine, disease, war and all the other pressing dangers have been alleviated. As a famous Chinese proverb has it: give a man a fish and you feed him for a day; teach a man how to fish and you feed him for a lifetime.[32] Providing the means for nations to become productive is the obvious way of ensuring their long-term ability to provide for their own people. This is a fact often ignored by those who reason that we should be unconcerned about world poverty because the idea of throwing money at the problem achieves little, or that providing aid creates dependency. As Thomas Pogge writes:

> If foreign donations of food depress demand, prices, and hence incentives for production in the target country, we can instead enhance the income of the poor. Where direct transfers to poor households create dependency, we can, targeting children especially, fund vaccination programs, basic schooling, school lunches, safe water and sewage systems, housing, power plants and networks, banks and micro-lending, and road, rail, and communications links. Such projects augment poor people's capacity to fend for themselves and their access to markets while also stimulating local production. Such projects, publicly funded, played an important role in the eradication of poverty in the (now) developed world. And in the developing world, too, such projects have been successfully realized by UN agencies, NGOs, and individual donor states.[33]

Pogge's point is that assistance to the poorest people in the poorest states of the world does not simply mean throwing food bundles at them. Creating the necessary social infrastructure to allow them to participate in world markets would be a massive step towards making them self-sufficient and eradicating poverty. As we have seen, in the modern world, access to ICT is central to productive activity. If the poorest populations are to gain access to economic markets in order to provide for themselves, then they must not be excluded from the technologies upon which the operation of those markets is founded.

All well and good, but this still leaves the question of why we should feel compelled to assist those who are currently excluded from the world of ICT. Why do *they* place a moral burden on *us*? After all, we're all competing under the same rules or system, aren't we? If some lose out while others benefit, isn't that just the way things are? Everyone has the same opportunity to win, don't they? Actually, no, we're not competing under the same rules; that's the problem. Or, at least, we're competing under different rules in the same system. The system that exists – the global system – is one that has, by-and-large, been created by the developed countries of the Western world, and it is one that benefits them disproportionately. The system that has grown up is one that is skewed. In this sense, it is like a group of tall people creating a sport where the rules disproportionately favour height. Unlike this sporting example, individuals cannot simply refuse to participate in the global system. A lack of alternatives compels participation.

Let us be clear here, this is not some ultra-radical or left-wing assertion about the evils of global capitalism, or the like. Even on the most moderate, or widely accepted, understandings of international politics and economics, the biased nature of the current system is difficult to deny. As we have already seen, there exists, at least at the economic level, a set of truly global institutions. The increasingly integrated global market exists beyond the ambit of the nation-state, but its effects reach down to every individual. We all share a common set of institutions. The consequence of this is that nation-states are no longer, if they ever were, autonomous and isolated political and economic units. Different nations have a greater or lesser voice in the governance of such global institutions. The United States, with its giant economy, speaks loudest; for example, it is the major shareholder in the World Bank. But even the US cannot go it alone, reliably, all the time. In 2003 it was able, with the support of the United Kingdom, Spain, Italy, Poland and a small number of other countries, to ignore the hostility of the UN Security Council to its invasion of Iraq; but it still worked to bring evidence of Iran's nuclear programme before that very same institution in 2005. Very poor nations have great difficulty getting their voices heard at all.

Political philosopher John Rawls provides a useful conceptual tool for thinking about these shared institutions. Within individual states Rawls refers to the existence of what he calls the *basic structure* of a society. By this, Rawls means a certain set of social, political, legal and economic institutions and rules. The basic structure has a profound influence over the lives of the citizens that live under its reach. The shape of an individual's life is deeply influenced by the type of goods, opportunities, liberties and so forth that the basic structure makes available to that person. It is because of these significant distributional effects that the basic structure is considered by Rawls to be the primary subject or focus of justice. As Rawls writes:

> The basic structure is the primary subject of justice because its effects are so profound and present from the start [of a person's life]. The intuitive notion here is that the structure contains various social positions and that men born into different positions have different expectations of life determined, in part, by the political system as well as by economic and social circumstance. In this way the institutions of society favor certain starting places over others. These are especially deep inequalities.[34]

Rawls's aim – particularly in his work *A Theory of Justice*, from which the above quote is drawn – is to specify an arrangement of the basic structure according to principles of justice that would remove the arbitrary inequalities that often exist within individual societies. Recognising the immense importance of the basic structure in shaping the lives of individuals, and recognising that some people may enjoy privileges or advantages because of things such as differential levels of bargaining power, Rawls seeks a fairer or more just set of procedures for allocating benefits and burdens within a society.

But Rawls's analysis of the basic structure within society applies equally well to supranational institutions and rules.[35] There is, in effect, a global basic structure. Such global 'institutions' as the European Union and the World Trade Organization, as well as the World Bank and the International Monetary Fund, do appear to have significant influence on both the internal structure of individual states and the lives of individual people all over the world. If Rawls is correct that the criteria for inclusion are the profound effects of institutions as well as those effects being present from the start, then there are good reasons for thinking that a good many global institutions ought to be included in the specification of the basic structure. In a recent work, Allen Buchanan picks up on this line of reasoning. He is worth quoting at some length:

> [T]here is a global basic structure – a worldwide cooperative scheme consisting of a complex pattern of institutions, including the international legal system, whose workings have profound, pervasive, and lifelong effects on individuals and groups. The global basic structure contains many elements, among which are a widely recognized system of private property rights (including intellectual property rights), the law of the sea, financial and monetary regimes, basic trade regimes, and the systematic patterns of interaction among states under various aspects of public international law ... [B]ecause the workings of the global basic structure have such profound and enduring effects on individuals and groups – and because these effects are for the most part neither chosen nor consented to by those affected – the

global basic structure is subject to assessment from the
standpoint of justice. The intuitive idea ... is that justice
includes the fairness of distributions of benefits and burdens,
at least so far as these are both subject to human control and
not chosen or consented to by the individuals or groups who
receive them.[36]

So, given that the system of global finance and commerce has been
created for the benefit of the developed world (perfectly properly),
given that the development of the developing world depends on its
successful participation in that system and given that ICTs are
important for such participation, then it seems to follow that
provision of ICTs may well be helpful, rather than a distraction. If we
think about this from the impersonal standpoint we described in the
previous chapter – i.e. without knowledge of those features about
ourselves that would introduce bias into our reasoning – then we are
likely to support some form of scheme that ensures a fair set of rules
for all. If there was a chance that we might be part of the group that
fares least well under the world system, we would surely argue for
provision of an adequate level of resources to be a basic feature of
any such rules. The next section will look at some of these ideas in
more detail.

The alternative would be to develop some other notion of global
economic governance, such as George Monbiot's recent 'repulsive
proposal' put forward in *The Age of Consent*.[37] In the absence,
though, of any very practical ideas for implementing such schemes,
however brilliantly conceived, we will not consider them further. The
anti-capitalist movements, happily celebrating diversity and 'rainbow
coalitions' as they do, tend to unite only in opposition, and squabble
as soon as the time comes to table any positive programme. This is,
of course, their right, and it would be churlish not to wish them joy of
it, but equally the amount of help that this gives to the poor is
precisely zero.

Can ICT make poverty history?

Given the assumption that we have to work more or less within the current framework of international relations (which does not preclude consensual incremental reform of that framework, but does preclude Utopian schemes to overthrow capitalism), is it possible that ICT might actually be helpful to the poor? There are many theorists who claim so. In that event, then the ongoing and self-supporting provision of ICT to poor regions or countries would be eminently justified.

This means two things. First, the support for the measures needs to go beyond aid. The user community needs to be able to access the ICT independently (eventually). If they are reliant on handouts from aid agencies or others to support the ICT, then 1) donors are likely to start to wonder, at some point, whether they could spend their grant a little more constructively elsewhere; and 2) such handouts have a habit of being withdrawn when fashions in funding arrangements change.

Secondly, it implies that the products that the users consume must have a commercial life of their own. They must be capable of earning someone, somewhere a profit. If not, we would have a situation where special purpose systems were developed for particular communities. This may be aid, or charitable giving, but as development costs are one-off, this would not fall foul of the sustainability argument; it would be an investment. But in general, such systems would be developed by non-commercial developers – academic computer scientists, say. Using non-commercial sources of software tends to increase innovation, but at the cost of a glitch-ridden system that is hard to update and maintain; non-commercial outfits tend not to have the resources and expertise for providing simple user interfaces, testing and market research.[38] Besides, innovation is not at a premium here. Open source software, however, could be a possibility, based on a sound enough model. On at least an intuitive level, these types of consideration suggest a prioritarian underpinning, as opposed to a more egalitarian position.

At present, though, there is little evidence that such a sustainable market sector is appearing in the ICT world. As Jon Guice and Kyle Eischen argue:

> If IT for development will be supported through revenues collected for commercial products, entrepreneurs will probably play an important role in creating the enterprises that sell them. As it currently stands, however, the field of IT for development does not have the structure to foster new enterprises … While some products and services may appear on the market in the next few years, they will be unusual, representing rare combinations of favourable circumstances. The reason is that the field of IT for development has yet to develop many market-oriented innovations and the associated organizational infrastructure for taking the innovations to market.

- Basic research: there is virtually no fundamental information technology research focused on developing world needs and potential markets;
- Applied research: there is almost no effort toward technical innovation, but a great deal of activity in applying standard technology in new settings such as rural community centres;
- Commercial development: there are very few new, small companies with non-philanthropic backing and target markets that expect paying customers and address needs among the world's poorest four billion.[39]

They conclude that the mechanisms that will produce a properly sustainable ICT solution to problems of the poor are simply not in place. Given that, is it possible that ICT can be used to address problems of impoverishment? To round up this chapter, we will briefly sketch a couple of case studies, one broadly negative, one broadly positive, from one particular developing country, India. Neither study is conclusive one way or the other, but we hope they illustrate some of the difficulties and issues that present themselves in this context.

Our first study concerns a series of innovations in governance in Andhra Pradesh, a large, relatively poor state on the East Coast of Southern India, with its capital at Hyderabad. In 1994, the state government was captured in a landslide election by a regional party, the Telugu Desam Party (TDP), headed by a former film star N.T. Rama Rao, or NTR as he was known. NTR's government was of a type very common in India, a welfare government that courted popularity with handouts for the poor. Examples of its populist policies included subsidised power for farmers, and a scheme selling rice for 2 rupees per kilo (less than 5¢).

However, NTR was toppled in the mid-1990s in a palace coup by his son-in-law, Chandrababu Naidu.[40] Naidu abruptly switched the tone of the TDP's policies by moving in the direction of liberalising the economy. At the time, India's national governments were gradually stripping controls from what was a rigidly planned and bureaucratic economy that had nearly bankrupted itself in a currency crisis in 1991. The Congress Party government of the time had, under its reformist finance minister Manmohan Singh, argued strongly that populist policies were unaffordable, and indeed helped no one. In particular, free or cheap power for the poor was seen as a major cause of the massive power shortages plaguing Indian industry and shackling development.[41] Naidu attempted to cut back the TDP's populism – in the teeth, ironically, of the local Congress Party's opposition.

Naidu's stated aim was to improve governance in Andhra Pradesh by deregulating: cutting the number of interfaces between citizen and government in order to reduce opportunities for inefficiency, complexity and, at worst, corruption.[42] So, for example, he launched a number of self-help programmes; Water Users' Associations managed water supplies and Forest Protection Committees ran forestry. Women's groups were promoted under a number of schemes, including the Development of Women and Children in Rural Areas programme. Among other ideas explored were *Deepam*, which provided cooking stoves and gas cylinders, *Adarana*, providing toolkits for artisans, *Roshini*, which made financial provision for artisans to develop their skills and set up in self-employment, and *Cheyutha*, which promoted the interests of the handicapped.[43] But these self-help schemes were all to take place in the context of an ambitious programme of economic development and growth.

> Andhra Pradesh has set itself an ambitious vision. By 2020, the State will have achieved a level of development that will provide its people tremendous opportunities to achieve prosperity and wellbeing and enjoy a high quality of life.
>
> To attain this level of development, the State will have to embark on a vigorous effort to create economic growth. Development, particularly social development, will require the creation of economic opportunity, mainly through the growth of the economy. Economic opportunity can be created even in the most adverse circumstances. Japan and Germany created great opportunities in the post-war era by developing excellence in manufacturing. Singapore, with minimal natural resources, raised the standard of living of its people by creating a free port and a trading hub in its island nation. In the same way, through innovation and resourcefulness, Andhra Pradesh will have to stimulate the growth of the three major sectors of its economy: agriculture, industry and services.[44]

Reform was a theme in much of Indian politics throughout the 1990s; economic reform led to an increase in underlying growth rates in India, accompanied, as ever, by increasing inequalities that encouraged a populist backlash. To that extent, the TDP's pro-reform policies were nothing special, but Naidu placed his reforms in a larger ideological framework, specifically one of globalisation and liberalisation.[45] Competitiveness, efficiency and good governance were to be benchmarks, and the development of the state was specifically tied to the opportunities that globalisation presented.[46]

> [T]o promote rapid development, the State Government will need to transform itself and quickly adopt a new role: from being primarily a controller of the economy, it must become a facilitator and catalyst of its growth.

How will Andhra Pradesh be able to do all this? Today, global forces are creating unprecedented opportunities for growth. Many growth opportunities have also emerged from India's ongoing economic reforms. Andhra Pradesh is in a good position to capture these opportunities – and has already made some breakthroughs in doing so. Going forward, the State can capitalise on its many strengths to create strong and rapid growth.

- Global forces are throwing open new avenues to growth. The world economy is becoming increasingly integrated. Realising that significant economic growth can now come from participating in world markets, nations are increasingly opening up their economies and doing away with barriers – trade, regulation, and other – which hamper the flow of investment or goods between markets. Companies are constantly looking for new markets in which to sell their products and new regions in which to locate their businesses so that they become more and more competitive. Investors are searching the world for profitable investments, providing capital to anyone who has the best returns to offer. Tremendous advances in knowledge and information technology are driving this process even faster:

companies (and governments) can now make quantum leaps in productivity and efficiency, leapfrogging several stages of development their predecessors had to undergo.

- India is opening its doors to growth. Realising that it too can make this quantum leap, India has started its transition into an international, market-based economy: it has initiated the opening of its economy to foreign investors and, to some extent, its markets to the products of foreign companies. It is gradually removing barriers to trade and industry. Along with these changes in the economic sphere have come changes in the political one: power is increasingly devolving from the Centre to the states, allowing India's states to become more self-reliant in the true spirit of federalism.[47]

In the context of such rhetoric, it is perhaps not surprising that Naidu seized on hi-tech as part of his drive for development; ICT and biotechnology became priorities. He aimed to provide every village with a computer in order to bypass conservative bureaucrats and make government more open; many government services were provided online by the APonline website.[48] Services are structured around the 'e-citizen lifecycle' – a particularly ironic notion, as the site borrows the metaphorical lifecycle from theories of software development, which itself was originally taken from biological development. The lifecycle of the e-citizen therefore looks remarkably like the lifecycle of the offline citizen – 'child', 'student', 'youth', family', 'old age'.

In the cities, so-called e-Seva centres were set up, in which clerks sat at computer terminals, able to complete several government services under the eye of the recipient. By 2003, 600,000 people per month were using e-Seva centres in Hyderabad (out of a population of six million) – though their popularity led to tedious queues.[49] In accordance with the liberal ideology, the e-Seva centres were partnerships between the state government and private firms. Services were good – customers were spared the bureaucratic tedium of several visits to government offices. Corruption fell too, as Naidu's theory predicted; the system bypassed the common problem of governance in the developing world, where underpaid bureaucrats administering complex regulations find plenty of opportunity for graft. The World Bank forked out money for more such schemes across the state.[50]

The TDP argument is that rural computerisation improves administration and enables villagers to get information about services they may not have known existed, and indeed access the forms and application methods for those services. The counter-argument is that, in a state of seventy-six million people, of whom 40% are illiterate, computers are the last things that anyone needs; in 2003, two opposition politicians went on a symbolic hunger strike because 600 villages in the Nalgonda region about 100 km from Hyderabad had no drinkable water.

The involvement of the World Bank, companies like Microsoft and the support of various international politicians, including Tony Blair (whose government's Department for International Development was prominent amongst donors), raised the suspicions of anti-globalisation lobbyists. The Andhra Pradesh Coalition in Defence of Diversity called Naidu's reforms 'the path to disaster', and British Overseas Development Minister Clare Short (no supporter of Blair) came under fire for funding them.[51]

There were other reasons for thinking all was not well in Andhra Pradesh. A long-term guerrilla insurgency by a Maoist group known as the Naxalites (whose grievances predated the TDP governments) threatened order, culminating in a failed assassination attempt on Naidu. The region of Telengana, which played host to many Naxalite groups and where agriculture has suffered from poor irrigation in drought-prone land, also formed a strong separatist movement. And Naidu's reforms, which were designed to lower the percentage of people working in the agricultural sector, led to an agrarian crisis; many farmers committed suicide across the state.

The opposition Congress Party, led by Y. Rajasekhar Reddy, managed to develop a consistent and damaging critique of the Naidu reforms' neglect of the common person, a neglect that had culminated in the wave of suicides,[52] which were widely reported elsewhere.[53] The villages had been left behind in the hi-tech scramble, and the digital divide was 'fast becoming a chasm'.[54] As a result, Naidu's TDP government got a walloping in the 2004 State elections, falling from 180 members to a mere forty-seven, and losing power to a Congress-dominated coalition led by Reddy.[55]

Anti-globalisation campaigners in the developed world were gleeful. George Monbiot even enjoyed a moment of pleasant fantasy, seeing the dispossessed rural farmers of Andhra Pradesh as proxies for the armchair guerrillas and indoor Marxmen of the rich world.

> Tony Blair has lost the election. It's true he wasn't standing, but we won't split hairs. His policies have just been put to the test by an electorate blessed with a viable opposition, and crushed. In throwing him out of their lives, the voters of the Indian state of Andhra Pradesh may have destroyed the world's most dangerous economic experiment ... We can't yet vote Blair out of office in Britain, but in Andhra Pradesh they have done the job on our behalf.[56]

The general feeling was that the TDP – as with its coalition partners the BJP, which lost the national election that took place simultaneously with the state election – had underestimated the extent to which most rural, poor Indians had bought into the reforming narrative. This seemed to chime in with experiences in other states that had tried to use technology as a development tool. Even Karnataka, whose capital Bangalore achieved world fame as the centre of the Indian business process outsourcing industry (and as such was frequently vilified by both sides in the US Presidential election of 2004), rejected its pro-tech government in a rural backlash against the urban elite.[57]

Nevertheless many academic commentators on the situation in Andhra Pradesh avoid the conclusion that the reforms are finished. The blame is partly due to an anti-incumbency bias in India, where governments often fall after failing to live up to expectations. But the special character of the Andhra Pradesh campaign suggested alternative hypotheses too.

> The policy discourse in [the] 2004 election in AP displayed a plebiscitary character. This was because of the dominance of the TDP by the persona of Naidu and political investment of the party in terms of its image, resources, choices and risks in him. For this reason the defeat of Naidu's regime, which gained an iconic status with regard to the State-level economic reforms, has been interpreted as a 'vote against anti-people reforms.' The discourse analysis of the election campaigns of different parties clearly shows that except for the Left no mainstream party made this election a contest on reforms.[58]

Furthermore, it does not seem that Reddy's Congress government is making any strong attempt to unravel the infrastructure or shift government back offline,[59] unlike in Karnataka, where the infrastructure of Bangalore, already creaking under the strain of years of economic growth, has been allowed to deteriorate further.[60] The administrative changes and the e-Seva centres have become much too popular to remove.

One effect of Naidu's putting the ICT infrastructure in place has been to raise the audibility of many of his constituents and their representatives (both elected and self-appointed) in the way that he intended. For example, in April 2005, the international environmental NGO Greenpeace was able to take 'cyber-action' against Naidu's successor Reddy, whose government had taken a decision to allow ship-breaking units at Kakinada port. These were allegedly threatening the livelihoods of local fishermen and the integrity of an ecologically sensitive nature reserve. Ramapati Kumar, Greenpeace's Toxics Campaigner, was quoted as saying 'one powerfully written email is worth 100 votes to a politician'.[61] It is ironic that it is the NGOs' *bête noire* Naidu who was responsible for making that powerfully written email possible.

However that may be, it is very clear that both the TDP's election campaign and its general campaign to reform governance were driven very much from the top down, and specifically associated with the person of Chief Minister Naidu himself. The amount of good that the hi-tech part of the reforms achieved is a matter of dispute, but there is clearly no doubt that the voters, even if they did not reject it, certainly felt no overwhelming enthusiasm for it.

Why might that be, and might there be an alternative route? In a generally positive analysis of the development of an 'informational society' in Andhra Pradesh, sociologist and entrepreneur Kyle Eischen argues that ICT-focused development is still not fully understood, in terms of its relations to other development efforts, the relation between global and national trends and the regional imperatives, and the impact of ICT initiatives on social and cultural structures.[62]

The structures and methods of ICT-based industries are different from other industries, and so impact on societies in different ways. In particular, the automatic production of information requires the definition of information-processing patterns. It is important to realise that, even in offline societies, there is a lot of processing of information going on. Most of that processing is done by individual people, and sources of that information can be verbal or, perhaps more likely, written down.

Writing down information transforms its properties. For example, it can move easily from person to person; it can be transferred at any time (as opposed to information in someone's head, which requires the physical presence of that person to articulate it); it can be formalised. This formalisation process is very important indeed. Consider the filling in of a form. By being directed to answer particular questions, the form forces the information provider to give information of a particular type, which is desired for a particular purpose; the provider is not at liberty to give his or her own narrative spin to the information he or she is passing on. In the information transfer process, a form, or other structured device, shifts power from the provider to the inquirer.

In the context of ICT, this shift is even more marked. Indeed, it may become worthwhile for an organisation to formalise entire chunks of expertise that previously resided only in experts' heads;[63] this would certainly tend to remove the competitive advantage of those experts.[64] This process of externalisation profoundly affects the properties of that expertise.[65] The production of expert performance will become much less fluent, as people have to consult the manual or learn how to use a computer system that has replaced the expert. On the other hand, the expertise will become much more available, because so many more people will be able to recreate it using ICT. Indeed, as we noted earlier (following the perspicuous Luddites), technology makes production routine – products become much less handcrafted and individual, but more people can produce them. The fate of experts, who will have spent a lot of time and effort at university learning their business, is a hot political potato.[66]

Furthermore, as Eischen argues, information processing patterns must be integrated into a society to be effective. Flexibility of organisational forms is a key. He argues that 'because it is socially structured and often determined, the production of predominately information-based products will take the form of craft-like production where tacit information and synergies are essential'.[67] Regional planners in Andhra Pradesh tried to adapt existing resources and build local models to fill in gaps in India's national ICT strategy, while also focusing on regional initiatives, because the long-term viability of ICT-based development requires 1) that the development fits into local patterns of life; and 2) creates competitive advantage for that region so that its fledgling ICT industry can continue to develop once donor interest, funding and government subsidy dry up.

However, points 1) and 2) above may jar against each other. In Andhra Pradesh, the more outward-looking aspects of Naidu's Vision 2020 cut little ice in the face of a series of farmers' suicides. It is certainly, and undeniably, the case that development requires the movement of people from unproductive economic sectors, such as agriculture, to more productive sectors, of which ICT is one. It will be a painful process; most industrial countries have gone through it at some point. But it can be managed more or less sensitively. The shift away from the land in the nineteenth century was quite painful in Britain, as many classic works of literature and *reportage* testify. On the other hand, many other European countries, such as France and Germany, and certain states of the United States have resisted the shift for as long as they can, saddling the world with indefensible policies to guarantee inflated incomes for farmers – in effect, trans-ferring resources from productive people to the unproductive. There is no right way to go about this, but the decisive rejection of Naidu's government at the polls in 2004 strongly implies that his way was less well advised than it might have been.

There is no easy way of resolving the dilemma of managing the transition of an economy from reliance on less-productive industries to reliance on more-productive ones, because the winners live mainly in the future while the losers are in the present. But equally, we can spot some pointers. For example, if we take the WWW as an example, it is worldwide in that anyone with the right equipment can access it and, indeed, publish on it. But the content is hardly 'worldwide' in the same sense. We have noted many aspects of the global digital divide – most Internet users are from the rich countries in the world, most English-speaking. In this book we have so far tended to assume, with most commentators, that the chief result of this is a lack of access in the developing world to information, to their detriment. But a second effect that we should note is that most information online is aimed at the main users – young, wealthy English speakers. Pictures of nude women, detailed accounts of the latest bands and loving write-ups of the latest gadgets are there aplenty. Access to this sort of fluff is hardly going to be terribly meaningful to the poor farmer in Andhra Pradesh. Even were the WWW to reach the poor effectively, there is not necessarily very much on it to excite them. The poor might need information about, say, weather forecasts or ranges of market prices; furthermore, even if such information was available, they would need it to be in a form which was legible to them.

But the Internet isn't everything. There are many ICTs that are more useful and important than the Internet in the development context. Mobile phones allow information to be pooled and passed around easily, without the need for expensive equipment; they are often shared between people in a village, and can bypass the traditionally less stable lines of communication (road and post, as well as land lines) that exist in the developing world. Information can also be tailored to the requirements of the recipient and can be up to date and exact (tracking market prices, for example). There is strong demand for mobile phones in the developing world, and the rates of ownership are increasing. It has been argued – admittedly in research sponsored by the world's largest mobile operator Vodafone – that there are strong links between economic growth and mobiles. An increase of ten mobile phones per hundred people in a typical developing nation could boost GDP growth by 0.6%.[68] And the good news is that, although half the world's population has not as yet made a phone call, three-quarters live within the range of a mobile network.

Our second case study explores this 'bottom up' philosophy. Giving people the information they need in the form they need it, rather than simply supplying 'access', has been attempted in South India by the M.S. Swaminathan Research Foundation (MSSRF), which supplies 'knowledge centres' to villages in the region of Pondicherry;

it hopes to export the idea across India.[69] The knowledge centre in a village is a solar-powered computer centre with wireless Internet connection. It offers villagers a range of information, including market prices, welfare schemes, job listings and health and veterinary advice. Enthusiasm for the scheme seems to be mixed,[70] although people from surrounding villages often come to get information from the knowledge centres, and they seem also to have raised the status of women, who are, of course, just as adept at using the machines as the men.

But much of the value-added from this scheme comes not from the use of the computers themselves (many potential users are, after all, illiterate), but by the pooling of information. Useful information is taken from the Internet and transferred in the local context by distinctly lo-tech means – broadcasts by loudspeakers, or distribution of a rudimentary newsletter. The result is a hi/lo-tech hybrid that looks like a very useful model indeed for development.

On 26 December 2004, a giant tsunami killed hundreds of thousands of people across South East Asia, including on the coast near Pondicherry. Many villages (mostly fishing villages) suffered heavy casualties, but the coastal village of Veerapatinam, which has an MSSRF knowledge centre, got away relatively lightly – only one person killed out a population of 6200. Opinion seems to be divided about whether the warnings came from the centre or from the local temple deity,[71] but whatever the ultimate truth of that, we might postulate that the presence of the knowledge centre there was not a coincidence.

There is no doubt that ICT investment can help close the global digital divide (as long as it keeps pace with growth in investment elsewhere). There is no doubt that ICTs can help poor and rural populations in developing nations. Cost, of course, is a major factor in whether such investment will take place. The real question is whether the investment in ICT will produce greater benefits than investments in health, clean water or education. These questions are unresolved at the moment. Since the collapse of rich world stock markets after the telecoms boom, ICTs are much less fashionable than they were in the heyday of Mr Naidu. Even computer mogul and philanthropist Bill Gates, who was courted by Naidu in the boom years, has refocused his philanthropic efforts towards combating AIDS. These are fine decisions, requiring complex calculations on insufficient data.

What does seem clear, given the arguments we have set out in this chapter, is that ICTs have a role to play in promoting development and closing the (general) divide between the rich world and the poor. The extent of that role, and the exact form it should take, are as yet unclear. But simply rejecting the use of ICTs in the developing world as covertly promoting the cause of globalisation is not a tenable position.

6:>
Democracy, Deliberation and the Virtues of Denizenship

Consumers and/or citizens

Adam Smith's *Wealth of Nations* is better known for its celebration of the onset of industrialism and the rise of capitalism than for its concerns about the deleterious effects of modern society on individuals and communities. Yet Smith's praise of free market economics – which has endeared him to libertarians and free marketeers worldwide – is tempered by a strong concern that a society founded upon such a base will not generate a level of civic engagement amongst its citizens sufficient to keep it stable and flourishing. What Smith was worried about was that the new society was an individualistic one, where the ties of community, even the social fabric itself, were broken by the isolation created through economic competition in a free market. In this, Adam Smith and Karl Marx shared a surprising observation: capitalism creates its own gravediggers. But for Smith the answer was not working class revolution to create a communist society, but the correction of these defects by the state to create a fairer market-based society.

Bearing witness to the Industrial Revolution in England, Smith observed how the rise of productive technology had begun to change the very shape of human existence. The industries that drew upon technical innovation began to gather in various advantageous locations. The cotton industry developed most extensively in Lancashire, where there was easy access to ports and an army of wage labourers, amongst other things. Cities grew out of the ground to house the exodus from the country – as in the developing world now, romanticisation of the joys of the quiet rural existence counted for nothing against the demand for jobs in the metropolis. Two problems arose from this.

First, the type of work that accompanied industrialisation was, according to Smith, so mind-numbingly simple that it removed any intellectual stimulation or extension from the 'great body of people' – the labouring poor. The blind repetition of one or two simple operations turns the brains of individuals to mush, rendering them ignorant and stupid, subject to delusions of 'enthusiasm and superstition', and lacking the capacity to unmask the 'interested complaints of faction and sedition'. The survival of the new society is therefore less than secure. Smith employs the example of a pin factory to illustrate his point.

> The man whose life is spent performing a few simple operations, of which the effects too are, perhaps, always the same, or very nearly the same, has no occasion to exert his understanding, or to exercise his invention in finding out expedients for removing difficulties which never occur. He naturally loses, therefore, the habit of such exertion, and generally becomes as stupid and as ignorant as it is possible for a human creature to become. The torpor of his mind renders him, not only incapable of relishing or bearing a part in any rational conversation, but of conceiving any generous, noble, or tender sentiment, and consequently of forming any just judgement concerning many even of the ordinary duties of private life. Of the great and extensive interests of his country, he is altogether incapable of judging ... His dexterity at his own particular trade seems, in this manner, to be acquired at the expense of his intellectual, social, and moral virtues. But in every improved and civilised society this is the state into which the labouring poor, that is, the great body of

the people, must necessarily fall, unless government takes some pains to prevent it.[1]

Smith is not decrying the working classes; he is genuinely concerned that the roles handed to them are destroying their intellect and moral fibre. His concern about the mental well-being of the working masses is founded neither on instrumental reasons about the importance of a healthy, keen workforce for industrial capitalism nor on general humanitarian principles of concern. Rather, his justification for such concern is about legitimate and stable government in the face of dehumanising toil:

> In free countries, where the safety of government depends very much upon the favourable judgement which the people may form of its conduct, it must surely be of the highest importance that they should not be disposed to judge rashly or capriciously of it.[2]

To be legitimate and stable, government requires popular consent. This must be genuine and informed consent, rather than engineered via coercion or ignorance. But if the conditions prevalent in society – specifically, in this case, the tedium of the available work – make it harder for people to exercise judgement and make informed decisions to give or withhold that consent, then the government of that society will lack legitimacy.

The second problem concerning Smith was the isolation of dislocated individuals in a city. The migration to the industrial heartlands removed individuals from close-knit communities, where they would interact daily with people who knew them and whose views they would need to consider in daily life. For Smith, this meant that cities were a potential breeding ground of vice because individuals lacked support networks to socialise them. Such socialisation helped create reasonable, virtuous people, predisposed to behaving in a 'proper' manner. One's visibility to others helps ensure good conduct and dissuades certain vices and flaws of character that can manifest in anonymity. Unlike the well-to-do (who are always in the public eye),

> A man of low condition, on the contrary, is far from being a distinguished member of any great society. While he remains in a country village his conduct may be attended to, and he may be obliged to attend to it himself. In this situation, and in this situation only, he may have what is called a character to lose. But as soon as he comes into a great city, he is sunk in obscurity and darkness. His conduct is observed and attended to by nobody, and he is therefore very likely to neglect it himself, and to abandon himself to every sort of profligacy and vice.[3]

Adam Smith's concern for the character of citizens in a democracy is not unique. Aristotle and Plato both highlighted the problem of citizens who did not 'pull their weight' in the enterprise of democratic governance, but who instead opted out of public business in favour of their private concerns. It is by no means accidental that the English word *idiot* derives from the ancient Greek term designating those who preferred private pleasure over public endeavour. An idiot was a 'free-rider', in modern parlance. Similarly, the Founding Fathers of the American Constitution displayed this awareness of the need for citizens who were willing and able to engage in public deliberation and action, rather than incapable and withdrawn. Writing of the importance of a free press for a republic, Alexander Hamilton asks in *The Federalist Papers*:

> What is the liberty of the press? Who can give it any definition which would not leave the most latitude for evasion? I hold it to be impracticable, and from this I infer that its security, whatever fine declarations may be inserted in any constitution respecting it, must altogether depend on public opinion, and on the general spirit of the people and government. And here,

after all, as is intimated upon another occasion, must we seek the only solid basis of all our rights.[4]

In short, the political institutions of a democratic society – Rawls's basic structure – no matter how perfectly designed, are worthless if the citizens who live under them do not actively support and uphold them.

Whilst Adam Smith is not the first thinker to worry over the character of a society's citizens, he is the first to point out how industrial capitalism exacerbates this particular problem, in advance, for example, of Blake and Dickens. The destruction of rural communities and the anonymity and individualism created by the cities that fuelled industrialisation provided a new breeding ground for selfishness, apathy, suspicion, intolerance and other vices. This is made worse by the type of work performed under the new technologies, where the division of labour has removed any creative or intellectual component from the vast majority of jobs. Individuals become mere automatons in their public life, and isolated atoms in their private lives.

The type of society that horrifies Smith can easily be imagined. All we need to do is think of a society where fair democratic institutions and procedures exist. Such an imaginary society would have much to recommend it. Achieving such a state of affairs would be a marvellous accomplishment for virtually every country in the world today. But, as it stands, the picture is incomplete. Imagine further that, when it comes to matters of everyday politics in this society, such as voting, running for office, calling officials to account, deliberating and speaking out against injustices, citizens refrain, out of a general apathy, from participation. Apathetic citizens do not even participate at the grass-roots level, the affairs of their own communities, posting leaflets, voting, serving on PTAs, writing letters to local newspapers and so on.

Public matters in this imaginary society do not rank highly on anyone's agenda. Individuals prefer to dedicate their efforts to the pursuit of their private ends, and this is, of course, permissible within a free society. Politics becomes merely an arena for bargaining at the level of group- or self-interests because individuals are either so unconcerned about matters beyond the satisfaction of their personal preferences or so ardently affirm a particular view of what makes their life valuable or worthwhile that they view interaction with others who fail to share their view as pointless. When circumstances necessitate contact across religious, cultural, racial or interest divides in this society, individuals respect the formal rights of others, but see such contact as a bargaining procedure, the object of which is to maximise one's gain within the confines of the legal framework.

Something is clearly absent from this imaginary society. Democracy (or politics more generally) has been reduced to a mere mechanical application of the formal rules. Democracy, in this sense, is fully compatible with the existence of self-interested, self-absorbed and unsympathetic individuals. Democratic arrangements become nothing more than a machine for calculating the sum of individual preferences. Deliberation, engagement and participation are all absent from such a model. We might wonder how far removed such a polity really is from our own supposedly democratic societies.

In fact, Smith's worries have reappeared in recent years, as the politics of the free market have become more common. The US Republican Party, under George Bush's presidency, teeters precariously between conservative concern for 'culture wars' issues such as the breakdown of the family and libertarian concern for issues such as tax cuts, and unites best when blaming Bill Clinton for the mess. On the other hand, on continental Europe, right wing parties in France, Germany and elsewhere eschew 'Anglo-Saxon' economic rigour for a social concern anchored in Christianity.

The United Kingdom is an interesting example: her politics were dragged from a relatively left wing, corporatist consensus in the 1970s, to a much more market-oriented view in the 1980s, by Margaret Thatcher, Prime Minister throughout the latter decade, thereby creating a new consensus that several years of nominally leftist government under Tony Blair have not dented.[5] Indeed, Britain's ideological journey through the 1980s was probably further than that of any other Western democracy. Though the ability of free markets to generate growth remains unchallenged by serious commentators, there has been collective hand-wringing from all sides about the social effects of the new British market philosophy. One might expect artists to oppose the vulgar effects of commercial pursuits, and Thatcherism has been roundly condemned in works ranging from half-witted knee-jerk attacks to thoughtful and amusing satires such as Jonathan Coe's *What a Carve Up!* and Alan Hollinghurst's *The Line of Beauty*. Many in Mrs Thatcher's own party, such as Sir Ian Gilmour, a minister in her first cabinet, disassociated themselves from her proudest achievements as they happened,[6] and others, such as David Willetts, while not repudiating her work, think that her governments focused too much on the economy to the detriment of society.[7] Other, fiercer, commentators on the right, such as John Gray, blame the perceived break-up of British society squarely on markets.[8] One would expect leftist academics to oppose free markets in all their guises, and so they do.[9] But even so, there are commentators on the left, prominent amongst them Polly Toynbee, who worry about the disengagement and irresponsible retreat to cynicism of the poor, and their willingness to ignore the demands that responsible citizenship creates.[10] Similar debates are to be had in many of today's insecure democracies. Smith's concerns remain as relevant now as they were in the eighteenth century.

Deliberation

What has that got to do with recent developments in ICT? Well, the types of concerns that Smith raised about the social effects of technological advances are starting to reappear in the more modern context of the effects of ICTs on democracy and democratic deliberation.

Admittedly, democracy was not Adam Smith's primary concern. Democracy in the Britain of Smith's day was largely unrecognisable by today's standards. The working classes (let alone women) were largely disenfranchised. The aristocracy still nominally held political power, but it was the middle classes – the bourgeoisie – that held the real reins of power through their grip on capital. The middle classes were, however, a liberalising class, and it was with the status of a liberal society that Smith was primarily concerned. Liberalism and democracy, though not synonymous, are sufficiently allied that Smith's observations and concerns apply to democratic societies.[11] The worries about participation in the face of technologically driven social and political change that occupied Smith are still present today. Indeed, the fear is that problems of participation – what we might term the decrease of levels of 'civic virtue' – are exacerbated by the rise of the new technologies. How is this so?

It is often assumed that the Internet is a boon for democracy. It brings colossal quantities of information within reach of virtually everyone in the developed world, and a large (and increasing) number of people in the developing world. It is hard for governments to police. It allows effective and targeted publishing by many more individuals. Not only is it difficult to keep people with a grievance quiet, but they can now send their complaints to an infinitely wider audience. Surely that is one up to the citizen?

This assumption has recently been the subject of a number of challenges. A more pessimistic view has begun to emerge from the disciplines of philosophy, law and political science, to counter wide-eyed geeky optimism. Like Adam Smith's view that a liberal polity must be based on a shared set of (liberal) civic virtues, the argument behind this pessimistic view is that democracy, to be successful, needs to be based to some extent on consensus, however virulent the arguments beyond that consensus. Serious citizens need to deliberate, see opposite points of view, genuinely engage with others, see opportunities to compromise. Positions need to be argued for, arguments need to be proved against their competitors. The democratic process is at least as important as the institutions of democracy, as our example of the hypothetical society demonstrated. Merely setting up media for making decisions is not enough; the process of making and establishing one's case is essential.

This view, which concentrates on the importance of consensus in the process of democracy, has been labelled *deliberative democracy*. Compare deliberative democracy with a contrary view that the purpose of democratic institutions is largely aggregative: they add and subtract the individual preferences or interests of citizens or voters as part of some immense calculation in order to decide upon a particular political outcome. In such a system democratic decision making is understood as relevantly similar to the economic market. Citizens are like consumers in that their preferences are largely set; it is the job of democratic institutions to calculate which preferences are most popular.

Deliberative democracy, however, does not assume individual preferences to be fully set, but instead considers them open to recon-sideration and change on the basis of genuine deliberation of alternate viewpoints. In a public forum, complex decisions are discussed and different approaches canvassed. Citizens are not assumed to be entirely self-interested, but to have some concern for the good of their society (as well as their own interests). Argument, undertaken by serious-minded people, should change minds, as Thomas Christiano argues.

> Discussion and deliberation play three main roles in the democratic process. First, they play a role in helping individ-uals learn of their interests and those of others, as well as the extent to which these interests do or can converge. Second,

they play a role in deepening citizens' conceptions of justice by informing them of each other's interests and by subjecting their views of justice and the common good to debate. Third, they ensure that the conflicts among citizens are tempered by the strengthened social bond arising from the increased understanding each has of others' interests.[12]

Note how these roles are premised on the idea that the members of a democratic society, despite having 'diverse preferences, convictions, and ideals concerning the conduct of their own lives', nevertheless share 'a commitment to the deliberative resolutions of problems of collective choice'.[13] That is, the idea of a common good (rather than naked self-interest) is the foundation of their democratic institutions, and what gives those institutions their legitimacy. Citizenship in such a society includes, therefore, deciding upon the aims of that society overall, and from a viewpoint on the whole of society. Thus, the role of the citizen 'is not to organize local areas of policy wherein they are most affected but to put together all the interests and activities in the society in a coherent framework that balances the activities and interests of all'.[14]

For example, if the question before a polity were about major reforms to healthcare provision, then the role of the citizen is to consider and make a decision upon the aims of the health care reform. This might include, for example, choosing whether society should have a nationalised, universal health care service such as Britain's National Health Service or a system based upon a regulated market of health care provision such as exists in New Zealand and the US. The organisation of specific policies to achieve these ends is, by contrast, a separate matter, and one that by and large is formulated in a different manner, such as via the input of citizens, user groups, policy experts within political parties or other interest groups.[15]

Deliberative democracy places certain demands upon citizens. If deliberation is central, then citizens must be willing and able to deliberate. What, exactly, does this mean though? For a start, it means that individual members of a society must be genuinely willing to engage with others in a reciprocal enterprise of discussion and consideration of alternative views. This cannot be merely hollow lip-service. Rather, it has to be undertaken on the basis of a genuine desire to understand alternative viewpoints, to consider their merits and drawbacks, and to review and revise one's own views where good reasons exist, in the spirit of poet Richard Wilbur's exhortation to 'Go talk with those who are rumored to be unlike you'. In general terms, this democratic virtue is one instance of what we might call 'fair mindedness' in the process of reasoning. As Richard Paul writes, fair mindedness includes:

> Willingness and consciousness of the need to entertain all moral view-points sympathetically and to assess them with the same intellectual standards without reference to one's own feelings or vested interests, or the feelings or vested interests of one's friends, family, community, or nation; implies adherence to moral standards without reference to one's own advantage or the advantage of one's group.[16]

Similarly, Eamonn Callan explains this virtue to deliberate genuinely thus:

> Your viewpoint is as important as mine to the fulfilment of that hope [a common perspective acceptable to all], and only through emphatic identification with your viewpoint can I appreciate what reason might commend in what you say. For if I am to weigh your claims as a matter of fairness rather than a rhetorically camouflaged expression of sheer selfishness, I must provisionally suspend the thought that you are simply wrong and enter imaginatively into the moral perspective you occupy.[17]

Or, as John Dryzek writes:

[D]eliberators are amenable to changing their judgments, preferences, and views during the course of their interactions, which involve persuasion rather than coercion, manipulation, or deception.[18]

The Internet may be all that the geeks claim, but it does not support reasoning and argumentative processes such as these. It presents information – which, to be sure, is no bad thing – but it bypasses the essential deliberative processes that give a democratic forum life and legitimacy, and thereby exacerbates the fissiparous tendencies within society. Furthermore, the Internet's content, as above often blandly characterised as 'information', really consists of a rumbustious mixture of truth and lies, often slanted and placed in suggestive contexts.

As a result, philosopher Gordon Graham, no fan of democracy anyway, expects the Internet 'to promote reinforcement of interest and opinion among the like-minded'.[19] Cass Sunstein, a leading thinker on free speech, the First Amendment and constitutional law, argues that regulation is needed to ensure that as many strands of opinion as possible get as general a hearing as possible.[20] To evaluate this sort of argument, we need to look at why deliberative processes are restricted online, consider whether proposed solutions are necessary and, if they are, determine how best, technologically, to deliver them.

Customisation and its discontents

Automatic filtering is an intense area of research.[21] The use of technologies that enable the computer to understand what a piece of information is all about, and of models of the user that enable a machine to understand what preferences the user may have (models that could be developed automatically in the background by, for example, logging what is on the web pages that the user downloads) will make it possible for one's computer to tailor the content that one receives. At the extreme, one need never receive information in which one has no interest.

Developments of automatic filtering are of enormous potential importance in both business and academic research. As a side-effect, they have also been of interest for recreational use of the Internet. One can avoid the financial news, or news about labour disputes, or everything except the football scores. One can generate personalised TV schedules that seek out the programmes one actually wants to watch. This is a communications package Nicholas Negroponte called the *Daily Me*.[22]

Commentators such as Cass Sunstein worry that, because of this filtering ability, a key prerequisite for the functioning of democracy will then be lost, which is that one should be exposed to alternative views to one's own. In the political sphere, it is possible that most voters will deliberately filter out articles and documents of opposing views. After all, why should someone of basic liberal hue force themselves to read white supremacist propaganda? Instead, we can ensure that we only read things that reinforce our own viewpoint. This will mean, says Sunstein, the loss of one of the basic components of a deliberative democracy, the public forum.

On the speakers' side, the public forum doctrine thus *creates a right of general access to heterogeneous citizens*. On the listeners' side, the public forum creates not exactly a right but an opportunity, if perhaps an unwelcome one: *shared exposure to diverse speakers with diverse views and complaints*. It is important to emphasise that the exposure is shared. Many people will be simultaneously exposed to the same views and complaints, and they will encounter views and complaints that some of them might have refused to seek out in the first instance.[23]

Hence, for Sunstein, the formation of reasonable, realistic views about the world – views that will support a pluralistic polity in which differing sets of ideas can coexist with minimal strain – depends on these chance encounters with alternative ideas and topics. The control of the content that Internet technology promises will tend to filter these alternative views away from the reader, with the result, say Sunstein and Gordon Graham, that people will only read news items that reinforce their prejudices and points of view. White supremacists will read white supremacist material, Conservatives Conservative material, Greens Green material and so on. And this will lead to a polarisation of views away from the all-important consensual base that underpins a properly functioning democracy.[24]

It might be asked why the Internet in particular is being singled out as a special area for investigation and worry here. After all, there are other high-penetration media that alter the distribution of heterodox views, television being an obvious example. Gordon Graham puts the potential radicalism of the Internet down to two factors: the increase of power it affords to spread views and cultivate personal autonomy, and its subversion of certain deeply entrenched attitudes, in particular ideas of national insularity.[25]

There are other arguments for the importance of the Internet. First, as we have seen, it is very empowering for individuals. Unlike television or radio, it is relatively difficult, though not impossible, to censor, and the barriers to entry are very low indeed. Hence more people's voices can be heard. Furthermore, more people can receive whatever information they need; for example, the possibilities for distance learning are vastly increased from the days of television, as the experience of Britain's Open University makes clear.[26]

Secondly, the amount of information made available by the Internet is colossal and flexible. Not only is the quantity of material many orders of magnitude greater than that of any other medium, but also there are many fewer delivery restrictions – you can access any page on the Internet at any time without having to wait for someone to broadcast it to you. You can use the Internet to target particular audiences very effectively. Messages can be read by interested parties, without having to consider wider audiences (as with television and radio) or limits of geography (as with newspapers or speech). And so instantaneous is the Internet that it functions as a communication medium for bringing people together and organising.

Hence the Internet has a connection with democratic pluralism, in that it removes many of the restrictions that have historically been exploited by states to restrict debate and preserve power. Not only does this have the potential to increase political participation, it also raises the possibility of increased democratic oversight of political processes via greater transparency – for instance, there is no reason why public tendering processes should not take place online. If knowledge is power, the Internet sends more to citizens, and governments' monopoly of it is correspondingly reduced.

Regulating the Internet

As we have pointed out before, we do not want to claim that the Internet is intoxicatingly novel. Many of the changes it has called into being are part of more general trends towards openness, individualism, greater use of communications, etc. We do wish to argue, however, that it is producing a series of small incremental changes whose cumulative effect may in time become very large. In that sense, the Internet may be a transformative technology rather like movable type – a series of improvements to existing technologies and practices adding up over time to a very large change indeed.

We also would not want to claim that the philosophical problems relating to the Internet are newly minted with the technology. Thinkers such as Smith, Marx, Plato, Mill and Machiavelli remain relevant in the cyberage. The problems that arise are familiar ones for historians of the philosophy of liberty – how to reconcile liberty and privacy, how to balance reasonable state interference with free and fruitful discourse, how to ensure that citizens earn their rights by performing their duties.

It is therefore a fairly natural thought that the Internet should be regulated in some way to ensure its democratic potential, partly by analogy to older media. Cass Sunstein argues this in *Republic.com*, in which he suggests the regulation of websites, rather as television stations are regulated in many countries. Political websites would have to contain links to sites that contained different viewpoints, and so people visiting a conservative website, for instance, would have easy access to sites containing liberal or socialist philosophies should they wish to follow the links.

There is a range of interpretations of Sunstein's proposal, from self-regulation through to quite strict requirements.[27] We will focus here on his strongest proposal, the 'must carry' rule – i.e. political sites must carry such links by law – as the threat of such a rule being imposed would always stand behind any weaker measure of light or self-regulation.

Though this seems at first blush to be an odd idea, it is not impossible. As the Internet is 'bedding down', it is becoming clearer that regulation of cyberspace is not as difficult as was first envisaged. True, a web page can be placed on a server anywhere in the world. But anywhere in the world is somewhere in the world, and not too difficult to trace. Geography is reasserting itself in cyberspace, and Internet regulation is becoming easier and more widespread as greater advances are made in firewall technology.

Neither are there simple and decisive free speech arguments against the proposal. The use of free speech as a principle to prevent any regulation of discourse at all, for example preventing the imposition of caps on political funding, is a peculiarly American legal phenomenon, because free speech is enshrined in the constitution in the First Amendment. However, Sunstein shows that any US government bent on mild regulation of websites would at least have a prima facie case[28] that such regulation was constitutional, added to which the extreme libertarian interpretation of the First Amendment is fairly recent and certainly not uncontested. And anyway such regulation would be small potatoes for relatively illiberal centralising European states such as France or the UK.

Despite all that, is regulation necessary? What can it do? And what can the technology make possible?

Freedom in cyberspace

Is such regulation premature? First of all, there are surely questions as to 1) how many of us get all our information from the web; and 2) of such people, how many of them deliberately filter out inconvenient views. Though it is obviously true that some people conform to Sunstein's stereotype, it does not follow that such people are sufficiently numerous to threaten the foundation of deliberative democracy. We have not, for instance, seen the numbers of votes for extremist parties rise significantly everywhere since the introduction and popularisation of the WWW in the mid-nineties (although we have seen a decline in support for mainstream politicians and parties, and a corresponding rise in the fortunes of single-issue groups).

Secondly, electronic sources of information only supplement the existing sources. We still have newspapers, we still have general interest television and radio, and we still have the public forums and places where we can encounter physical demonstrations and expressions of other points of view. There is no evidence that cyberspace will replace these traditional sources, although no doubt usage patterns will be affected in unpredictable ways. In fact, the Internet, as we have argued, opens up a whole new space for politics, one that allows more interaction and does not always privilege the rich and powerful. More discussion is possible now than before its invention, as even press barons such as Rupert Murdoch are willing to admit.[29]

Similarly, the Internet is likely to increase its importance in terms of politics. However, it is unlikely to replace totally other media and forms of communication with regard to politics. The same worry was originally aired with regard to television. TV was heralded as ringing the death knell of radio, public meetings and local politics, not to mention other forms of entertainment, such as theatre, live sports and cinema. Has it? No. These things continue, some stronger than before. TV has taken some of the audience from these other media, but, more accurately, it has opened up a space for entertainment and politics alongside them. Early indications are that the Internet will do the same. For example, despite early predictions that online publishing would kill off the printed book, sales are still buoyant. After all, you, the reader, are still reading this in book form, or if not in book form then on printed paper.[30]

The question becomes, then, one of how much influence the Internet will have on citizens and their political views. Online discussion – even with like-minded people – is a new phenomenon, but it is unlikely to form, for most people, the exclusive source of their exposure to politics and other political views. Moreover, with more traditional media – such as CNN, Sky News and the BBC, as well as a host of newspapers – now providing their services via the Web, many individuals sufficiently motivated by politics and current affairs are likely to have bookmarked some of these sites simply because their coverage is virtually instantaneous.

It should go without saying that filtering occurs here all the time – for example, newspaper editors and TV programming chiefs filter information before it reaches us. The nuance is that with the Internet we'll soon have autonomy in this regard. Although the technology does not yet exist to filter perfectly according to things such as political views (for instance, if I say I am interested only in the Middle

East or Democratic Party politics, my Web filtering program is just as likely to produce documents that I would disagree with as it would ones with which I would concur), it may well do soon. The main thing is that it is us who are likely to be able to control what information we receive, rather than someone else. The argument cuts both ways: it may mean a narrowing of our viewing space, but we might also be exposed to things that, previously, editors had declined to make available to us. Without evidence to the contrary, this possibility is difficult to deny.

Thirdly, even without regulation, it is clear that reasonable access to opposing views can generally be found. For instance, if I do a search on Google for 'White Supremacy', I will no doubt come up with a number of white supremacist websites, but I will also come up with sites that oppose the ideas (in fact, at the time of writing, most of the sites at the top of the Google ranking either oppose white supremacist ideas, or analyse it objectively as a social phenomenon). And Google presumably would be the first port of call for a budding racist. Anyway, on Sunstein's own account, even the most virulent racist site is not far from links to a nice liberal one. He produces a table[31] quantifying links among hate sites to like- and unlike-minded sites. Apparently, the website of Skinheads of the Racial Holy War contains 100 links to other hate sites, but none to non-hate sites. OK, but suppose that one of these 100 links is to God Hates Fags. That gives three links to opposing sites. Or the Adelaide Institute, a holocaust revisionist site, provides six links to opposing sites. In other words, even in these – presumably appalling and senseless – sites, we are only a couple of mouse clicks away from someone opposing them. Of course, one is at liberty to click on such links or not, but for Sunstein it is the presence of such links that counts, not their actual use.

Regulation and technology

It may not be the case, therefore, that regulation such as Sunstein's 'must carry' rule is properly justified by the empirically determined facts. It is also an interesting question – and instructive, given our purpose of establishing an overview of the properties of cyberspace as a political space – as to how such regulation could be implemented, as a matter of technical arrangement. Let us accept that, contrary to the arguments in the previous section, some form of regulation is required. Some sort of navigational route is needed from sites with overtly political content to sites with opposing views. If we now put on our techie hats, how does Sunstein's practical proposal measure up?[32]

One problem with Sunstein's proposal is that the onus is on the content provider to place the weblinks in the page. So, for instance, an American white supremacist site would have to put some link in to, say, the National Association for the Advancement of Colored People (NAACP). Fair enough, but this is irrelevant if the reader happens to live anywhere other than in America, as the NAACP is an American organisation. For a link to be relevant to a British reader, it would need to be to, say, the UK's Commission for Racial Equality. And similarly for surfers of other countries.

So our putative American white supremacist would have to do some dramatic research, and list organisations promoting racial equality in every country in the world. That would be a hard enough task, and we might smile at the thought of the efforts it would entail. But actually, the task doesn't stop there. Organisations appear and disappear. They change their names. Websites close down, or they move to different addresses. If there is any kind of responsibility on the part of the content provider to keep these weblinks up to date, then the research would not only be massive, it would be continuous – our supremacist would have to monitor the links to check that they worked at regular intervals. Failure to do so would eventually mean that a number of the links would not get through to websites at all (they would be what are called dangling links). The overhead on the content provider would be massive, not just in writing the site in the first place, but in maintaining it as well. OK, we may not worry about the white supremacist having to do all that, but to be properly just, political sites of every type, from Greens to Conservatives, Marxists to Liberals, would have to do the same thing.

Another problem is that Sunstein – who focuses strongly on the American case – does not address the different requirements in different polities. There is a clear pattern in the US, where unsocialised, immature people develop particular hatreds, often though not always via the Internet, and then set off on a shooting spree. But access to guns is easy in the United States. This is not the case in, for example, the UK, where most guns are banned, and as a result this sort of mass killing, though certainly not unknown, is a much rarer event, and much less often associated with the Internet. Hence what might seem like a sensible regulation from the American point of view would look like bureaucratic overkill in the UK.

Thirdly, there is an issue of definition: framing such a regulation would be extremely difficult. For instance, though few legislators would worry about making a white supremacist place a link to an anti-racist group, one would hope that they would be squeamish about making the NAACP include a link to the Skinheads of the Racial Holy War. And fourthly, there is the obvious problem of the inability to legislate in the US with respect to a site based abroad.

Nevertheless, while we are thinking along these lines, it is interesting to note that actually new technologies, particularly the customisation technologies that so exercise Sunstein and others, could, if need be, be applied to the regulatory problem that Sunstein's proposals engender. Sunstein's suggestion places the onus on the content provider, which is reasonable because that is the general model for media regulation. The key to avoiding these pitfalls is to note that the beneficiary is not the content provider, but the reader (and the reader's democratic polity). The problem with static weblinks is that they are created not by the reader, but by the author. Furthermore, static weblinks are static – they need to be updated regularly to keep track of changing addresses.

There are technologies, such as open hyperlink technology,[33] that are reader-based and dynamic, and hence are a possible alternative. Such technology creates appropriate links for a reader at a particular time. Business and scientific applications work on the assumption that the links created will be for sites that the reader wants to see. However, in the sort of regulatory regime imagined by Sunstein, one could imagine a system built into proprietary browsers, extracting useful oppositional links from a centrally held resource discovery service (which in this case could simply be a database) that would link to sites that the reader ought to see (in the regulatory authorities' opinion). This would meet, to an extent at least, the above four worries.

First, the content and maintenance of the database of sites would be the responsibility of the regulatory authorities. Secondly, different countries could have different regulatory regimes, and so software sold or licensed in the US might have different link creation procedures from software sold or licensed elsewhere (some countries would not require automatic link creation at all). Thirdly, the detail of the actual links to be featured would be an administrative matter for the database manager, rather than a hot political potato dependent on the artful framing of legislation. Fourthly, a link provision service operating in the US could operate on any site wherever it was based, because it would be operating from the computer receiving the content; so American legislation would apply to American users, British legislation would apply to British users, and so on.

There would still be issues to resolve. Sunstein's proposal is based on known standards, whereas open hyperlink systems remain a maturing research topic. The technology would have to be proved on an Internet-wide scale. Nevertheless, if regulation is really necessary, surely it is better to focus it on the reader rather than on the writer, particularly given that the technology is already in place. Then we could enjoy the benefits – which we have argued are essential – of filtering technologies, whilst still keeping a lid on all the crazies.

We are not arguing for regulation in this form. However, the example is instructive. Thinking in this sphere shows us the extent to which the new technologies on the horizon shift emphasis from writers to readers. It will not just be publication that will have to be managed, but reception as well. It will take many years for the full benefits to be realised and for the unintended pitfalls to become evident. But we should not underestimate the extent of the paradigm shift.

Cultivating democracy on the seedbed of civic virtue

The points made above are empirical claims and the technologies described already in existence, but it is also possible to question some of the underlying assumptions relied upon in the claims about the effects of filtering on the process and procedures of deliberation. Here we want to look at just one such assumption, and show how it develops into a claim about the deleterious effects of information customisation on deliberative democracy.

Many views of the relationship between deliberative democracy and lower-level sites or places of civic participation tend to assume what Nancy Rosenblum terms a 'logic of congruence'.[34] In existing democracies this means that, following observer and theoretician of democracy Alexis de Tocqueville's early lead, the associations and groups of civil society are often seen as 'seed-beds of civic virtue'. For example, associations ranging from the overtly political, such as local branches of political parties, trade unions and political pressure groups, right down to non-political groups, such as bowling leagues and amateur dramatic associations, are seen as fertile grounds for cultivating the skills and virtues of democracy in citizens.[35]

For de Tocqueville, cooperation increases familiarity with networks of similarly cooperative persons, and the virtues of trust, reciprocity, tolerance and so forth that are so created have a spillover effect with regard to participation in wider social processes.

> Certain men happen to have a common interest in some concern; either a commercial undertaking is to be managed, or some speculation in manufacture to be tried: they meet, they combine, and thus, by degrees, they become familiar with the principle of association. The greater the multiplicity of small affairs, the more do men, even without knowing it, acquire facility in prosecuting great undertakings in common.[36]

All well and good, but many of the pessimistic views regarding the effects of the Internet on democratic deliberation seem to assume further that there must be some form of congruence between the internal workings or processes of small-scale groups and wider democratic procedures. In other words, secondary associations should be democratic and deliberative in form if they are to create and foster the virtues required for democratic society.

Several things can be said here. First, participation in associative relationships – even ones that are organised along lines amenable to democratic deliberation – does not guarantee that individuals will take on those norms. For example, the mere fact that you take an active part in your local amateur dramatic society, that you coordinate well with, and show a friendly disposition toward, fellow members of that society, as well as witnessing and being party to the high level of mutual trust that helps your dramatic efforts come to fruition does not necessarily mean that you (or any other amateur thespian) will display an increased willingness to become engaged in political matters, to deliberate more earnestly or to display any of your acquired virtues in another context. It is entirely possible that your membership in fact fosters particularism, intolerance and mistrust of those outside the group. You might, for example, see non-actors as beings of less moral worth, because they have not recognised the seminal importance of acting and drama. One might turn out to be a luvvie but not a democrat.[37]

Secondly, the converse may also be true (i.e. the logic of congruence may simply be false). The disposition to participate in and support democratic processes, as well as to engage in genuine deliberation, may have little connection to the internal structure or content of other groups. Individuals may acquire important virtues from narrow, non-democratic groups just as easily as they do from groups that mirror society's own democratic structure. How might this be so? Well, even in the most extreme, undemocratic groups – think here of, say, Aryan supremacist groups or paramilitary groups such as the so-called State Militias that exist in the US – individuals are combining and cooperating, albeit for purposes that many of us would find unsavoury. They are learning skills that are useful for the democratic process, if such spillover does indeed occur. More importantly, however, these groups, in order to increase their numbers beyond a small fanatical membership, actually have to engage with others who do not share their own views. For sure, extremist groups pick up members from outside, but evidence shows that these are largely people who already share similar views. They are preaching to the converted. Doing this will mean that their membership base is always restricted.

In order to increase membership size, extremist groups have to attract those who do not normally share similar views. They have to preach to the unconverted. This, however, is a very different game from their core belief. They have to engage in public argument, to offer reasons that stand a chance of persuading others of their cause (assuming, of course, that methods of violence, coercion and deception are largely unavailable to them). But once they begin to do this, then they are actually engaging in the deliberative processes of the democratic enterprise, rather than attacking it from outside. An inevitable consequence of this is the moderation of the message being offered. It is a well-worn fact of political science that to increase membership size a political party or group has to moderate towards the centre ground, for this is the terrain occupied by the vast majority of individuals. Those who refuse to give up their extremist positions will always remain marginalised.

A similarity exists here with the position articulated by Adam Smith with regard to the social usefulness of churches and religious sects. Faced with the problem of the anonymity created by the industrialised society outlined above, Smith searched for other associations or groups that could fulfil the task originally held by the close-knit rural community, of instilling virtuous behaviour. Smith soon settled his gaze upon the institutions of the Christian religion. Here he found that a variety of small religious sects could perform the same educational role within society. Smith's interest in the Church was not religious; rather, his praise of religious sects was purely instrumental: they were means to a socially valuable end. Smith's focus on churches is not surprising, given that they were the main form of secondary association in existence at that time. Churches, according to Smith, are crucial substitutes for the small-scale face-to-face communities of the pre-industrial era. It is not the spiritual ends of religion that are important to Smith, rather it is the moral, social and political benefits that are the by-products of religion and religious groups that matter for civic purposes.

Whilst Smith's churches provided a civic education conducive to a flourishing liberal polity, he was acutely aware that it is only a certain pattern of churches that can play this role. For Smith it is a multitude of small-scale churches and religious sects that will guarantee that citizens develop the right kind of virtues. Religious liberty, that is, helps ensure the perpetuation of civic morality and civic peace. Religious diversity, if properly ordered, can ensure civic virtue. Smith acknowledges that religious sects have displayed a tendency to slip into extremism or fanaticism with regard to virtuous human behaviour. Religious groups provide the perfect site for fostering dispositions beneficial to the polity, but extremism has to be guarded against lest it seize hold of citizens and turn moderate values into extreme ones that would be harmful.[38]

Smith's recommendation for achieving this is that all religious sects should exist without state funding or support. Instead, they should depend purely on private support, even for the payment of the clergy. This was a radical suggestion for Smith's day, when state-sponsored religion was the norm. Smith bases his suggestion upon his analysis of the position and workings of the Roman Catholic Church during the Middle Ages. In particular, he notes the incentive structure that existed for the Catholic clergy to expand their sphere of influence. 'In the church of Rome, the industry and zeal of the inferior clergy is kept more alive by the powerful motive of self-interest, than perhaps any established Protestant church.'[39] It pays, therefore, to be proactive in increasing the size of one's flock when one's livelihood depends upon the voluntary donations of that group. Smith's description of the incentives is magnificent: 'It is with them as with the hussars and light infantry of some armies – no plunder, no pay.'[40] Unlike his friend David Hume, who defended state support of the Church on the grounds that to do otherwise would encourage the clergy to continually invent more and more extreme methods for enticing adherents, Smith is arguing for the disestablishment of the Church on the ground that this will result in a multiplicity of small religious sects, and these, in turn, will be moderate in terms of the views they foster amongst their adherents.[41]

But why would a large number of small sects produce moderation? Smith's answer is an early version of a phenomenon well known in modern political science: gravitation towards the centre ground. Smith advises that the state ought to deal 'equally and impartially with all the different sects', and in this way allow individuals to choose the church they wish to attend.[42] As a consequence of this free competition between religions there will arise a multitude of small and relatively equally balanced (in terms of power) religious groups. Smith's reasoning that state neutrality will give rise to such a situation is based on his assessment of the inevitability of religious disagreement. Smith observes that one's acceptance of a religious view is largely connected to one's personal history, psychological makeup and socio-economic background, as well as the rhetorical skills of the clergy. These factors dictate that disagreement will exist and persist. The inevitable result is a multitude of different sects.

Once we accept the fact of religious pluralism as a permanent feature of a free society, then it is easy to see how this creates moderate values. For, in order to ensure their survival, these little sects would have to adopt a stance of moderation and mutual respect.

> The teachers of each sect, seeing themselves surrounded on all sides with more adversaries than friends, would be obliged to learn that candour and moderation which is seldom to be found among the teachers of those great sects, whose tenets being supported by the civil magistrate, are held in veneration by almost all the inhabitants of extensive kingdoms and empires, and who therefore see nothing round them but followers, disciples, and humble admirers. The teacher of each little sect, finding themselves almost alone, would be obliged to respect those of almost every other sect, and the concessions which they would mutually find it both convenient and agreeable to make to one another, might in time probably reduce the doctrine of the greater part of them to that pure and rational religion, free from every mixture of absurdity, imposture, or fanaticism, such as wise men in all ages of the world wished to see established.[43]

In the context of online extremism, the point is that, even given that someone may develop extreme views thanks to too much positive feedback, that doesn't matter much as long as he stays in his bedroom and surfs the Web. The moment he tries to put his views into practice, he must, in a democracy, persuade voters of his views (or, in a totalitarian state, persuade key bureaucrats). Then he may become dangerous. But to carry out that persuasion, he must enter some sort of public forum, and his views must be presented alongside alternatives. Voters (or functionaries) are presented with a range of views, so for a view to carry it must be persuasive. Furthermore, when our extremist enters the public forum, he will be exposed to the alternative views himself. Hence the engagement of our extremist with the policy formation process – independently of whether such a process is democratic – will produce exactly the result that Sunstein wants to encourage.

The Nihilists: from Columbine to the World Trade Center

It has to be admitted, however, that this is not the whole story. Sunstein cites the phenomenon of school shootings, a common pathology of mass murder in the USA (a recent count found sixteen such events between 1996 and 2003[44]). The pattern is fairly simple: one or more children, usually mid-to-late-teens, who is a loner, who enjoys shoot-'em-up video games, gothic music or science fiction films, who mixes badly with his (occasionally her) classmates and is often the focus of bullying or verbal abuse, suddenly turns up at school one day carrying some of the extraordinary arsenal of weapons that Americans seem to think essential for daily life (or to protect themselves from one of the most hands-off governments in the developed world), often having slaughtered members of his own family first, and then opens fire on his classmates and teachers, ignoring pleas for mercy, often smiling, and usually killing himself before he can be disarmed and captured by the police. We have never seen a really convincing explanation of such events, though the desire for notoriety on the part of these people may be fuelled by commemorative pop songs such as The Boomtown Rats' *I Don't Like Mondays* or films such as Michael Moore's *Bowling for Columbine*, plus the many websites devoted to antisocial posing.

As we saw above, Sunstein argues, not unreasonably, that the fevered online atmosphere will tend to encourage such people in the development of their beliefs. The Internet has a tendency to encourage the development of extremes. In late 2004, a craze called 'happy slapping' began in South-East London, where teenagers would slap adults on buses or other public places while their friends would record the incident on their mobile phones. The videos of these mild, if disturbing, attacks would then be exchanged via the Internet, rather as previous generations used to swap football, baseball or Pokemon cards. By mid-2005, however, the craze had spread far beyond London, and the attackers were prepared to conduct very serious assaults.

A similar effect seems to happen with some disaffected students at school; finding themselves unusual and often the target for bullying, they find a group of like-minded people online who are fantasising about revenge. Most of them, of course, will ultimately knuckle under to the weight of the system, get a job, get a partner and leave behind their urges to shoot everyone in sight. But as long as young, impressionable and bitter people (their bitterness is often more corrosive for being grounded in nothing other than adolescent rage, and therefore for being impossible to address) have access to this rage-fuel and are allowed to imbibe it undiluted by any common sense from any other source, then a very small minority of them will eventually cross the line between unpleasant fantasy and murderous reality.

As hinted above, this argument, even if true, is hardly decisive. In the first place, the problem is a peculiarly (though certainly not exclusively) American problem, caused by the particular tensions in the American constitution. The First Amendment allows almost unlimited free speech (and, as we have seen, technical considerations make censoring the Internet hard enough anyway), while the Second Amendment is often interpreted to render any attempt to limit access to weaponry unconstitutional. The First Amendment lets people poison their minds and the Second allows them to blow everyone away. A more realistic interpretation of the Second Amendment – whose purpose is to prevent government encroachment on the citizen's domain, not to allow the detritus of the 'me' generation to pretend they are Arnold Schwarzenegger's Terminator – would reduce access to guns, which is directly correlated to the number and severity of such incidents.

In the second place, the scale of these (admittedly horrific) incidents hardly implies an adjustment to the arguments we adduced above. Of the sixteen school shootings between 1996 and 2003, three were specific attacks with motives of revenge or gang warfare, while another was carried out by a six-year-old boy on another six-year-old, so presumably the Internet was not to blame there. The other twelve incidents saw forty people dead, excluding the suicides of the murderers. Five people per year is too high a number, but whether it is high enough to demand constitutional change is not clear.

Why might school shootings matter? Because the assumption of our counter-argument is that, in order to be effective, those extremists who wish to engage in political action in democracies need to gain a hold on the levers of power, which means either standing in elections (and thereby engaging with others in the inevitable debate) or convincing bureaucrats (and thereby engaging with them through argument). Either way, they must take part in the very deliberations that Sunstein worries that they avoid.

But there are some who are so extreme that they become nihilists; that is, they offer no positive programme whatsoever. In which case their political action need only be destructive, and they therefore have no need of the levers of power. When such nihilism is combined with a disregard of personal safety, such people can become very dangerous indeed.

Until recently, this combination of traits was fairly rare. There were people who were willing to die for a cause, and sociopaths who opposed everything, but no sociopaths who were willing to die for nothing, as Yundt the terrorist laments in Joseph Conrad's great novel *The Secret Agent*.

> 'I have always dreamed,' he mouthed fiercely, 'of a band of men absolute in their resolve to discard all scruples in the choice of means, strong enough to give themselves frankly the name of destroyers, and free from the taint of that resigned pessimism which rots the world. No pity for anything on earth, including themselves, and death enlisted for good and all in the service of humanity – that's what I would have liked to see.'[45]

Yundt could never find three such men together. But if such men were abundant, then their destructive political action could become very dangerous to society indeed. Terrorist organisations, such as the IRA or ETA, were never a serious challenge to the principles of liberty because it was their desire to bomb their way to the negotiating table; even though their methods were violent and ruthless, they framed their purpose within a recognised set of assumptions, and so the possibility of political progress was always there. On the other hand, how can you address similarly violent and unscrupulous people who have no recognisable end purpose, who promote terror for terror's sake, who wish to blow up negotiation and compromise itself?

Such people are the school shooters, but devastating on small communities though their attacks can be, their combined effects are pinpricks compared with other types of criminal. However, another group of nihilists has managed, in a few short years, to change the entire world.

It is often thought that neo-fundamentalist terrorism,[46] most notoriously supported by al-Qaeda and Osama bin Laden, is an attempt to create Islamic states; actually it is no such thing. There certainly are people who wish to set up Islamic states; they are adherents of the ideology known as Islamism.[47] Islamists can be uncompromising, but can equally well be moderate and democratic.[48] They provide no weight to Sunstein's argument, as they are willing to enter into whatever political processes are available to them in the societies in which they are located; they join in the deliberations in the democratic space. Fear of such people smacks rather more of xenophobia than the preservation of democracy.

However, neo-fundamentalist thinkers are not interested in the political. That does not mean that they are necessarily extreme; philosophers such as Tariq Ramadan, drawing on Islamic thought and civilisation, aim to provide some sort of *modus vivendi* for Muslims to retain their identity while integrating into Western society.[49] But there is no doubt that the fiery rhetoric of the terrorists and their apologists is gaining support amongst some communities.[50] And the neo-fundamentalists have no interest in politics; their activities in Iraq, for example, have been entirely destructive and their alliances (most obviously with the pro-secular Baathists loyal to the deposed Saddam Hussein) purely pragmatic, while elsewhere, in the British general election of 2005, the Muslim Council of Britain and the anti-war party Respect, an alliance with plenty of Muslim representation which made a strong play for the Muslim vote, found themselves under attack from radical Muslims opposed to elections per se.[51] As Olivier Roy explains:

> Beyond their religious radicalism, neofundamentalists tend to ignore or despise politics, which paradoxically pushes them to accept the present political order without bestowing any legitimacy on it. Their religious radicalism pushes them

towards political neutrality (except for the jihadists, even if they do not have a political agenda either). This may explain why they accept and even support regimes like that of Saudi Arabia, but also why they are more adapted to living in the West than true Islamists.[52]

When neo-fundamentalists bother to make an argument, they dissent from the Islamist view on the ground that an Islamic state should result from the Islamisation of the world. They say it should be the other way round.

However that may be, the serious issue for us is whether such neo-fundamentalist Muslims are a danger to the political process. As they wish to bypass politics, to avoid the deliberative political space, and as they wish to play a part in politics by rendering places ungovernable (very successfully in a number of instances), then they must be. We can argue that the school shootings, dreadful in themselves, are irrelevant compared with the annual American gun-related carnage, and therefore not worth altering important points of political principle over; but no one can argue that Islamic neo-fundamentalism is politically insignificant. Indeed, all over the Western world, and in the US in particular, political principles have been altered, generally away from the pursuit of liberty and towards ensuring security, explicitly on account of the threat from international terrorism.

For Sunstein's point to be valid in this context, it also needs to be shown that neo-fundamentalist thinking is warped by the excessive feedback effect of an online community only reading its own literature and avoiding the unwelcome criticisms of political opponents. Olivier Roy's surveys imply that indeed it is.

As usual the internet serves as a circulatory system of ideas that are reaffirmed by dint of repetition: the same set of references reappear again and again, while some authors are mentioned systematically.[53]

Most quoted are extreme, puritan Wahhabis from Medina. Their texts are often designed to circulate easily. They carry relatively populist, anti-intellectual messages (which challenges Adam Smith's argument that churches greedy for new members must be tolerant and respectful; it is the crudity of the messages that helps their word to spread).[54] They often appear in English rather than Arabic, to reach the large number of Muslims in the West.[55] Furthermore, the Internet and, perhaps more importantly, satellite television have created a sense of Arab unity that politicians throughout the twentieth century failed to do. Modern standard Arabic, taught in schools but non-colloquial and over-formal, is becoming a genuinely spoken language. And Muslim ritual is becoming more similar the world over, thanks to the increasing number of experiences held in common.[56]

Clearly neo-fundamentalist terrorism is a greater threat to security and democracy than school shootings. This is the most extreme example where regulation of the Internet could be called for. Add to that the pragmatic consideration that the United States calls many, if not all, of the shots about the Internet's governance, and given its so-called war on terror, we might expect some kind of action.

But even in this case, we should pause for thought. First, to frame the question in a practical context is to doubt its feasibility in that context. When so many websites are here-today-and-gone-tomorrow, and so many of them are based in places that are relatively hard to influence (though admittedly a surprising number of Islamic websites are based in the US), it is hard to quantify the effort required to keep track of and regulate them, and police the regulations adequately.

Secondly, the Internet is only part of the telecommunications web. There are many other forums for disseminating this material, in particular satellite TV. So regulating the Internet may not actually be as effective as one might hope.

Thirdly, the victory in the propaganda war, at least in the Middle East, might have been conceded by the Americans rather than won by the neo-fundamentalists. During many of the momentous events in the Middle East between 2000 and 2003, about fifty million viewers got their news from the Arabic satellite channel al-Jazeera. But the US never tried very hard to get its message across on that channel. Instead, it bombed al-Jazeera's Kabul office. Its tactic was to set up a rival channel, al-Hurra, in Washington. Not surprisingly, no one watches it. The US government – and this really *is* incredible – still, at the time of writing, has no spokesperson capable of defending the American line in good Arabic.[57] And al-Jazeera was actually more than willing to interview US officials, and to show such interviews uncut. The problem often was that official American views tended to reinforce the fears of Arab audiences, rather than alleviating them.[58]

Fourthly, though there is evidence that the vicious information feedback loops that Sunstein referred to exist in the neo-fundamentalist world, equally there is evidence to undermine suggestions that such loops cause dangerous apolitical nihilism. For example, a series of public opinion surveys conducted in the Arab world by Shibley Telhami, an expert on Arabic media in Washington's Brookings Institute and a fierce critic of the Bush administration's media policies, found few correlations, and indeed some of those few were surprising and counterintuitive.

> The aim [of the surveys] is to find out whether there is a real direct relationship between people's opinions on the issues of the day – particularly in foreign policy, political reform and the role of Islam in politics – and what they watch on the news. And let me briefly tell you the findings of that aspect of the research: there is a minimal – absolutely minimal – impact on matters relating to support or opposition to the US for example. The lack of trust in US foreign policy among people who don't watch Al Jazeera or people who don't have satellite is very similar to those who watch Al Jazeera and have satellite. On matters related to the Arab–Israeli conflict, the views of those who watch one station or the other are minimally different. In fact, sometimes they go the other way

than you might think. Those who watch CNN tend to be more anti-American in some countries than those who watch Al Jazeera. So it is very difficult. I have done some correlation studies, statistical analysis, controlling demographics. I see no major impact on those opinions. It tells you that for these opinions, their sources are somewhere else.

The media is an intermediate factor. It does influence on the margins, but it is not the driving force for these opinions.[59]

To sum up, the arguments against restricting free speech online have a certain intuitive force, but upon examination they are less practical and less theoretically inviting than they seem at first sight. Such restriction and regulation can only be effective against murderous nihilists – of whom there is an increasing number. But even in that case, the evidence is not unequivocal. The control the rich nations, and the US in particular, exercise over the Internet is large enough that if there were a head of steam behind the drive to regulate it, it could happen. And such regulation may help moderate the information environments of potential terrorists (which is the aim) without disturbing harmless users too much. Or it may not. At present, we contend that the balance of the argument is still firmly against regulation.

7:›
Cutting Out the Middleman:
e-Government, e-Democracy

Democracy online

While the WWW strongly affects the environment of the deliberations through which opinions are formed and democratic decisions are influenced, it is also true that the machinery that ICT makes available can be adapted to provide a mechanism for democracy itself to be carried out. As the technology used for any kind of service provision affects the quality of service provided, as well as the demands made on it, this will be as true for democracy as it has been for telecommunications, education or the media. In this chapter we will look at some of the areas where ICT is being applied to gauge how important or desirable such changes might be. We will focus on the use of ICT for providing voting systems, and then look at its use for spreading information through a democracy, and for the process of governance itself.

The decline and fall of direct democracy

The instantaneous communications that the WWW render feasible have opened up the possibility that, for the first time since the fall of the ancient Greek *polis*, a truly direct form of democracy is on the horizon. The origins of democracy lie in the small, face-to-face communities of cities such as ancient Athens, where citizens convened together to take shared political decisions. They met together, they deliberated together and they decided together. They also implemented their decisions together, especially when the decision was to go to war. The role of being a citizen in a *polis* was one filled to the brim with positive political obligations. For the ancients, politics was inseparable from their day-to-day lives; they could not dip out of their public duties and focus only on their private interests. Their liberty came at a price: every person (barring slaves, women, and others of lower class) was a politician, a public servant and a soldier.[1] As historian of political thought Paul Rahe writes in his majestic *Republics Ancient and Modern*:

> Modern liberal democracy and the ancient Greek *polis* stand, in their fundamental principles, radically opposed. The ancient city was a republic of virtue – first by its very nature, and then also because it had to be one in order to survive. Its cohesion was not and could not be a mere function of incessant negotiation and calculated compromise; it was and had to be bound together by a profound sense of moral purpose and common struggle.[2]

The ability to abdicate from political duties in modern democratic societies is closely related to the different model of democracy that currently operates; one that has enabled the near total separation of public from private matters. Modern liberty is largely viewed as freedom from state institutions, rather than the freedom to participate in those institutions. John Locke captures this modern idea with his view that the law 'hedges us in only from bogs and precipices'; it is a framework within which to operate as private citizens, not something that forms part of our daily life or something to be operated on.[3] Part of the reason for this is that the model of democracy born in those ancient republics did not scale; it did not transfer easily to large communities, where face-to-face meetings of the entire citizenry were a physical impossibility. The rise of the modern nation-state pretty much put paid to the direct form of democracy as self-governance on the Greek model was incompatible with the sheer number and dispersal of citizens in the new political format.

The heyday of direct democracy was in the fifth century BC, in the Athenian city-state. This small area, populated by maybe a hundred thousand people, produced such figures as Pericles, Socrates, Sophocles, Euripides, Aristophanes, Thucydides, Praxiteles and Plato (whose influence on philosophy is still vast two and a half millennia later[4]), and such wonders as the Parthenon and the extraordinary sculpture of the time. It is certainly safe to say that no other culture has produced such a concentration of genius.

The direct democracy of the *polis* worked in ancient Athens because the concept structured most public activity in the state. The Athenian assembly was the cornerstone of the democracy; every citizen (native adult free male, which of course ruled out a very large percentage of the population) who had not been disenfranchised for some offence was a part of it. There was no property qualification at all. The assembly met in a mass, and was the sole legislative institution. It met once a month routinely, although it could be called more often in the event of an emergency; anyone could speak at any time (though getting people to listen was a trickier matter). A smaller council, of five hundred men, arranged business – but even these could not act as a powerful clique, as it was made up of fifty men from each of the ten tribes chosen by lot. The assembly even meted out justice.

The implicit theory of the *polis* was that the individual owed a duty both to it and to himself. The life of the individual was structured around this more or less formal set of requirements to ensure that the high quality of life in Athens continued; as such, the *polis* theory came as close as humankind has ever come to defining the relationship between the individual and society in a mutually supporting way. Self-rule was vital to freedom; a sophisticated society with plenty of cooperation was vital to a properly full life. In many societies, these two imperatives can interfere with each other (does the individual suppress his or her own desires in the public interest?), but the *polis* system made them, for a short period at least, magically mutually supporting.

Why, then, did the system break down, after perhaps a century and a half of successful government? The answer seems to have been specialisation and, indirectly, growth. Government and administration in the Athenian *polis* was essentially amateur, which is not to say amateurish, as it managed to conduct a couple of wars (not always successfully), recover from the occasional lapse into oligarchy, collect taxes, maintain justice and keep a strong currency. But eventually the system collapsed. Larger states, such as the Persian empire or, later, the Macedonians, who ended the city-state system forever, managed a coherence of affairs at the cost of freedom and self-rule for their citizens. The small democratic *polis* struggled against these larger units. In the fourth century a more individualistic frame of mind developed; the balance between the citizen and the *polis* began to fail. Citizens who were more individualistic were less likely to contribute their labour and their time to the needs of the *polis*; they would rather pay a waiver fee or tax. When the great orator Demosthenes warned the Athenians of the danger that the barbarian Macedonians posed, he was forced to try to persuade the people to pay for a national defence by diverting money away from the fund that enabled all citizens to go to the theatre for free. There had been no such complacency to overcome a century and a half earlier, when the Athenians had recognised the threat from the Persians and organised an effective defence. When states need to grow beyond a certain size, in order either to realise the benefits of cooperation or to protect themselves against larger rivals, the *polis* system's requirement on everyone to play their part in government becomes unrealisable.

Nowhere is this more evident than in the founding of the republic of the United States of America. When the colonists finally shook off

British rule they needed to install a new political system. The hierarchical systems of monarchical and aristocratic Europe were unattractive as models for obvious reasons. Instead, the Founding Fathers deliberately reached back over two millennia to ancient Greece for their model. However, the model did not translate to the new situation without some difficulty. Much of the constitutional wrangling of this period revolved around the implicit question of how Greek democracy could be adapted to the American situation, with its large population and massive geographical context. To overcome the problem of direct deliberation and decision making, the framers of the Constitution put in place a system of representation. The views of citizens were to be represented by their (usually) elected officials in the democratic chambers of their state.

The Founders struggled with the various secondary problems this solution caused – factions, separation of powers and so forth – but the model stuck. Indeed, it is difficult for citizens of modern democracies to conceive of any system of democratic decision making other than the representative one. However, the perennial problem of the system is that it removes citizens from politics by one step. This can fuel perceptions of uninvolvement, disempowerment and so forth. For many theorists of democracy the aim of institutional reform should be to bring our modern institutions as close to possible to the core ideals of the direct form of democracy found in ancient Greece.

e-Voting

The beauty of the Internet is that communication with many people is relatively straightforward and instantaneous. Communicating a message, however, is not so immediate, at least if we wish our audience to take proper notice of what we have said; chapter 6 demonstrates that. But if the content of the message is highly structured or is intended to be informative rather than persuasive, then the Internet comes into its own. If you want to buy or sell an item on eBay, for example, then all you have to communicate is your decision to exchange and the price you are prepared to pay or be paid, and even if there are a lot of people in the marketplace, your voice will be heard and taken account of.

Voting is similar to buying and selling – basically, your preference needs to be registered at a certain agreed point and a tally made of the various aggregate strengths of the different options. This is an ideal domain for ICTs, in that, effectively, all that is involved is message passing and counting. Can it really be that simple?

Obviously there is more to it than that. Elections are gateways to power; they are often the subject of fraud and error. A voting system is an end-to-end security problem, from registering votes to counting. The integrity of the system is essential, and the need for honest and committed election administration officials is neither removed nor lessened. Furthermore, the security problems are not merely technical, but are sociotechnical; that is, they require integrity of technology and the way it is used in actual social contexts. Voting is governed by large codes of law, and when the code that governs the voting software is designed and written, it has to be mapped onto the law; in other words, the information processing systems have to be congruent to the systems of government, exactly as discussed in chapter 5 with respect to mapping information processing onto other social processes in the development context. In particular, as election laws vary dramatically across countries as a result of historical, geographical, political and social factors, it is highly unlikely that a 'one size fits all' approach to e-voting will work. Early hype about e-voting is giving way to a more measured set of expectations and experiments that will, with luck, aid efficiency and fairness.[5]

Two general classes of measure are possible to ensure the integrity of elections. First, there are preventative measures, such as voters having to identify themselves, that are intended to make the election as fair as possible. Secondly, there are auditing measures, to ensure that, once the election has taken place, fraud can be discovered and, hopefully, remedied. Indeed, there is some crossover between the two, as auditing measures can be preventative if their being made routine acts as a deterrent.[6]

Auditing is a complex process. One key factor is the ability to reconstruct the election. For instance, in the United Kingdom, the Secret Ballot Act of 1872 makes each voter's ballot a state secret. This means that it is perfectly legal in the UK to link every vote to a voter, and the UK system, largely paper-based, allows just that. The British voter has a number on his or her voting card, which is taken to the polling station; the voter is then given a voting form which is stamped with the number. It is then theoretically possible to trace the vote back to check with the voter if fraud is suspected. This traceability makes auditing possible. In fact, it is more than theoretically possible. In the past, for instance, this auditing measure has been used by state surveillance services to find out who has voted for political parties such as the Communist Party. As we shall see later, surveillance and privacy overlap in many interesting arenas. On the other hand, there are places where secret ballots are absolute, such as in Iowa, where it is illegal for officials to mark ballots to make their provenance identifiable. In such cases, votes are not traceable back to voters, so auditors have to be more cunning if they are to audit without actually invading voters' privacy.[7]

In the context of using ICT for voting purposes, there is a number of things that can be done to aid this. One possibility is to have a paper printout of the vote that the voter can see and check him- or herself. This, however, can only aid the voter to check that his or her vote has been correctly recorded. Without such checks, though, the results can be farcical. In a local election in Florida in 2004, 10,844 votes were cast, the winner won by twelve votes and a recount of some of the votes was required. But because the vote was done on paperless touch screens, and the only paper printed contained each machine's final tally, the recount simply involved each machine printing out its tally again. Congressman Robert Wexler pointed out – correctly – that a reprint is not a recount.[8]

These are the problems set by the possibility of e-voting. Is a change to electronic systems justified? Let us look at three sets of issues: first, the problems associated with the instantaneity identified earlier, especially in the context of the discussion in chapter 6; secondly, the difficulties of security of the auditing process; and thirdly, the issues of fairness that arise.

Responsibility

It has long been thought that one of the roles of the political class was to protect the general population from its own irresponsibility. Certainly Plato's *Republic*, written in democratic Athens and clearly intended to be relevant to its politics, envisaged such a role. Another, related, idea is that politics demands a great deal of research and thought, and it would be impractical for everyone to devote that amount of time and energy to internalising the issues and reflecting accordingly. Hence the political class is just a part of that well-known phenomenon, the division of labour; we have carpenters to specialise in work with wood, plumbers to work with the mechanics of the water system, mechanics to keep our cars going, builders to build our houses, and politicians to run the country. We all specialise in something, and we trade our time and our labour for the services we want.

A British film, made at the end of the 1960s, called *The Rise and Rise of Michael Rimmer*, starred Peter Cook as a public relations executive (eerily reminiscent of Tony Blair) whose ability to play businessmen and politicians off against each other by his grasp of public opinion allows him to take more and more power for himself. He becomes Prime Minister by offering to use the best of modern technology (then-impossible but now-feasible set-top boxes for the TV) to consult the people on every issue. Overwhelmed by the tedium of having to make all sorts of boring decisions, the people vote to end the consultations, and instead give Rimmer all the power he wants by making him President of Britain. That, it is often thought, would be the result of too much public consultation: a weariness with power which eventually would play into the hands of professional politicians and populists.

Is this a reasonable view? It has to be said that when consultation is not part of a recognised political process within a country, then imposing such consultation upon it is unlikely to have entirely happy results. Also, the very idea of a referendum cedes a lot of power to those who control the process of generating the question, deciding how the campaigns are resourced and when the vote takes place.[9] However, when the culture and history of a country support consultation, then there is no need to think either that people will get fed up of doing much of the political work or that they will make ridiculous or unwise choices.

The Athenians were very keen on participation in politics – indeed, the *polis* system could not have flourished otherwise. The democracy was all the more thoroughgoing in that there was no large officialdom to put plans into action, so that decisions made by the people in the Assembly were ultimately to be carried out by the very same people. A sense of realism had to ensue. The idea that a direct democracy will lead to irresponsible edicts is associated with a quite separate idea, that the people making the decisions (the legislature, management) will not be the people who have to carry it out (the executive, the workers). It is well known that a people can be whipped up into a war-like fervour in certain circumstances, but they are less likely to go to war if they themselves will be the people who would walk onto the battlefield.

The ancient Athenians did not seem to have begrudged the time involved in politicking, although, as classicist H.D.F. Kitto points out, they had somewhat more time to spare.

[W]hen the reader has calculated how much of his working time is consumed in helping him pay for things which the Greek simply did without – things like settees, collars and ties, bedclothes, laid-on water, tobacco, tea and the Civil Service – let him reflect on the time-using occupations that we follow and he did not – reading books and newspapers, travelling daily to work, pottering about the house, mowing the lawn – grass being, in our climate, one of the bitterest enemies of social and intellectual life ... We envy, perhaps, ordinary Athenians who seem able to spend a couple of hours in the afternoon at the baths or a gymnasium ... *We* cannot afford to take time off in the middle of the day like this. No: but we get up at seven, and what with shaving, having break-fast, and putting on the complicated panoply which we wear, we are not ready for anything until 8.30.[10]

Thucydides' *Peloponnesian War* provides, perhaps wittingly, a commentary on the decline of Athenian democracy, as it came under increasing pressure from the war with Sparta, which shows how experienced assemblies can react. Sometimes the results were first rate: Athens, under its democratic leadership, managed to repel superior Persian forces, build up an impressive navy and amass an empire in all but name, without any kind of direction or government from a named political elite with recognised authority.[11]

However, later in the war, the weakness of direct democracy was exposed somewhat with the revolt of Lesbos. Defeated, Lesbos had no choice but to submit once more to Athens, and in the ensuing Assembly debate a populist called Cleon won a vote to send a ship to Lesbos's capital Mitylene to execute all the men and sell the women and children into slavery. However:

The morrow brought repentance with it, and reflection on the horrid cruelty of a decree which condemned a whole city to the fate merited only by the guilty. This was no sooner perceived by the Mitylenian ambassadors at Athens and their Athenian supporters, than they moved the authorities to put the question again to the vote, which they the more easily consented to do, as they themselves plainly saw that most of the citizens wished someone to give them an opportunity for reconsidering the matter.[12]

Cleon was appalled by this.

I have often before now been convinced that a democracy is incapable of empire, and never more so than by your present change of mind in the matter of Mitylene.[13]

The lie was given to Cleon's contention not only by the fact that Athens had built up an empire (not without a little bullying, but in general through persuasion rather than force), but also by the fact that the debate in the Assembly on the next day reversed the harsh decision about the Mitylenians. The statesmanlike decision was made after a marvellous speech by one Diodotus[14] – but required no statesman to either propose it or enact it.

Nevertheless, the Assembly also made some awful strategic decisions. Cleon's aggressive populism gradually persuaded more and more people, and, as is always the way with populism, the decisions made got worse, both for Athens' material well-being and for its spiritual and moral health. One decision that went very badly was the attempt to open a second front in Sicily

with a greater armament than that under Laches and Eurymedon, and, if possible, to conquer the island, most of them being ignorant of its size and of the number of its inhabitants, Hellenic and barbarian, and of the fact that they were undertaking a war not much inferior to that against the Peloponnesians.[15]

This foolish campaign undermined the Athenian cause and led to its eventual defeat. It also lost its moral compass; the island of Melos, a neutral non-combatant, was infamously dealt with.

> Reinforcements afterwards arriving from Athens ... the siege was now pressed vigorously; and some treachery taking place inside, the Melians surrendered at discretion to the Athenians, who put to death all the grown men whom they took, and sold the women and children for slaves, and subsequently sent out five hundred colonists and inhabited the place themselves.[16]

The Athenians, although culturally and morally a long way from ourselves, clearly provide equivocal evidence for the effectiveness of direct democracy. Are there modern examples of direct democracy that we can consider?

Offline direct democracy, on the Athenian model, would be pretty well impossible in the modern world, as has often been pointed out. But there are nations where democracy flourishes and representation takes something of a back seat, at least some of the time. Consider, for example, Switzerland, a landlocked, mountainous, relatively fissile country. Centralisation in such a country would be doomed; Switzerland's 1848 constitution is aimed at ensuring that democracy is as direct as possible.[17]

Indeed, there are nearly 3000 communities in Switzerland, each of which has some sort of consultation system. Some opt for parliaments, but the majority have a traditional Assembly on the Athenian model (some even meet outside), where anyone over the age of 18 is allowed a say over local issues such as schools, social services and energy supplies. Over the local level is the canton, and above that is the actual federal government. Unlike other hierarchical systems, much of the government is devolved down to the lowest possible level; this idea of subsidiarity, supposedly enshrined in the European Union but rarely implemented there, is what makes the Swiss system stand out.

Most big decisions are taken by referendum. So, a decision with a large local impact, such as building or closing down a school, would be decided by a local referendum, while a decision with national repercussions, such as whether to join the EU, is decided nationally. Large changes to the constitution are decided by a dual majority of individual voters and of cantons. New laws can become the subject of a referendum if fifty thousand signatures can be raised in a hundred days. One hundred thousand signatures in eighteen months will give you the right to hold a referendum of your own. About one in ten of the latter type of initiative gets through, though Parliament gets its way about two times out of three. Turnout seems to be about 40% for a federal referendum, a big decline from a few decades earlier, but hardly disastrous given the large number of times the Swiss are expected to vote, and the effort involved in understanding the issues.

Do these referendums result in decisions that are uncivilised or hasty? Would the Swiss have saved or massacred the Mitylenians? Well, there have certainly been some dubious decisions; for example, women were denied the vote in 1959. On the other hand, such results are often overturned; women received the vote in 1971 thanks to a two to one majority vote from their menfolk. Sample referendum results from recent years on potentially populist issues are given in table 1; one may agree or disagree, but the decisions are hardly mad or unimplementable.

So direct democracy, understood as something that bypasses representatives, does not necessarily produce populist or direction-less government. However, it is worth pointing out that in an offline referendum the effect is to slow decision making down, as questions are framed, debates are undergone, campaigns are fought and so on. This process fits into the deliberative model of democracy that we discussed in chapter 6. Online, the result might be very different indeed.

The advantage of online processes is that it is possible to consult a population immediately; a question framed in the morning can be

Table 1: Recent Swiss referendum results

Year	Issue	Verdict	Winning vote (%)
1998	Road charges for heavy lorries	Yes	57.2
1999	Heroin on prescription	Yes	54.4
2000	Immigration controls	No	63.8
2001	Join European Union	No	76.8
2001	Abolish the army	No	78.1

answered by lunchtime. No one should assume that such a narrow timeframe would be satisfactory; the enforced pause in legislation to allow time for thought, which is a by-product of paper-based consultation, has to be *designed* into online systems. The whole point of the Swiss system is that snap judgements cannot be made; the ever-present danger of any online system is that they can. And if snap judgements act in a party's interests, it is also in that party's interests to reduce the amount of debate that takes place. The Swiss system is cleverly designed to exploit the inevitable delays of paper and the physical location of ballot boxes to prevent unworkable legislation getting through without proper scrutiny and debate; online, only artificial measures could perform the same function.

Is it possible that such measures could stay in the system? It is relatively easy to whip up hysteria in the press nowadays, be it about dangerous dogs, paedophiles, immigrants, reds under the bed or whatever. If enough people felt frustrated by a system designed to bog down debate, it seems almost impossible to imagine such a system remaining in place for very long. The argument that online direct democracy will coarsen debate and lead to populism and unwise legislation cannot be ruled out of hand, despite the admirable, if different, examples of direct democracy in ancient Athens or modern Switzerland.

Security

There are two different types of e-voting system that could be used. A system might be free standing, that is, it might be a standalone machine that is self-contained. Such a system would be more or less identical with a ballot box so far as the electoral process is concerned. Instead of putting paper votes into a box which is then sealed, voters would touch a screen or click a mouse to put an electronic vote into a memory, which is then isolated by a firewall. The voter would still have to walk to some sort of voting centre to cast the vote – to interact physically with the machine in the same way as is now done with the ballot box.

The second type of system is more flexible, and would involve interaction by voters with a central system, with the voters choosing their method of casting a vote. For instance, one could imagine a system of voting via a website on the Internet; voters could then register their vote from their own computer, say, or from some other convenient point. Such systems are often seen as being a remedy for the low turnouts that are worrying many democrats today, on the rationale that making it easier for people to vote, and allowing them to vote using trendy hi-tech methods rather than old-fashioned pen and paper, will increase the likelihood of them actually voting.

Unfortunately, ensuring the security of either type of system is not straightforward. Let us begin with the Internet-based systems.[18] First of all, there is the obvious problem that the Internet is international. An offline election (usually) takes place within the borders of the government being elected, and is therefore overseeable by officers of that government. This may create a conflict of interest, which is why there are international election overseers, but in general a government can defend its own national interest by securing the local election. However, an online election can take place anywhere in the world, and hence it will be extremely difficult to police against hackers, election fraudsters or even terrorists. Such hacking is not terribly difficult. Furthermore, the election officials have very little control of the voting environment. With a paper-based election the authorities can determine where the election takes place and with what equipment; with an online election voters will use their own PCs, laptops, mobiles etc. If some hostile third party controlled enough equipment, attacks on privacy, attempts to disenfranchise voters or attempts to alter votes could be quite common without anyone noticing. Computers (particularly corporate-owned computers that voters use at work or in a cyber-café) can be subject to hacking or automated attack; software downloaded or read from a CD-ROM could allow attacks thanks to poor security (a common problem with proprietary software).

To vote in an online system, the voter would go to the voting website. A so-called spoofing, or man-in-the-middle, attack inter-poses another site between the voter and the website the voter wants to visit. Thus, instead of logging on to the voting website, the voter actually logs on to the hacker's site, which looks exactly like the voting site. It might be, then, that the vote never registers, in which case the voter has been disenfranchised. Or, worse, the site may be used to glean the voter's password and other identifying details, which are then used to place an apparently genuine vote on the real voting site.

Another common kind of hacking attack on websites is the denial of service attack. In such an attack, the hacker automatically places software on one or more computers, which then send lots of messages to the attacked website. The website is overwhelmed by the message traffic and is effectively blocked or crashes; genuine users then cannot log on to the site. In such a circumstance in an election, voters would be unable to log on within the correct time in order to register their vote.

We will discuss privacy in more detail in chapter 8; however, to anticipate that discussion, the information stored in any online system needs to be secure if it is not to be misused. Sensitive information, such as one's vote, is a particular issue here. In an Internet-based voting system, each vote is stored in a memory, and because the system is connected to the outside world, it is theoretically possible for a hacker anywhere in the world to get into that memory and extract the voting information. Encryption systems are employed to circumvent this problem. A ballot is easily encrypted for transmission from the voter's computer to the system's server. The ballot contains two components: a record of the voter's identity, and the actual vote itself. Once the vote is received, the server decrypts it and separates the two components, and then re-encrypts them and sends them to two different parts of memory, one of which tallies the votes while the other keeps a record of who had voted. At least one of these parts of the memory must shuffle the data in a random order, so it is not possible to correlate who voted with the actual votes themselves.

At all these points there are substantial privacy risks. When the votes are decrypted, they could be intercepted. If the stored votes were intercepted and downloaded quickly enough – and with a computer such speed is possible – then each vote could be paired with the voter's identity and potentially decrypted (if the hacker had sufficient skills, or had access to the key of the encryption process). Perhaps more plausibly, if the encrypted ballots were stored for a long time after the election – as they might well be for auditing purposes – then that would provide a large window of opportunity for potential hackers. These reasonable auditing measures would be nightmarish in the wrong hands; the British auditing system, where the entire election could, if necessary, be recreated, is hardly a threat in a paper-based world. It would be too much work. But electronic machinery could exploit such auditing flags in the twinkling of an eye (this, incidentally, would be true of standalone machines as well as Internet-based ones).

Another problem with voting on the Internet is vote selling. The US Presidential election of 2000 saw vote-swapping websites proliferate as voters for Al Gore and Ralph Nader tried to keep George Bush out of office. In Dorset in the United Kingdom, pop singer Billy Bragg sponsored a website (http://www.votedorset.net/) where Liberal Democrat and Labour voters could pledge to swap votes tactically to keep Conservative candidates out. The scheme could claim to have had some success: in 1997, all of the county's eight MPs were Conservatives; in 2001, Labour gained one seat while the Liberal Democrats gained another, both on wafer-thin majorities; in 2005, despite a small Conservative recovery nationally, not only did they fail to win back either seat, but also the two non-Conservatives increased their majorities. Neither of these initiatives is illegal – they are vote swaps using an honour system. But the online auction house eBay has been used for a number of auctions of votes.[19] More to the point, an online system could be used to ensure votes changed hands in sufficiently large quantities to sway election results.

If we look at electronic systems that are not based on the Internet, in other words, systems that are merely electronic replacements for ballot boxes, then these problems do not generally apply. However, they still have some problems, and most of these also apply to Internet-based systems as well.

We noted earlier the importance of including a paper printout of the vote to provide an audit trail for the voter to verify. Sadly, and almost incredibly, very few voting machines in use allow paper printouts of the vote recorded. Furthermore, the voter's check is only that the interface is correct; it may be that the machine's storage or counting system has been undermined, in which case the paper printout cannot help detect fraud or error. It can also only be used to check a correctly registered vote; it cannot detect whether phantom votes have been added to the count. This latter is an obvious source of fraud; a group of undergraduates from Yale University recently proved that a very small level of alteration to voting machines (of only one vote per machine) could swing an election result, particularly one as close as the 2000 US Presidential election between George Bush and Al Gore.[20]

Indeed, this sort of subversion of any electronic voting system is likely to be much more damaging. With a paper-based, geographically dispersed system, vote-rigging requires at a minimum some effort and lots of people. As we know, it is not beyond a sufficiently corrupt government to do that – stuffing ballot boxes is a well-known method of ensuring victory. But at least that is visible, and it is very hard to avoid detection; indeed, it is very rare that rumours of large electoral fraud do not get reported. With an electronic system – particularly online systems, but also standalone machines – very large numbers of votes can be switched, removed from or added to the tally. It would be as hard to detect a large-scale fraud as it would a small-scale one.

Fairness

Is e-voting fair? We want a just distribution of cyberspace, and an important aspect of democracy is that everyone's opinion is taken equally into account. Under what circumstances will e-voting be fair?

One important point is the access one gets to the vote. If the provision of electronic voting services does not make it easier for some people to vote than others (so their voice is more likely to be heard), or helps previously disenfranchised people to make their voices heard, that is a desired result. If, on the other hand, e-voting raises the prominence of some groups above others, that is a result to be avoided.

So there are three cases. The first case is where offline electronic machines simply replace ballot boxes in polling booths. In such a case, the machines are as fair, or as unfair, as the paper-based system, so that provides no argument against e-voting.

The second case is where voting is over the Internet for a general population. Such a system, given the existence of a digital divide in Internet access, may well propagate that divide into democratic political institutions. Assuming an Internet-based system went on in parallel with paper-based voting in the first instance, one can see that, for example, wealthy voters and their families could simply log on to their PCs or laptops when they got up on the morning of voting day and vote easily enough while they were waiting for their overnight emails to download. Poorer urban voters might have to trek down to the library, a cyber-café or a dedicated voting terminal, perhaps in the council offices – clearly a more tedious process (if not prohibitively so). The geographical layout of the city will determine how difficult this is; in the city centre, there might be many government and commercial buildings which could host terminals, but in the suburbs or the urban housing projects facilities tend to be more spread out. In relatively wealthy suburbs and exurbs the general assumption is that everyone has a car, so there is very little within walking distance; in the inner city residential regions, the general assumption is that no one has any money, so there are few facilities because of low demand. Poorer rural voters might find themselves miles from any public access to the Web, reliant on the sporadic public transport that isolated locales have to live with. So it is quite possible that the net effect of having an online system is to increase the weight of votes from the wealthier and more urban parts of the electorate while decreasing that from the poorer and rural.

There is also another digital divide, that between the elderly and the younger – the 'digital immigrants' versus the 'digital natives'. Young people who have grown up with the Internet and ICT are completely comfortable with it. Middle-aged people tend to be much less excited by techno-stuff, but have often been forced to learn,

perhaps through their jobs, and so are quite OK with ICT, if not necessarily enthusiastic. Older people, not attracted by the content and
having missed the IT revolution in the workplace, tend to be less
wired. In which case, it may also be that an online system would give
extra weight to the votes of the young.

Note that these worries remain true even if the Internet-based
system runs in parallel with a paper-based system. Of course, the
existence of the lo-tech system will mitigate the worst effects, but the
possibility of Internet voting as an alternative will still lend further
weight to the votes of various privileged groups: the wealthy, the
urban and the young. The Internet has long been used as a medium
for opinion polling, and the same problems crop up there – it is
important that an opinion poll sample is representative of the
community as a whole, whereas Internet access is not evenly spread.
However, for an opinion poll it is possible to control for that, and if a
large enough panel is selected, then any reasonable demographic
profile can be achieved.[21] But an election is not an opinion poll, and
the voting 'sample' cannot, and of course should not, be controlled
for demographic fairness.

The third case, however, is where some groups are under-repre-
sented in a society, and Internet voting might help to improve their
access to the polls. For instance, in some countries with very remote
areas, Internet voting might help those who live a long way from
polling stations to vote. Some experiments have been made to help
those on military service, although the satisfactoriness of the security
arrangements is still an issue.[22]

But a fraught situation, midway between the second and the third
cases, is where there are groups who might be helped to vote via the
Internet, who have not been voting in the traditional system, and
whose voting would be desirable. For instance, in many Western
democracies, young people vote less than others. In the United
Kingdom there are fears that young people are turned off from the
processes of politics, and there have been calls to reduce the voting

age to 16 (despite its not being terribly clear why this will turn young people on to politics).[23] In advance of the 2005 general election, only 31% of first-time voters claimed they would vote.[24] Voting has been made easier in response: there have been experiments with voting by mobile phone, and a postal voting system has been set up with security flaws so glaring that no Internet system would ever be able to get away with them. But there surely is a serious issue as to whether a system should pander to those who, having a perfectly good opportunity to vote, do not choose to do so. We certainly agree about the importance of engaging as many people, from as many representative groups, as possible in the democratic deliberating process. But merely making it even easier for disengaged people to register their votes is not necessarily engaging them to any useful extent. These ideas need very serious thought; in the UK, one wonders how far such thoughts are driven by a government confident that younger people tend to vote for it (as when a reduction in the voting age from 21 to 18 was rushed through in the late 1960s by the Labour government prior to what was forecast to be a close election in 1970).

A second important issue is the fairness of the process of obtaining the result. This will, of course, depend on the alternatives; what was the system like before? Different countries have different problems, different ways of subverting the system. In some countries, using the Web to bypass corrupt election administrators is clearly a winner. In others, the government might well have control over the machines themselves, in which case it may well be that electoral fraud becomes easier, not harder. As noted, rigging elections is not difficult, but at least with paper so many people and lorries are needed that it is hard to do it without being detected. Who commissions the machines? From whom? Is there a paper printout? For example, in the recall referendum on President Hugo Chávez of Venezuela in 2004 (which was declared to be clean by the Carter Center[25]), the vote was intended to be fully automated. The touch-screen machines, supplied by an unknown company run by Venezuelans from an apartment in Florida, had never been used in an election before. The software supplier was a firm part-owned by Sr Chávez's government, with a government appointee on the board.[26] There was a big argument over the auditing of the results,[27] although Chávez was almost certainly popular enough to justify his victory and suspicions about the referendum appear to be unfounded. But it does little for trust in the electoral process (in a country whose politics at the time were very polarised) to have such arguments or room for suspicion.

A third issue, which has not been explored in depth, is the issue of whether e-voting provides any particular means to produce a fairer result than paper-based systems. Most debate in this area concentrates on the fairness to parties and candidates – getting a parliament or assembly whose makeup is broadly representative of the voters – but that is a question that is independent of e-voting as an issue (it is a question of how the votes are translated into seats, not about how the votes are garnered). In the context of our enquiry, a more pertinent question is that of how one's preferences are converted into votes (which are then aggregated to produce a result).

Paper systems allow a number of ways of registering one's preferences, depending on the system – some of these are sketched in table 2. The fourth column of this table suggests some problems that might make it very hard for an individual voter to make a decision. Sometimes one has a clear preference for a candidate or a party, but sometimes one's loyalties are stretched. For instance, in the UK general election of 2005, there was a general sense that Tony Blair's Labour government was the best potential government available, although it had done some very unpopular things (not least supporting the American invasion of Iraq in 2003). A remarkable amount of debate during the election focused on the problem, given the UK's first-past-the-post system, of how voters could 'deliver a message' to Blair without actually deposing him – perhaps one of the

Table 2: Some voting systems

System	Your vote	Procedure	Problems
First past the post	For the individual candidate you prefer most out of those standing.	Winner is the candidate with most votes.	There may be a range of candidates you like. A small minority of voters may pick the representative. The results can let in a government on a very small proportion of the national vote. If your opposition to one candidate is important, your incentive is to vote tactically for the best person to beat that candidate, rather than to vote for your preferred candidate.
Party list	For the party you prefer.	Each party puts forward a list of candidates. The percentage of votes for each party translates into a given number of seats. This number of candidates is taken from the top of the list.	You may not like the candidates at the top of the list. There may be a range of parties you like.
Run off system	For the candidate you prefer.	A first ballot is conducted of all candidates. The first two then compete in a second run off ballot.	If your party puts up more than one candidate, you may not feel able to vote for your preferred candidate, because it is bad to split your party's vote. In the final ballot, you may not like either candidate. Again, there are incentives for tactical voting, rather than expressing your preference.

Table 2: Continued

System	Your vote	Procedure	Problems
Alternative vote	You list the candidates you prefer in order.	The votes of the candidate at the bottom of the poll are redistributed according to next preferences, until someone has over 50% of the vote.	Ordering candidates may be hard. The point may not be placing them in order, but rather the amount you like them. You may prefer one party's candidates (unordered) a little bit more than another's, and a lot more than a third's.
Single transferable vote	You list the candidates you prefer in order.	Similar to the alternative vote, except that the aim is to elect a number (usually four or five) of representatives. Therefore the votes of winners and losers can be redistributed. The method is often fiendishly complicated and time-consuming.	As with the alternative vote.

most bizarre aspects of the campaign. All the parties entered into the debate. The left-of-centre Liberal Democrats urged voters to give Blair a 'bloody nose', while the right-of-centre Conservative Party exhorted them to 'wipe the smirk off his face', each message careful to suggest the possibility of discomfiting Blair without actually damaging him too much. Even Blair's own Labour Party entered into the spirit, with Blair promising to step down from the leadership before the next election, and hinting strongly that he would hand over to the more trusted Chancellor Gordon Brown.

So no paper-based system will be entirely satisfactory. However, if it is possible to recalibrate democracy through modern ICTs along the axes of deliberation and directness, then it is also possible to conceive of recalibrating the actual aggregative function of democratic decision making. ICT can offer radically new possibilities for revolutionising the process of voting.

Consider just one of these possibilities. This is a purely hypothetical example, general in nature, but it is an interesting illustration. One of the mainstays of democracy has been the dictum: 'One person, one vote.' What you do with that vote is entirely up to you. You choose which party best represents your views, add a few other things into the mix, such as whether the candidate has a beard or not (because, for many, looks do matter), and then cast your vote (or not). But table 2 shows us that, even though you can do what you like with your vote (given the constraints of the voting system), it may be hard to convert your preferences into a voting strategy. What you cannot do, for example, is vote for two people. You can, of course, arrange for your vote for one person to be transferred to another in the event of the former being eliminated, but that is not what we mean. Specifically, what you cannot do is cast half a vote for one person and half for another. With modern ICTs a system that would allow this is easy to imagine.

But why would you want to split your vote this way? Well, one reason might be that one candidate better represents your views about, say, taxation policy, whilst another better represents your views about crime and punishment. There is no reason, even, to limit it to just half votes – arbitrary specificity could be supported. Imagine an ICT-mediated system where you can allocate your single vote in any fraction, however infinitesimal, you wish. You could give, for instance, 0.25 of your vote to the person who best represents your views on taxation, 0.15 to the person who best represents your views on crime, 0.01 of your vote to the person who best represents your views on, say, overseas investment and so on. You decide who best captures your views on specific issues and you decide how much of your vote to give them based upon how you weight the relative importance of the issue. You could even discard some or all of your vote – you could give 0.75 of your vote to one or more candidates and 0.25 to nobody. All this can be done without superseding the one vote per person requirement. Individuals would still have the same (i.e. equal) level of influence in the formal voting process, it would simply be that they could apportion their influence in a way that is finely tuned to their views.

The knock-on effects with regard to the wider political system would be huge. The current voting systems in the UK and the US, for example, have generated particular systems of party-based politics; there are clear incentives for those who organise themselves into parties. Under our hypothetical system it is not so obvious that parties would spring up, or continue to exist; at least not in the same form as now. Individuals could stand on single issues, or a set of issues. They would not have to hold a party line on things that they disagreed with, and voters could select whether to support their choice or not. This may well give rise to a more issue-based form of politics. Similarly, there is no automatic requirement that elections need to be held on any specific date under such an ICT-based system. Rolling elections could be feasible, where those in government are selected and de-selected on a more frequent basis depending upon how public opinion changes regarding the performance of those elected.

e-Voting: the disappointment

Voting electronically has been touted for some time as the answer to a number of problems, although whether such problems are seen as such has varied from country to country. In the United Kingdom, for instance, the elections of 2001 and 2005, which were both hoped to be electronically enabled by a self-consciously modernising and 'hi-tech' government, both turned out to be paper-based affairs where votes were counted by hand, although it is still claimed that the first post-2008 election (probably in 2009 or 2010) will be e-enabled.

Much of the argument in the UK, as with other rich democracies, is based around the claim that e-voting will increase turnout. We have already argued that, even though low turnout may be a symptom of a malaise in democratic societies, it does not follow that addressing that symptom is either pointful or a good use of governmental and technological resources. If people do not like politics, forcing them to vote is hardly going to make any difference (any more than you can cure measles by painting out its characteristic spots). Anyway, it turns out that, according to the Electoral Commission, on the basis of a large-scale experiment in local government elections in 2003, e-voting could increase turnout by between 0% and 5% – hardly worth the effort.[28] In Paraguay, participation was about 67% for those registered for e-voting in its general election of 2003, against 61% for those not – once more, hardly startling.[29]

A very negative report on a US initiative to allow its military personal to vote online anywhere in the world revealed endemic failures in security and the preservation of privacy.[30] One of its arguments was that the experiment, limited as it was, could not be allowed to go without criticism, because even a limited success would increase the momentum behind the e-voting lobby. Indeed, there was some evidence that insecure systems were being used by some American states on the back of the mere fact that the experiment had taken place at all. The authors of the critical report felt obliged to be very harsh, to stamp down any lingering hopes for voting over the Internet.

Politics is a complex business, and democracy doubly so. Democracy involves deliberation, argument and sometimes messy compromise. There is nothing wrong with that – when tens of millions of people share a territory, they are bound to disagree about some things, and there needs to be a decision procedure short of civil war that helps the best responses to problems to be chosen more often than not. There is a Utopian fantasy that the Internet can achieve this, by allowing either great technocratic solutions to emerge or (more realistically) direct consultation of people in order to cut out our representatives, who, in this fantasy, are generally seen as venal, corrupt, incompetent, overpaid and more concerned with political point-scoring than with doing the 'right thing'.

In fact, our representatives are like that less often than the fantasy makes out.[31] And there is remarkably little evidence to suggest that elected representatives are less likely to make good decisions than technocrats or 'the people'.

The possibilities of direct democracy vary dramatically depending on the way that the consultation system works. We saw, for example, that the extended referendum campaigns, together with the ethos of public service, in Switzerland made that system work pretty well, if somewhat conservatively. And in some countries, such as Brazil and Paraguay, e-voting has helped reduce electoral fraud.[32] However, the Internet allows very different models of consultation. Most importantly, these models are independent of the amount and quality of deliberation that takes place. 'The people' can be consulted immediately, in the flush of temper or the throes of an early reaction to a few possibly skewed presentations of very complex and nuanced situations. We are sceptical that the best decisions can be made under such conditions,. Longer and more thoughtful campaigns can also be launched, but even then there is nothing particular to link the process to any meaningful attempt to deliberate. Political discussion, as the Athenians realised – indeed, as we discussed in chapter 6 – is essential to accompany the process of aggregating preferences.

To flip the argument, any process of consultation surely has to be meaningful. It has been known for a long time that consultation exercises are often just a way of enabling people to let off steam, and that they often get in the way of good government.[33] It has to be possible for people's views to be taken into account – if they just sound off on some topic into some deaf ear, then cynicism will result.

Equally, citizens must accept the limitations on consultation – in a situation where there are two diametrically opposed views available, one or other of those views has to be disregarded, and the possibility of defeat must be accepted by those who wish to take advantage of the opportunities for complaint that democracy affords.

New technology provides many methods for consulting, but it is essential that such exercises are not spurious. Tony Blair's government set up a 'Big Conversation', where people could write into websites and attend meetings and explain their gripes to the government. Very little happened (the government still went to war, for instance). It seems to have been a waste of time (although it is claimed that much of the discussion fed into the Labour Party's policy-making process, and indeed rather less convincing claims have been made that it was a new way of making contact with the people).[34] Rather like being made king for the day at a Maytime festival, one's ability to post some complaint onto a government website was largely ceremonial. It is such empty exercises that bring cynicism.[35]

Better not to consult than to consult spuriously. Better not to use new technologies until a way to use them to improve the political process genuinely can be found.

Spreading the word

Of course, the computer and the Internet are of use for much more than collecting and aggregating opinions. Let us close with a quick look at a couple of ways in which ICT could be used effectively in politics. One important use of the Internet is for spreading ideas – a view that has been called 'viral politics'.[36]

> It is the nature of a virus that it requires a host to incubate it and spread it. That's how it thrives. It must be so in the era of new media. New media is characterised by fragments and

flickers accessed through multiple channels. For a virus to thrive in this uncertain, conditional and user-empowered environment, it needs hosts. The problem that you have in politics is that if your 'messages' – the language, symbols, and celebrities of your political narrative – kill off their hosts then your messages will just rattle around the hollow tin that is the 'Westminster Village'.[37]

However, it is not clear that ICT changes politics all that much. The suggestion in this paragraph is rather buried in the somewhat odd mixed metaphor. But it seems that, in the Internet age, one's message has to be passed on via rather shadowy routes, and therefore must be tailored to be passed on that way (or, put another way, those messages that are tailored in such a manner will tend to survive and those that are not will not). Argumentation, rather than being a quasi-rational process, becomes a process of passing on impressions.

The major parties seem to have got the idea here, although the Internet has been exploited best by mavericks such as John McCain and Howard Dean, who have failed for one reason or another to capture the big party machines. And we should not forget, in this viral politics, that it is those big party machines that have the power – it was George Bush, not John McCain, who was the Republican candidate in 2000, and John Kerry, not Howard Dean, who got the Democratic nomination in 2004. In the UK, both the Labour[38] and the Conservative[39] parties claim to be using the Internet extensively and effectively for campaigning. But, in a country where only 3% of voters look to the Internet to inform them about politics, the effectiveness of this strategy seems hardly guaranteed.[40] Indeed, it may be partly because his modernising Labour Party always had the new messages about networks in mind, even before the Internet took off, that voters have long seemed puzzled about what Tony Blair stood for. For the 2005 general election, the Conservatives narrowed their message down to five policies, all of which had been road-tested by focus groups. No doubt this was a good example of the new viral politics. However, in the real world, the message failed to get across – one of their themes, immigration, took over the whole campaign, as the traditional media stuck to the themes that they preferred.

It may be, as no less a luminary than Rupert Murdoch has claimed, that interactive media, blogs and other forms of communication will take over from the old media.[41] However, there is as yet relatively little sign of this happening in any significant way, and anyway the old media control the important news brands (for example, the BBC's website is one of the most significant).

The more realistic danger, surely, is that, given that the medium shapes the message, using the Internet as a communication method will tend to produce messages that Internet users – an unrepresentative lot – will appreciate, at the expense of those who do not consider the Internet as a place where politics get done (and therefore will, to borrow a phrase, rattle around the hollow tin that is cyberspace). Very large swathes of the population will be ignored by politicians' messages. Indeed, messages are so very well tailored to particular demographic niches nowadays that this is already happening.

Given the short attention span that the Internet encourages, and the personalisation of content that it allows, is there a danger that the more thoughtful messages, the more nuanced approaches, the less sweeping generalisations, will get crowded out? Our politics will be trendier. Will they also be healthier?

e-Governance

If we are sceptical of e-voting, and of viral politics, is there a definite contribution that ICT can make to the practice of politics? We have tried to make clear that what works will depend on the polity in question; if a country's politics aren't broke, why should they be fixed? And if something does need fixing, we cannot really be sure of the unintended consequences. For example, in the UK, a worry (perhaps exaggerated) about low voter turnouts led to moves to make voting easier (mainly, though not exclusively, focused on postal voting). This reduced security and enabled a number of postal voting scams to be carried out. Was the malaise really worse than the cure?

Where ICTs seem to work very well in government is in the rather less romantic area of the actual delivery of services. We saw in chapter 5 how popular the e-Seva centres have been in Andhra Pradesh, even though the government that implemented them was not. As another example, in Latin America a number of countries have made inroads into implementing governmental processes online, with considerable success in countries that have not traditionally been particularly democratic or well governed. In Mexico, CompraNet, an online public sector tendering and procurement system, removes some opportunities for graft by eliminating supply chain intermediaries and opens up procurement to a wider range of suppliers; the increased transparency has generally improved matters (and also made one or two scandals easier to expose).[42]

Again, we must be sure that e-government is really helping, not hindering, and that the reasons for deploying ICT are the right ones. In Chile, for example, their Agenda Digital programme has made the Chilean government one of the most e-prepared in the world, although the reasons behind it seem to be slightly skewed. One of the aims was to realise ICT's potential nationwide, while the other was that Chile was falling behind its regional competitors.[43] All well and good, and Chile remains a relatively well-run country, but it surely has to be understood that 1) the potential for ICT is important for ICT professionals, but secondary for politicians; and 2) falling behind in a race you do not need to win is not a problem.

There is clearly a place, particularly where bureaucrats, officials or politicians are unable or unwilling to deliver government services cheaply (or legally), for ICT to bypass some layers of government. As in industry, the cheap provision of services will save money, which means that an activist government can do more and a liberal government can reduce taxes. Service provision can be made more responsive to citizen demand (for example, a citizen could get all of his or her welfare payments through a single website, rather than going separately to a number of offices). In areas such as these, there are quick wins for ICT. However, ICT service provision needs to be costed and targeted at those who can best use it, and it has to be realised that ICT is not the magic bullet that will slay the vampires of inefficiency and corruption overnight.

Quick, strong or thick?

To sum up, there are a number of institutional effects that ICT can have on democracies, at varying levels of development. ICT will transform the ways that political business gets done, possibly unpredictably. Political scientist Ted Becker has claimed that ICTs can produce various levels of increase in democratic decision making. The following categories, in ascending order of transformativity, are accompanied by edited quotes from Becker himself.

- *Cyberpolitics as usual*. In representative democracies, a cursory glance at the Internet in any country, state, city or town will reveal a myriad of Web sites belonging to governmental and establishmentarian political interests addicted to that system. The main purpose of these Web sites is to make the government look as though it is cyber-hip and thus help legitimize it as being modern and responsive to the demands of the information age. Other purposes are to help cut costs of daily government business by automating services and being more convenient by being online. Another goal is to make the government look more responsive by allowing feedback via email.

- *Strengthening the present system*. Web sites that truly enrich citizens within the present system are ones used to inform about the wealth of alternative ways to look at issues involving the present political economy (globalization). The email capabilities of the Web are even more significant since they add something lacking in all representative systems: a cheap and rapid way to organize resistance to established power centres and interests. Examples abound: the WTO protest in Seattle; the IMF protest in Washington, DC; the Million Mothers March in DC in favor of gun control; and worker organization to pressure both their unions and employers prior to and during strikes.

- *Changing the representative system to give citizens more power: toward a stronger system*. Combining new ICTs with face-to-face deliberation and a promise of representatives to bow to the will of their constituencies produces a much stronger linkage between the citizenry and their government and gives much more power to the citizenry in the representative system.

- *Transforming representative democracy into a participatory democratic state*. The real key to a transformed system of participatory democracy into a teledemocracy using ICTs is to afford citizens the right to be law makers directly.[44]

It is, of course, a moot point as to which level of transformation is desirable, if any; it is clear that Becker favours the highest level. Indeed, as we have argued, ICTs can cut both ways, and there are flipsides to Becker's arguments; we have already shown that increasing participation and consultation can produce less effective government, and the dangers of populism are ever-present. The procedures that Becker collects under the heading of 'strengthening the present system' focus almost entirely on resistance to current ways of doing things, and seem not to allow governments to put their point of view. The utility of resistance to established power centres depends entirely on whether those established power centres exploit their power unjustly. Some do, some don't; there are strong arguments that gun control would improve many aspects of American life, but equally there are strong arguments that the WTO is the key to lifting a number of developing states out of poverty. If ICT gets associated strongly with resistance, politics may well be paralysed. To repeat, the power to resist is vital, but equally not all establishments deserve resisting.

At the lowest level, cyberpolitics as usual, Becker's concerns rather cut across ours. We have argued that the best use of ICTs, at least in the short to medium term, is to boost current systems by interpolating processes where they host breakdown, inefficiency or even corruption. Becker rather looks down on these initiatives. We certainly agree that many initiatives aim to make governments look cyber-hip, and it will already have been seen that we deplore this as much as Becker. Similarly, we have made our disdain for spurious consultations clear. But can Becker really be dismissive of attempts to govern more efficiently? Can he really not care when a government puts a process online to save money?

A better way of looking at things is a three-way distinction set out by Joachim Åström between quick, strong and thin democracy.[45] The best way for ICT to aid democracy will depend a great deal on the type of democracy we are trying to develop. Quick democracy involves speedy consultation of the citizen – lots of referendums, direct democracy, the Athenian model (or the *Michael Rimmer* model for those less enchanted). Politicians cease to act as intermediaries between citizens and decision-making; ICT systems do that job instead. Strong democracy is where public debate is enabled, and citizen participation no longer ends once the vote is cast. Legitimate decisions are made at the end of long deliberative processes. The aim is not to glean raw public opinion, but public opinion only when it has been shaped by argument and confrontation with opposing points of view. People are given power by such deliberative processes, but only as they receive an education, through debate, leading to increased understanding of society. Here, ICT provides forums for these debates to take place. Finally, thin democracy does not try to increase the level of citizen participation, but makes it easier for citizens to hold political elites to account. ICTs, in such a system, need not provide the citizen with the information relevant to the making of particular decisions, but rather are there to give them the information they need about how the system is intended to work, and what entitlements are available. ICTs are used to give feedback, and provide useful connections for the elite to the outside world. The three types of democracy are summarised in table 3.

All of these models have their supporters. Quick democracy generally appeals to radical democrats, whereas thin democracy appeals to neo-liberals. It is probably fair to say that, of the three, strong democracy appeals most to the current authors. But the choice of which model to take is a political choice, and the debate must not be glossed over. Furthermore, the ways in which ICTs can help will vary depending on which of the three models is chosen. But the

Table 3: Characteristics of quick, strong and thin democracy[46]

	Quick democracy	Strong democracy	Thin democracy
Aim	Power to the people	Consensus	Efficiency/choice
Ground for legitimacy	Principle of majority	Public debate	Accountability
Citizen's role	Decision maker	Opinion former	Customer
Mandate of the elected	Bound	Interactive	Open
ICT facilitates	Decisions	Discussion	Information

converse of that is scarier – the uses to which ICTs are put now may well dictate whether democracy ends up quick, strong or thin. As we have shown, in a number of cases the uses of ICT for democratic purposes have not been properly thought through – the desire to be cyber-hip, to borrow Becker's phrase, has often trumped more mature considerations. ICTs are not just a neutral arena in which political debate takes place; rather, they are central in forming conceptions of how debate functions, what institutions should accompany it and how it should translate into government action.

8:>
Privacy

The technological threat

Bureaucracies thrive on information. They consume it ravenously. And bureaucracies are very powerful; their needs drive many social developments. It has been argued, for instance, that the strong and robust institutions of the Egyptian state developed as a side-effect of the great third- and fourth-dynasty Pharaohs' desires to build giant structures to house their remains and to host their preparations for the long journey into the afterlife. The network of officialdom that was needed to oversee the giant transfers of Egyptian GDP into the building programme soon took on a life of its own, and the profession of scribe became an important and valued one. Scribes are traditionally portrayed as leaning over their documents, scribbling away, with three or four rolls of fat showing the sumptuousness of their sedentary and well-fed lifestyles.

Knowledge is power, as the saying goes. A bureaucracy must have access to ways of making people part with information, whether that be a police force of its own, a legal framework or contractual authority. But once it has that information, it can use it in all sorts of ways.

Technologists have traditionally been more than willing to supply bureaucrats with the gizmos they need to extract and apply that information. From writing itself, double-entry bookkeeping, printing, typewriters, dictating machines, skyscrapers, telephones, photocopiers and faxes, the development and refinement of information technologies (broadly conceived) have often been conditioned by the needs, and supported from the pockets, of bureaucracies to feed their info-thirst.

Need always outweighs means. Bureaucracies demand a certain quantity of information, and generally that quantity takes more time to produce than is strictly worthwhile (all that triplicate form-filling). Eventually some boffin somewhere invents a way to provide or process the information more quickly. Hurrah! But celebrations prove to be premature, because, as the amount of information that the bureaucracy can process increases, it just as surely finds more ways of using that information, and develops new appetites for new types of data. So the information overload remains.

Britain's ID card scheme, long under discussion, is a case in point. There are many civil liberties arguments against the scheme, some of which we will canvass, in more general terms, in this chapter. But two things stand out about the evolution of the scheme under Tony Blair and his various Home Secretaries. First, the expensive and relatively flaky technology underlying the cards has not put anyone off; the projected cost to the citizen has risen, at the time of writing, from tens of pounds to hundreds without prompting any change of mind. And secondly, the aim of the cards keeps mysteriously shifting. Initially they were supposed to help with post-September 11 security. Then they would provide a bulwark against illegal immigration and bogus asylum seekers. Then they would prevent identity theft. Then they would sort out social security fraud. Mr Blair's government has the solution: it just isn't quite sure what the problem is. Very similar points can be made about the US scheme to demand biometric data on foreigners' passports – the technology is more likely to *aid* identity theft than hinder it by forcing people to make explicit records of their identities. The underlying driver of such schemes is quite obviously bureaucratic info-thirst, rather than any particular real or perceived problem in the real world.

The net result is that the bureaucracies know increasing quantities about us. We are open books to them. The extent of our private realm gets smaller and smaller. Our public face grows, and we have relatively little control of our public aspect. How many of us knows how much of our background, our habits, our history is known by whom?

Privacy is a casualty of the information age. It seems that ICT is killing our personal space. Information about many sensitive aspects of our lives is held by all sorts of people and organisations, public and private. It is, as we have argued, easy to set up different identities and personas online, which may seem to aid privacy. However, this is only a veneer, as a sufficiently determined agency can do a lot of tracing, and records of online transactions are remarkably difficult to delete. In this chapter, we want to argue that this creates something of an unsolved problem particularly in the context of the incredible power of ICT today.

But there is no easy solution. We cannot just put a data-moat around ourselves and pull up the info-drawbridge. Nor can we not contribute information, because the benefits of gathering information together are so vast. One key area where the needs of bureaucracies, the needs of citizens and the issue of privacy are central factors is the thorny issue of ICT in health care.

An easy example: information in health care

Some years ago, the authors of this book made up 33.3% of a six-a-side football team, and during one match, one of us bravely (or stupidly) sustained breaks to his left wrist and his right thumb. A course of hospital treatment ensued, with the wrist falling under the aegis of the bone clinic and the thumb being a matter for the hand clinic. But there was a small problem, which was that the bone clinic was held in one hospital and the hand clinic in another some two miles away.

It was the information needs of the health care professionals that turned a minor inconvenience into a relatively major one. The information – X-rays, details of progress, previous health history – followed our author about. Perhaps surprisingly in a rich democracy in the twenty-first century, it was all in hard-copy (paper and X-ray print) form. None of the information was ever committed to computer, as far as our author could tell. So it was supposed to follow him around literally, in a big buff envelope with his name (misspelt, as it happens) written in big letters in green ink on a label.

All well and good. But our author began to spot a pattern. As he attended his weekly bone clinic at the one hospital and then the hand clinic a couple of days later at the other, the information was never there; when the author was in the hand clinic the information had remained in the bone clinic, and vice versa. The author's arrival at one clinic triggered the transfer of information, too late, from the other. It followed him around alright, but with a two-day time lag. A consultant or surgeon would turn up, with a nurse in attendance; he or she would always be very rushed, and his or her time was very expensive and scarce. But the consultation would always be imperfect, because the X-rays and other details were not present.

For our author, this was hardly more than an object lesson in the value of knowledge management, but for others it could be a matter of life or death. Someone with a serious allergy to certain drugs, for example, is at risk from hospitals that do not have access to full medical records. The figures are startling. Preventable medical errors kill over 50,000 people annually in the United States – some say well over.[1] That makes it the eighth biggest killer in the US, above the number of deaths in car accidents, for instance.

The reluctance of the medical profession to invest in ICT is odd, given their techno-fervour in other respects (MRI, nanotechnology, etc.). Technology is welcomed in treatments, but not administration. But admin is important; the costs to the hospitals treating our injured author in physically shipping piles of documents between them (however inefficiently) must have reached a tidy sum, especially when

special journeys had to be made to ship individual records. Duplication of the records would obviously have helped, but duplication is
not the answer to the problem. In the first place, duplication is a
waste of resources and also creates costs of its own (both production
and storage costs). And in the second place, unless all records are
duplicated everywhere they might be needed (within as well as
between hospitals), the transportation problem will not be eliminated
completely.

Furthermore, the administration costs we are talking about are not
insignificant. Round about one-third of the $1.6 trillion that the US
spends on health care annually goes on procedures that either dupli-
cate previous ones or are otherwise inappropriate,[2] and it is generally
thought that the US is about average in this respect. If we extrapolate
this figure to the whole world, which spends about $3.3 trillion on
health care, that makes $1,100,000,000,000 that could be eliminated
with decent ICT systems. Administration is often derided (and is often
the first to be cut in a squeeze), but it is necessary, and making it
more efficient would free up much more money to be spent on treatment, equipment and drugs.

No doubt it would be impossible to take all the slack out of the
system, and no doubt poorly designed ICT could as easily increase
waste as decrease it.[3] But even if only 1% of the potential savings
were realised, that would still be $11 billion saved worldwide, which
must surely be worth the investment.

Beyond admin savings, there are also important public policy
implications to using ICT in health care. Good and well-maintained
records would allow much greater understanding of general patterns
of public health; for example, disease outbreaks could be spotted
much more quickly. The links between geography and disease,
currently poorly understood, could become clearer – and then
resources for tackling individual diseases could be targeted at
particular neighbourhoods or communities.

What sort of systems would be required? They would need to be transparent and interoperable – which means that many people can interrogate the system and extract the information they need. Data need to be entered in a structured form – not too onerous a requirement, as all the paper information is entered on forms anyway. The structure would then also convey information to a properly programmed computer, so any correctly configured computer could extract information from it whenever it was needed. Furthermore, in such a system, new information (from tests or from clinical observations, or even quite complex data structures such as X-rays) could be added immediately it was available to update the records. So there would be no waiting for test results to come back from the lab – they would appear magically in the data system the moment they were written down.

To do this requires no great technological marvels; the difficulties are the rather more mundane ones of 1) developing the standards for such data structuring and transfer, including security standards;[4] 2) implementing large systems in giant organisations (Britain's National Health Service is the world's third largest employer); 3) implementing large systems across very fragmented sectors (as in the United States, where there are numerous service providers); and 4) getting the notoriously technophobic medical profession to learn new techniques for recording and accessing information, and integrating these techniques into their working routine. Mundane these tasks may be, but they are not easy. The UK is planning to spend £6.2 billion on rolling out ICT services in the health sector – and don't expect that to be the final bill.

So there are great gains to be made, both in terms of administration and the benefit to the citizen, in the centralisation of information storage and the interoperability of information systems. But the flip side is obvious: medical information is highly sensitive. There can be financial repercussions to people whose medical history is known (for example, particular genetic conditions might affect insurance premiums), or the possibility of social stigma or even just embarrassment. The tricky political problem is to balance the potential gains of information centralisation and storage against the potential loss of privacy.

Information and intrusion

Much of the information that gets stored is like this: its collection and storage is of great benefit to us, but equally its release and publication would be very invasive of our privacy. This is so not only in the health sector; financial information is perhaps most obviously like this. The distribution of credit in the Indian economy, for instance, is relatively poor because of a lack of information about credit histories. Default rates on credit cards are pretty high, at 6.3%, and banks are more reluctant to lend than they should be (thereby curtailing investment in the economy). The State Bank of India has set up a credit bureau, but relatively few banks disclose data to it. Sharing information is hard, because there is no unique proof of identity of each customer in India. All this suggests that data collection is important for the Indian economy, and indeed Parliament is trying to make information-sharing easier.[5] It should not be assumed that the collection of such information is frivolous, or designed merely to increase profits. On the other hand, credit histories are about as sensitive as information gets. Indeed, all sorts of information systems can, in the right (or wrong) context, be pretty sensitive; one could imagine information systems in one's car that broadcast and receive useful nuggets (e.g. an airbag that tells nearby cars when it has been operated in an accident). That information could save lives, but it could also be used to track your movements.

As Moore's Law (discussed in chapter 2) states, information storage is getting cheaper and cheaper, and more and more abundant, while information retrieval techniques are becoming increasingly efficient. A wealth of data logging our movements and transactions is now available – but this will be as nothing compared with what the situation will be in a few years' time, when computer technology has become integrated into our lives to a much greater extent. Our children, the first natives of the digital world, will leave even more of a footprint in the memory banks of the world's computers.

There is clearly colossal potential for misuse here, even while society reaps the gains. If the details of our lives are open to governments and others, then a number of requirements obviously arise. First, systems must be *dependable*; if vital information about us is filed under the wrong name, or is corrupted, then that could be a matter of life and death. Secondly, systems must be *secure*; if there is a criminal advantage open to the possessor of that information, then it is important that the information security industry has access to cutting edge prevention technology. Thirdly, the information gathered must not be *excessive*; there has to be enough for the benefits to accrue, but it is important that no more than that information is held. Fourthly, information must be *accurate*. And fifthly, storage systems must be *open* to the subject, both in the interests of accuracy (one should be able to check that one's records are correct) and out of fairness to that subject.[6]

Even if those conditions obtain, the quantity of information stored about us, and the much larger quantities expected to be stored in the near future, are clear threats to our privacy. Imagine if the government placed a CCTV camera in every living room and stored the output; even if it undertook not to look at the films (and even if that undertaking were believed by citizens), it would still be an extraordinary invasion of privacy. Yet that is the level of invasion that we might expect in the near future – a level of invasion that is technically feasible, and could well be extremely useful for certain aspects of government action. Already in the UK there are 2.5 million CCTV cameras keeping an eye on its citizens.

Politically impossible? Well, maybe. People have sleepwalked into undesirable situations before. If the government were to suggest that we all carried around a device that signalled our location to a central information repository which could be interrogated by the police and other government agencies with relatively minimal statutory safeguards, there would be an outcry. However, many of us happily carry around mobile phones, which are exactly such devices. It has been estimated that by 2007 the number of mobile phones in Europe will exceed the number of people.[7] So it's not so politically impossible after all.

We are often presented with complex choices or complicated trade-offs: preserve parts of our privacy or give aspects of that privacy away (allowing more surveillance into our lives) in return for some benefit, which is usually either material or to do with security. For instance, we use customer loyalty cards in supermarkets, which leave behind a record of our shopping habits. We earn some piffling quantity of points or stars or other typographical sweetmeat, which can be converted into a free meal,[8] free night in a hotel,[9] free CD[10] or whatever, while the store gets incredibly useful information about how, where and when people shop. (The information about individual expeditions may be fairly useless, but the amalgamation of information about a large number of shoppers reveals trends that are invaluable for planning stock levels.)

Alternatively, if we allow governments access to personal data, the idea is that ne'er-do-wells can be identified and caught by the various information trails they leave. Attempts to complain about such intrusion are standardly met by the stunningly false reply that 'if you keep within the law, you have nothing to fear'. A response that would be correct, but somewhat less persuasive, would be 'if you keep within the law, and the government keeps within the law, and its employees keep within the law, and the computer holding the database doesn't screw up, and the system is carefully designed according to well-understood software engineering principles and maintained properly, and the government doesn't scrimp on the outlay, and all the data are entered carefully, and the police are adequately trained to use the system, and the system isn't hacked into, and your identity isn't stolen, and the local hardware functions well, you have nothing to fear.'

What is privacy?

Privacy is an invention of post-Enlightenment modernity.[11] In ye olden days, the individual was subsumed within the life of an often large family, and family life in turn was subsumed by a public life in the community. Not even the top people had much of a private life; Louis XIV would perform his morning ablutions in front of an adoring aristocratic audience. Privacy had to be wrested from the community, after something of a low-level struggle; bedrooms, as chambers where one slept alone, with a partner or with a small number of family members, appear relatively late in architectural history. So privacy, which seems the most apolitical of concepts, actually began life with a political struggle to stake out some personal space into which only selected confidants were allowed to enter.

The private individual, then, emerged in politics and philosophy fairly late. As soon as he or she did, the big issue became the complex relation between the individual and the society which surrounds him or her. The interests of the private individual and society are bound to diverge. How should we conceptualise that divergence? And which should take precedence when?

Privacy has a number of forms – or, rather, the concept of 'privacy' covers a number of different restrictions appropriate for us to apply to others.[12]

1. Not being observed by others.
2. Restricting others' knowledge of oneself.

3. Restricting others from publishing knowledge of oneself.

4. Not being in a position to observe certain actions of others. There is surely no reasonable objection to an innocent passer-by being in one's visual field, but, for instance, an exhibitionist who insisted on displaying him- or herself nude in front of one would be invading one's privacy. More prosaically, how annoying it is to be bombarded, in one's own home, by someone else's loud music.

5. Not allowing others to meddle in one's affairs, to take decisions for one.

6. Not allowing one's affairs to be a subject of discourse, and preventing comment on the decisions one makes.

No doubt there are many more ideas of privacy around. Many of these senses of 'privacy' depend on social settings, but there can be invasions of privacy online too. All six of the above types of privacy can be (and regularly are) violated online, most of them in obvious ways. Perhaps the hardest to imagine *ab initio* is number 4, but one's privacy is invaded by people trying to display things which one does not want to see. The phenomenon of spam, the sending of unwanted emails (such as those offering Viagra or other prescription drugs, putting one in touch with fictitious girls, suggesting methods to increase the size of one's penis, or giving one the chance to help expatriate a giant sum of money from Nigeria), is an increasing nuisance online – 62% of emails in 2004 were spam, up from less than 10% in 2001.[13] Spam is an invasion of privacy, in just the same way as the streaker invades one's privacy.

Privacy is the concept that we use to describe the possibilities of one's personal space, whether that is real three-dimensional space or online. When one is in private, one should legitimately be able to retreat from public life.

Is privacy a bad thing?

Put like that, one would think privacy was up there alongside motherhood and apple pie as an unalloyed good. But there are many thinkers who reject the notion of privacy as being necessarily beneficial to society.[14]

1. Egalitarians oppose the idea of rights to private property being foundational. Someone who thinks that all should have equal access to resources presumably reserves the right to take some resources off the rich and give them to the poor; one should not, on this view, have unlimited rights to accumulate private property, even by means acknowledged to be legitimate. At the extreme of this view lie anarchists like Proudhon, who coined the catchy slogan 'property is theft'.

2. Communitarians think that privacy has anti-social connotations, and encourages a possessive individualism as opposed to a proper regard for community interests.

3. Some feminists think that the notion of a private sphere exacerbates inequalities and asymmetries between maleness (public) and femaleness (private). The patriarchal division between the public and private allows proper scrutiny of events in the public sphere, which can then be policed, criticised, etc. But there is an implicit assumption of a contrast with a private sphere which cannot be scrutinised or policed, where people can live by their own rules. If such rules include – as they often do – the subjection of women, then the claim is that even such intimate settings are characterised by injustice. Indeed, in many cultures (including those of the Western democracies, at least until fairly recently), domestic violence and child abuse were tacitly tolerated to some extent by the authorities.

4. An alternative feminist view contrasts the ethic of care with the ethic of justice. Justice implies the setting of rules which are then

applied impartially to all; care, on the other hand, implies making sure outcomes are properly fair, even if that involves treating some people differently. Justice is a rule-based notion characteristic of the public world; care is a case-based notion characteristic of the private world. By trying to make the public space more like the private, this view does the opposite of (3), which tries to make the private space more like the public.

We will not examine these four claims in any great detail. On the other hand, all of them have some measure of plausibility behind them, and draw attention to genuine problems with the use of private spaces, so we certainly do not wish to gloss over them. However, we should point out that the arguments they produce to criticise privacy are not sufficiently powerful to force us to reject the notion of private spaces altogether.[15]

The egalitarian view and the 'ethics of care' view, (1) and (4), can be met by very similar responses. The promotion of equality and the promotion of fair outcomes (as opposed to fair rules to achieve possibly unequal outcomes) are fundamentally implausible methods to order society, even given that they are morally superior principles. The toleration of inequalities and unfair outcomes allows resources that would otherwise be required to monitor and redistribute to be used in more productive ways. (1) and (4) are too expensive to operate. Having said that, when outcomes do go beyond some threshold where the inequalities or unfairness are too great to tolerate, then most societies have corrective mechanisms. Measures such as redistributive taxation in the case of (1), or new legislation to alter the operation of the rules in the case of (4), should prove sufficient to temper the worries of all but the most diehard ideologues.

With respect to (2) and (3), we can make the same point that privacy can be preserved as long as the ill effects of there being a private sphere do not cross some obvious threshold of injustice, be that antisocial behaviour in the case of (2) or domestic violence in the case of (3). But a further step is required. In both (1) and (4) implausible and impracticable ways of governing society were being proposed, but (2) and (3) are not like that. (2) requires merely the privileging of the interests of society over those of the individual; (3) suggests that public rules should apply, and be policed, in the private sphere. As neither of these positions is prima facie implausible, we need a positive argument to show that the private sphere has an important role to play and is therefore worth preserving. Can such an argument be found?

Is privacy a good thing?

We have discussed the importance of a deliberative democracy a number of times, the idea that the democratic processes and rituals themselves are of importance. People need to consult, to argue, to discuss, to root out the objections to their own positions and try to overcome them, and to deter others by pointing out the weaknesses in their views. Such is the rough and tumble of politics in a democracy.

But deliberation is not something that ideally always takes place in public. Of course, the final decision-making processes must be public, and involve a public display of argument, victory and defeat, and a public acquiescence by those who lost the vote. On the other hand, there needs to be a private space for discussions with friends and allies to draw up arguments, tactics and strategies for debate. One needs a private space to formulate one's own position on issues. One needs a private space, furthermore, in order to exercise one's right to autonomous action.[16]

George Orwell's *1984* is the classic statement of what a society without privacy would be like; recall the classic opening scene in Winston Smith's flat, where he finds a corner not monitored by the telescreen and begins his forbidden diary. That act of creating a private space for himself sparks off the events of the novel; without that space, without the ability to create an alternative truth for himself with the diary, Winston would be unable to challenge the authority of Big Brother (not that it does him any good in the long run).

So a personal, private space is essential to democracy in order to allow diverse opinions to flourish and to be developed into sufficiently persuasive lines of argument. This is not just a statement of psychological fact, that people by and large need moments of peace and seclusion to think things out for themselves (though that is true). The point is rather that a political argument, as with any negotiation, requires that each side remains in ignorance of at least some aspects of their opponents' position. Which is why Richard Nixon's Republicans bugged the Watergate Hotel where their Democratic opponents were headquartered in 1972.

Furthermore, opinions once aired become fixed. There can be fluid discussion in private, but once a statement of an opinion has been made in a public arena, there is no going back. Even when the circumstances have changed, it is not easy to retract a view. George Bush Sr's promise not to raise taxes in the 1988 election campaign was inconsistent with his later tax-raising. The promise broken, he failed in his re-election bid in 1992, despite the obvious fact that the tax rises were essential and sensible, given the ballooning US deficit at the time, and the unexpected circumstance of a pricy war to liberate Kuwait from Saddam Hussein's Iraqi invasion force. John Maynard Keynes's well-known barb that when the facts change, he changes his views is well known precisely because it goes against the grain of democratic politics; if one has promised to do something and been elected on that basis, then one should do it, however counterproductive it actually turns out to be. Again, this isn't just a contingent psychological failing; in a democracy, there should be a strong connection between what you stand for, what you promise and what you do. Even if voters were forgiving enough to allow the odd broken promise or two (which they are not), it is not clear how a democracy could function if promises were routinely broken by politicians. The private sphere of argument provides an essential shelter for deliberation to occur before fateful public utterances ossify the debate.

The other point that *1984* dramatises very effectively is that knowledge is power. A government that knows a lot is in a position to apply a large amount of pressure. Now, not being natural conspiracy theorists, or pessimistic glass-half-empty types, or the sort of people who compare Tony Blair with Stalin, we do not want to suggest that democratic governments are disposed to gain knowledge about their opponents, or about their voters, and apply it in a blackmailing fashion to ensure electoral victory. There is always a risk that this might happen, and that information might be misused in such a way, but the risk is relatively slight.

What matters here is not only the risk, but also the perception of risk. If people believe, however misguidedly, that information gleaned about them might be misused, they will behave in an unnaturally circumspect way. A government employee who realises that his membership of an opposition group is known to his superiors may well feel threatened, even if in actual fact he is not. A well-policed private space will enable him to pursue political courses that he thinks are correct in his private time, even while his work time is spent doing his job according to government specifications. It may be true to say that the relationship between our public lives and our private lives is much more complex than is generally thought,[17] but nevertheless this separation is more or less how it is supposed to work. Good fences make good neighbours, as the proverb has it, and when the neighbour is as big and as powerful as a Western government, the fence had better be pretty good indeed.

Furthermore, a government is a corporate entity. It can certainly be described as having views, ideas, plans and so on – we can treat the government, in some sense, as a 'person'. But that should not obscure the fact that it also contains within it several thousands of agents who are also persons. When we send information to the government, it also goes *ipso facto* to a human being, who may well misuse that information, even if the government will not, for criminal purposes, or maybe he or she will publish it either advertently (gossiping) or inadvertently (accidentally emailing it to someone).

Recall the bureaucratic thirst for knowledge that we described at the beginning of this chapter. That will always be unassuaged, however well-meaning the government. It will always be the case that: if a government wants information about some particular issue for some reason, it will get it, by hook or by crook; even when that reason no longer obtains, it will continue to collect the information; once some information has been gathered for some specific reason, it will be exploited for other purposes; and greater efficiency in gathering the information will be rewarded by demands for further information. Again, we do not want to argue that such 'function creep', as it is called, is necessarily pernicious, though it may be on occasion. But equally the overhead is pretty high, the benefits not always obvious (or even existing).

These reasons for privacy, though good, are relatively dramatic. At a more mundane level, in a properly deliberative democracy the individual needs privacy fundamentally in order to be able to carry out the duties and responsibilities that go with being a good citizen (or indeed consumer). Further, each individual will have different requirements for his or her private space, and is also the best judge of what those requirements are.

The post-privacy era

Even though privacy is important, and arguably essential, in a democracy, it is under threat, and increasingly so. Imagine a person who tried to avoid giving away any personal information at all. That person would never use a mobile phone (unless it was someone else's), always use cash, never fill in questionnaires, keep an unlisted phone number, never give it out and always withhold it when ringing anyone, badger credit agencies and marketing firms for any personal information they hold and constantly check it for accuracy, never use toll roads, never use the Internet without disabling cookies and encrypting emails, conceal his or her mother's maiden name, and at work would assume as a matter of course that all emails sent and websites visited were being monitored all the time.

Such a person sounds totally paranoid, though such actions would merely deliver the level of privacy that would have been routine in the 1980s. Privacy has been surrendered slowly but surely by a society keen to reap the benefits of ICT as discussed above. Although post-Enlightenment political theory endorses privacy as an important value, for the first time the privacy that it endorses is no longer possible to sustain.

The question, then, is: how do we ensure that sufficient private space is available for the political requirements of a deliberative democracy to be met? Let us quickly sketch two approaches that have been suggested.

PETs

PETs are privacy-enhancing technologies. This is to turn the problem on its head: if the problem is technology, then why not use the very same technology to fight back? The same technologies used to elicit information can also be reconfigured to keep it safe.

PETs come in two forms. First of all, there are communal technologies. These might be built into the operating systems of the computers we buy (such as Windows), or into the technical standards that the software and hardware obey. So, if there was genuine public disquiet about privacy, goes the argument, there would be a market to provide computers that ran operating systems that enhanced privacy; people would be prepared to pay extra to get such service. Actually, this is a little glib, since the operating system is a near-monopoly run by Microsoft, and a level of public ignorance means that demand may well be less than it would be with a higher level of public awareness.

Indeed, the problem is more complex than that, because the software industry is a fast-moving one. Microsoft is newly committed to security and privacy, and is trying to upgrade its software so that it contains lots of methods for enhancing these.[18] While concentrating on security, it has also been working on Longhorn, the successor to Windows XP; however, the commitment to security took development effort away from Longhorn to help repair the holes in XP, and as a result the launch of Longhorn has had to be delayed.

Worse, Microsoft has been on the wrong end of a series of antitrust judgments in the US and Europe, which penalised it for bundling its proprietary software in with its Windows operating system. This bundling, which helped preserve its monopoly, included such (free) software as Internet Explorer, the Windows Internet browser, and meant that the market for other browsers, such as those provided by Netscape or Mozilla, was correspondingly attenuated. Now that this practice has been ruled illegal, though, there is a legitimate question as to whether putting PETs into Windows is a repeat of the same antitrust behaviour, as there are many other firms selling PETs whose markets have traditionally relied on Windows' security failings.[19] The question of whether there would be a market for PETs if there was any genuine demand or need is much more complicated than it seems at first blush.

These independent PET initiatives, where individual users buy the technologies that meet their needs and then load them onto their computers, is the second form in which PETs can be distributed. Perhaps the best known is the Platform for Privacy Preferences (P3P), developed by the World Wide Web Consortium,[20] a set of standards for privacy protection that are intended to let users understand the privacy policies of their computer and easily adjust them according to their need.

Individual PETs abound, but their quality varies and they are hard to generalise about. In addition, with the world of computing changing incredibly fast, no single PET is able to keep pace; a privacy-aware person would therefore have to keep a suite of carefully chosen PETs on hand, and constantly update and maintain it. This is a large overhead, particularly for a relatively casual user (who may nevertheless have important security concerns with a home computer, which may be used for banking, work-related emails or commerce).

We also need to look closely at what infrastructure underlies PETs. Clearly it is important for both business and government to find and support methods of establishing identity, in order to enhance privacy. A central plank of any privacy-supporting method is to ensure that only authorised people get to see the information, which means being able to identify such people reliably. But there will always be a tension here: we are trying to ensure privacy, but in order to do that we inevitably need to gather a lot of data that can be used to confirm identities. To secure privacy, it may be necessary to take the risk of surrendering a lot of information about oneself.

PETs will no doubt always be part of the solution of the privacy problem, but cannot be the exclusive answer.[21]

Sousveillance

The second suggestion about preserving private spaces is a paradoxical one. As we have had cause to note before, there has been an important shift in the control of surveillance technologies; whereas relatively recently they were the preserve of governments, nowadays, from mobile phone to digital cameras, they are being democratised. Many, perhaps even most, of us have access to surveillance technology that the original James Bond could only have dreamt of. All the forces we discussed in chapter 2, making technology smaller, making storage larger and making search more efficient, work to make everybody a potential spy.

This has been a mixed blessing. On the one hand, there have been a number of cases of robbers being caught within minutes of their crimes, after having been photographed on mobiles and the photo emailed to police. On the other, there have also been cases of miniature cameras in dressing rooms and toilets. But the general pattern has been the use of surveillance by people and small organisations for their own protection, such as webcams in classrooms. Transparency seems to be growing as a result of public demand.[22] The attack on Rodney King and the abuse at the Abu Ghraib prison were both captured by amateurs, not the ever-snooping authorities. Surveillance is being replaced by sousveillance – the observation of us all from below by individuals as opposed to observation from above by governments and corporations – and the monitoring operation itself has been democratised without turning everything into a voyeur's paradise (yet).

The two situations cited above suggest that privacy can actually inhibit accountability. Openness is more liberating than secrecy, and the main problem with traditional surveillance is that its ownership is so narrow. However, in today's society, with the ownership of surveillance technology so widely distributed, anyone can see anyone – it is nowadays not just the rich and powerful looking at the poor. So, for example, if the police are watching us, why shouldn't we watch the police? If credit agencies gather information about us, why shouldn't we be able to see who buys it?[23]

This is a startling argument. The post-Enlightenment idea of privacy is something of a historical anomaly; the idea here is that we should build on that. As the Chinese proverb has it, we should welcome the inevitable. We should accept that we are living, in Marshall McLuhan's phrase, in a global village.[24] When McLuhan coined that phrase, it was widely thought that he was talking about a world in which events in, say, New York could affect affairs in London, Paris, Hong Kong, Cape Town and so on within minutes. Indeed so. But an extra twist, consciously intended by McLuhan, is that a village is an arena in which everyone knows everyone else's business. The world as a global village is a world in which you cannot expect your affairs to be concealed from anyone.

Startling the argument may be – but is it ultimately convincing? Consider the connection between privacy and ignorance. Much information has always been gathered, but – and again refer back to chapter 2 – searching through it is not always straightforward. Many organisations, particularly governments, have piled up huge quantities of data without ever budgeting for extracting anything useful from it. And data are not where it's at – it is knowledge, seen as usable information, that is important.[25] Recall from chapter 2 the example of the 'disappearance' of the Ark of the Covenant in *Raiders of the Lost Ark*. And there are many serious examples of that in real life: the FBI is sitting on thousands of hours of tapes of tapped telephone conversations between Arabic speakers, which may possibly contain a nugget or two of interesting information, but the information is not usable (it is not *knowledge*) because the lack of translators means that no one in the Bureau can understand them.[26] Remember Adam Smith, quoted in chapter 6, fretting that people can fall under the moral radar in cities.

There is actually enough information on record to make the lives of very many people uncomfortable. Given enough time and effort, it would be possible to find out whether someone has been evading tax from records of tax returns, bank statements and various company accounts. In practice, there are not enough resources to do that for everyone, although if there is a strong enough suspicion for the authorities to investigate, then it can be done in a few individual cases. Quite often, the preferred strategy of tax evaders, money launderers, organised criminals and their ilk is nothing more sophisticated than to complicate the scene with lots of sham businesses, temporary accounts, etc. None of these would be an insuperable obstacle to a well-trained forensic auditor, but put together they make it hard for auditors to understand what is going on and, more importantly, harder to create a criminal case that would be presentable to a lay jury. The authorities are very powerful, but their very ambition often causes them to overreach themselves.

Given the spread of sousveillance, can ignorance protect privacy? For instance, with the development of digital cameras and mobile phone cameras, a girl who sunbathes topless on holiday may well be photographed, innocently or otherwise, by other holidaymakers. Such a digital record may well be posted on a website. That need not be a malicious act; it may be part of the record of a holiday, and the girl may not mind her friends seeing her in her beachwear. Alternatively, the girl may just be, as far as the photographer is concerned, part of the scenic backdrop to the real object of interest, which might be the seagull eating Auntie Edie's ice cream. But if the photograph is discovered by one of the dedicated band of individuals who trawls the net looking for voyeuristic images, then he (almost always a he) can save it on his computer and post it on one or more of the many websites devoted to such images. The image has now changed from a jolly record of an incident to a piece of pornography. It is unlikely that the girl will ever discover what has happened; it is unlikely that anyone who knows her will ever see the photo. To that extent, the ignorance of the girl's immediate community saves her privacy; is that an outcome with which she should be happy?

It is certainly the case that, on occasion, malice can be involved. There are various stories, many no doubt apocryphal, of jilted lovers posting intimate pictures of their exes performing various sexual acts online. No doubt, in such sordid circumstances, part of the point of posting the pictures is that the friends of the ex get to see them.

Some of the cases have led to prosecution, but there may be many more that have not.

The malicious case, which has the connection of motive between victim and perpetrator, is actually less worrying, because there are trails of events that may be used to expose the damage to reputation. It is the random event that is harder to trace, and the only thing that saves the reputation of one who is voyeured upon in this way is the ignorance of her circle of acquaintances. That ignorance is here to stay, given the giant number of images online. However, if we take the sousveillance thesis seriously, it should be made harder for voyeurs to post (or view) such pictures anonymously, which might put some of them off. Nevertheless, even given the truth of the ignorance thesis, can we really say that this is a situation that is stable, or which provides many crumbs of comfort?

The ignorance thesis depends rather on a particular atomised view of society current in the West, but which does not necessarily translate easily into the experiences of non-Western cultures. The problems with the ignorance thesis have been highlighted by a recent case in South Korea, which is much less individualistic than the US or Europe, while also leading the world in broadband connection to the Internet. A picture of a girl who had failed to clean up after her dog on a railway carriage was circulated online, and a witch hunt to find her ensued. She became known as the 'dogshit girl', and such was the amount of hate mail sent to her that she was forced to drop out of her university. The government, reluctant to restrict free expression but equally concerned about online mob rule, is somewhat hamstrung.[27]

The steady improvement of information retrieval technology will also play a part. Initiatives like the Semantic Web, welcome and laudable though they are in context, will enable cleverer searches, multimedia searches and searches from amalgamated information stores, all of which will increase the possibility that one's minor indiscretion on the beach or at a party could be discovered by ill-wishers in later life – and, because these are digital records, they may well end up as memories for life that one would rather be forgotten.

Privacy and policy

Our discussion of privacy has been somewhat inconclusive. Indeed, technological and social aspects of privacy have developed in tandem and are so rapid that it would be unwise to generalise about either the theoretical difficulties or the actual, practical torts that could be exercised. For example, opinion is sharply divided over whether privacy is a right or a preference. Is privacy something that should be provided in a just society or is it merely a nice thing that we would, by and large, like to have (on a par with a Mercedes Benz)? As we have already seen, there are some people who think privacy is essential for democracy to function and others who think that it is a bad thing entirely. And online, there is always the perennial question of how the Internet can be policed at all.

If there is a right to privacy, then there are serious questions to be asked about whether privacy is properly and justly distributed; that is, whether everyone has enough privacy for his or her own legitimate purposes. Even if privacy is a preference, the distributional question comes into play. But the questions still pile up, as Charles Raab notes.

> Even to the extent that privacy is a value for individuals to enjoy, it would still be relevant to ascertain who enjoys what privacy, and why, and who does not. However, the knowledge basis for informing privacy policy is underdeveloped, although unequal distributions, if they exist, can be construed as worrisome. By failing to consider the social distribution of privacy, the conceptual apparatus and the paradigm it sustains are deficient. Is an uneven distribution of data protection justifiable on social and political grounds? Is

everyone's privacy of equal worth to protect, or should some receive greater protection than others, and how? There are few arenas in which such queries can be addressed.[28]

Part of the problem is that we don't really know a great deal about how privacy, or its lack, affects us in democracies, where governments, if not always well intentioned, are more often than not benign. More than most things to which we have rights, more than many things for which we have preferences, the extent to which we need or desire privacy really does depend on our personal makeup. The abstract individuals of political thinking may have abstract privacy requirements, but people differ radically in terms of their exposure to ICT, their online presence, and the desirability of any snippets of intrusive information about them. What is particularly ironic is that, with the wealth of information held about people by certain data management firms, that information is never used (for reasons of data protection) to find out (by analysing their socio-economic and demographic position) how private someone is likely to need or want to be. People are often categorised by policy makers in terms of their interactions with ICT, for example as credit-seekers, students, criminals or e-commerce customers, but not according to their interests, gender, age or income – factors that may well affect their attitudes to privacy just as much as the former set of categories.

Another question that raises itself when we think about privacy policy is that of the relation of the individual to the collective. We have already seen one tension here, the supposed (though often assumed without proof) trade-off between the need of a society to protect itself from its citizens and the need of the citizen to prevent intrusion from society. But there is a further issue, which is whether privacy can be provided for individuals separately (like houses) or whether it has to be provided for all (like street lighting). We have seen how some PETs can be bundled together, e.g. in operating systems such as Windows; if this is the best way to distribute privacy, then every computer user benefits from it (and pays for it) even if they don't want it. On the other hand, it may be that PETs have to be bought by individuals (and we have also seen how the antitrust judgments against Microsoft tend to make that a more likely option). In such a situation, we are likely to see distributional problems, in which privacy is unequally spread. There are at least two relevant dimensions here, creating a 2 × 2 matrix, as shown in table 1. There is the extent of a person's online presence and their ability to secure privacy, either through having the resources to buy PETs or to obtain advice or through having sufficient knowledge to keep up to date with the latest trends in technology. Market solutions to the online privacy problem depend on there being plenty of well-informed consumers ready to buy PETs, but not only is information relatively hard to come by, it also changes very rapidly, and the effort involved for experts, never mind laypeople, may well be too much for most people.

As society gets more and more technologically based, more people

Table 1: Dimensions of unequal distribution of privacy

	Can obtain privacy	Cannot obtain (sufficient) privacy
Strong online presence	Subject is informed about the latest trends, and needs to be, as he or she is very exposed to those who wish to gain information. His or her online life will be a long struggle to keep up to date, an arms race against the information gatherers.	Subject is most at risk, very much a privacy 'have-not'.
Weak online presence	The combination of a person exposing him- or herself to very few risks, and taking strong precautions anyway, means that Subject will be very safe indeed.	Subject will miss out on many opportunities, but equally is risking comparatively little. That little, however, may be exploited.

will move from the relatively safe bottom row of table 1 to the riskier top row. This is likely to happen to many of them without their consent and without their knowledge. Therefore, even if they did possess enough knowledge to protect their privacy to the optimal extent, and enough resources to fund such protection, they still may not realise that the threat applies to them and that they need to move themselves from the right hand column to the left hand column. Even worse, the effort required to stay in the top left box of the matrix is enormous – there will be an awful lot of running hard just to stay still. It may well be that many informed, rich consumers with a strong online presence just drift into the top right box of the matrix because it is too hard or too tedious to stay safe.

Empirical evidence backs this up. A survey conducted by the Oxford Internet Institute strongly suggests that the digital privacy divide is likely to widen if the technology develops as we think it might.

> People with the appropriate skills and resources to get online and to collate and interpret online information could enhance their ability to authenticate the value of products, services and information, thereby protecting themselves against cyber fraud and crime. However, others with less expertise remain offline, fail to experience the Internet and are more likely to distrust the technology.[29]

Particularly post-September 11, governments have taken it upon themselves to encroach upon our online privacy; the technology to do it is simple, the legal position unclear (making it easy to change the law) and public awareness of the developments small, so there has been little resistance. The net effect is to move more of us from the bottom row of table 1 to the top. Partly, this is bureaucracy's information thirst reasserting itself, and the dangers per se have not been evaluated very much. This may not be too much of a problem, because most Western governments mean no harm (which does not mean that they don't cause harm, of course). But though the risks to society as a whole of a transparent Internet may be small, it may still be that privacy is distributed unjustly. In such a case, governments surely have more serious thinking to do.

9:⟩
The Future is Here

A fair tomorrow

The future is here, science fiction writer William Gibson is reported to have said, it's just not evenly distributed yet. We have argued in this book that this is the case – our review of the science, much of which now seems terribly familiar and mundane, shows that the science fiction world envisaged two or three decades ago is now in place. We don't whizz off to faraway galaxies like Captain Kirk in the *Enterprise*, but then travelling faster than light was always a bit of a fantasy. But the smooth integration of personal communications and information processing is happening, and is proving to be much more powerful than anyone conceived (with the possible exception of McLuhan). Of course, when you see a teenager swapping inanities with mates over the mobile, it is less impressive than seeing Charlton Heston talking into a wrist radio in 1968. But if we focus on the substance, the power of information processing (which, basically, is what creates distinctively human civilisation) has increased by orders of magnitude in the last half-century.

Gibson's joke does have ramifications. Let's agree that the future is here, and now focus on the second clause – 'it's not evenly distributed'. A nice line, but it does raise a distributional question, which is a matter of fairness and justice. This has been the focus of this book, and in this final chapter we want to wrap up the arguments and debates.

The question we are left with is: what should we now do? Given the fast-moving nature of the technology, it is a very hard question to ask, and it is very unwise to provide a nailed-down answer to it. Here is a better question: How shall we decide what to do? Or: How should we develop just policies?

To answer this, we should consider a number of things. We need to look at the nature of the computing industry. How does it work? What would stop it working? That will provide natural limits to government or regulatory intervention. Not only that, the principles we find compelling, which are of course underpinned by *a priori* argument, also depend to a great extent on the nature of the world we live in. The way the world is also determines whether we are applying our principles impartially and fairly (in which case we can pat ourselves on the collective back) or whether we are being capricious and selfish. To shed further light on this issue, we need to revisit the digital divide, and question assumptions about its nature and extent. Finally, we need to firm up the prioritarian framework, defend it from potential counter-arguments and think how that framework can be applied to an industry like ICT.

Essential and innovative industries

By any standards, the ICT industries are as innovative as anything in the world. Flicking through any scientific journal will net you lots of stories of extraordinary things that are possible. For instance, it is now possible to transfer data using human skin. Matsushita's Touch Communication System allows users to pick up information from a device by touching it; the information is transferred to a wearable piece of memory (perhaps in a wristband or the earpiece of a pair of spectacles) using very weak currents across the surface of the skin, and then can be transferred to another device with another touch.[1] Extraordinary innovations, such as quantum computing, smart dust or digital ink, are routinely announced. Traditional industries have been transformed. And many ICTs, such as mobile phones, iPods or flash drives, are must-have items even for those fashionistas with limited pockets.

Capitalism is an engine for innovation.[2] No other system devised in human history has ever innovated so rapidly and effectively. Furthermore, it seems to flourish best in liberal societies where there is a premium on freedom. Innovation is, of course, possible anywhere. For instance, China was for many years the most innovative country in the world; however, those innovations never became suffused through society, influencing and enriching it, as has happened in Western capitalist nations. The Soviet Union, when pushed, could certainly outstrip the United States in certain areas of technological endeavour, but could not manage to do so across the whole range of scientific research; its collapse in 1989 revealed how backward it was, and how unproductive its people were. The US's moon landings in the 1960s and 1970s were arguably an unscientific digression in the history of its scientific progress (only one of the Apollo astronauts who landed on the Moon was actually a scientist). But the successful launch of Sputnik I in 1957, in retrospect, seems like the high point of Soviet science.

So, even if one does not subscribe to neo-liberal ideology in the spirit of Hayek, there are good reasons for letting free markets reign in the ICT industry. Without free markets, computing would be only marginally advanced from the days when academic research drove the industry and computers the size of wardrobes spread themselves round the walls of laboratories. If one does subscribe to neo-liberalism, then the free market is a no-brainer.

[P]olicymakers should let markets rather than governments address any problems associated with digital technology. Although the federal government initially financed the development of the Internet, the digital revolution is overwhelmingly a private sector phenomenon and should remain so. Efforts to regulate or tax electronic commerce and other digital technologies may be unenforceable. If they are not enforceable, they run a grave risk of stalling further tech-nological advance, to the detriment of citizens around the world. In fact, the great virtue of a market-based approach is that if digital problems are perceived to be significant by large numbers of users, then firms have strong market incentives to develop technological solutions that premature regulation is likely to preempt.

In fact, the pace of technological change itself favors market-driven over government solutions ... By the time government acts, the nature of the problem or the problem itself is likely to change radically. In contrast, corporations increasingly must live or die by Internet time, a reality that tips heavily in favour of market-driven solutions to problems in the digital environment.[3]

There is much in this that must be accepted. The extraordinary power of ICT is largely down to the lightweight regulation of the industry. Processing information, as we argued in the previous chapter, has been a general function, and desire, of governments throughout the ages, and it is next to impossible to imagine a government not pumping research money into the ICT industry. Giving that industry the leeway to make money through innovation has led to too big a bonus.

On the other hand, as the authors of the above quote are aware, government thinking, often at the strategic level, is useful for direct-ing research in interesting directions. The Internet itself came from a number of government-sponsored research efforts. We discussed a number of the components of Internet technology in chapter 1, but close scrutiny shows that they often stem from government, not the private sector.

Table 1 shows how little the private sector was involved with the development of the Internet, and how much is down to universities, government research agencies and the US military. Note in particular that the private sector did not put up the money for any of these

Table 1: Provenance of selected Internet component technologies

Internet component	Principal developer(s)	Sponsors	Year
Packet switching	Paul Baran (RAND, a government agency)	The US Air Force	1962
ARPANET (the first physical network of connected machines – all at universities)	BBN (private sector firm)	ARPA (the Advanced Research Projects Agency, a US research body set up after Sputnik)	1968
TCP/IP	Vinton Cerf (Stanford University) and Bob Kahn (DARPA)	DARPA (the Defense Advanced Research Projects Agency, the successor to ARPA)	1973
Domain Name System (DNS)		University of Wisconsin	1983
World Wide Web	Tim Berners-Lee (CERN)	CERN (Conseil Européen pour la Recherche Nucléaire)	1990

innovations. Once the infrastructure was in place, the private sector was able to build on it, but without the government as a driving force (particularly, though not exclusively, in the United States) there would be no Internet, or its equivalent, at all.

This is not merely an artefact of the long period over which these events took place, or the more corporatist age in which they occurred. For instance, one very forward-looking area of technological development is that of flexible display screens. The dominant form of display technology currently (i.e. of the essential screens which act as interfaces between you and your computer) is liquid crystal displays, or LCDs, but the heat these generate require a glass backplane on which the silicon used for the transistors is painted, and glass is extremely inflexible. However, it may be useful to have flexible computer screens, for example to reduce the size of mobile computers (you could unroll the screen when you needed to see it), to reduce the dependence on paper while on the move (imagine a designer being able to scribble on a smart design whilst travelling by train or when on site, and the changes and annotations being transferred automatically through a wireless connection to the database at the office), or even to provide wearable computing (imagine a motorcycle courier's leather jacket acting simultaneously as an advertising display, with the adverts changing according to the GPS location of the driver). In general, the trend towards miniaturisation and mobility that Moore's Law has enabled in the computing world has not been followed in the display screen world at anything like the same pace.

There are many small private sector firms doing excellent work in this area, and one may well provide a breakthrough discovery or, perhaps more likely, find a solution to a niche problem. But simultaneously with this, the government funding juggernaut rolls on, in the university/military nexus. For example, Arizona State University has opened a Flexible Display Centre,[4] bankrolled by various sources but most notably by the US Army Research Laboratory, which is donating $43.7 million over five years, with an option of a similar amount over the next five. Who would bet against such a site acting as an important centre of gravity for the research field given that amount of guaranteed funding over such a long period?

There are actually strong economic arguments that innovation does not happen optimally when private firms are the focus for research. Profit and loss criteria are less important than nonpecuniary incentives in ensuring that socially useful research gets done.[5] In addition, as we argued in chapter 3 and illustrated in later chapters, the importance of ICT is so great that questions of distributional justice have to be addressed. So it is not enough simply to wish away governments from direction and regulation of the ICT industry. The question is the balance between regulation and over-regulation. How to ensure, or promote, a just distribution of ICT without shackling this extraordinary innovative industry is a very tricky issue (and, as we argued in chapter 6, how to produce regulations that can be effectively policed is even harder). How can we learn the right lessons about regulating a sensitive, innovative industry?

ICT is not the only industry where such issues loom large; banking is another.[6] Most governments interfere with their banks, however liberal or free marketeering they are. There are two major reasons for this. The first is that banks play a central role in the economy of every country. They take in deposits, which are, in effect, spare cash that the owners have little use for at present, and lend the money out to others who have useful things on which to spend money they do not have at present, and for that service they cream a little off the top as interest payments. The second reason is that banks are central to people's personal financial strategies. Our earning potential peaks in our middle years, but our spending needs remain much more constant, which means that we have to find a way of spreading out our earnings, concentrated in the years from our 20s to our 60s, over a lifetime that may reach a century and beyond.

On top of this, some massive global banks are simply too big to be allowed to fail, because their health affects the system of banking across several different countries.

OK, so we can agree that allowing banks to fail willy-nilly would be disastrous, both for the economy, as the amounts of deposits would inevitably fall as trust in the system declined, and also for those unfortunate individuals who lost their life savings. Why then not regulate banks very tightly? There are two reasons for this.

First, there is always the problem of moral hazard. If a bank is sure it will not be allowed to fail, then it has little incentive to be careful. It can lend money to people or companies that are bad risks, and when they go bust (and cannot pay back the money that is ultimately due to the depositors) it can ask for handouts from the government. The risk is thereby transferred from the banks to the taxpayer, whereas the profits go to the shareholders. Not a great result.

Secondly, there is the importance – and here the banking industry is very like ICT – of innovation. Financial instruments, such as pensions, unit trusts, annuities and derivatives, are developed to add value to the funds from depositors. Such innovations are what helps the banking sector, and the wealth of the world, grow. Many of them are designed to help people spread the wealth they accumulate in their middle years over the whole of their lives (pensions, annuities), others are designed to insure customers against adverse economic or other woes (derivatives, hedge funds). These are both vitally important services in modern economies. Government control tends to stifle innovation while competitive markets foster it.

It is essential that regulation be light enough to allow innovation to happen, and to curb moral hazard as far as possible, while simultaneously protecting economic interests and ensuring that people's life savings are safe. It is essential to avoid both cartels that damp competition down and competition so cut-throat that failures are frequent.

Another such industry is pharmaceuticals, which is somewhat different, but has a similar too-important-to-be-left-alone quality to it. Obviously drugs are needed to make or keep people well, but there are also important questions of justice concerning whether the wealthy have better access than the poor, and questions of safety of pharmaceuticals, which are dealt with by strict licensing systems, usually following the lead of the US Food and Drug Administration. However, the most important parallel with ICT is to do with innovation.

Developing drugs is a hit-or-miss business. Of all molecules screened, about 2.5% make it through to pre-clinical testing. Of those, 4% make it through to clinical trials. And of those, 10% are approved by the FDA or other regulator. Do the maths and it will be clear that only one in ten thousand molecules screened becomes a saleable drug – and that number is on the decline. So the total R&D spend has to be covered by a relatively small number of drugs. Averaged out, the cost of bringing a new drug to market is close on $1 billion.[7]

Furthermore, the testing process is a matter of decades rather than years, and so new drugs reaching the market now reflect the state of science in the early 1990s. The fruits of the latest developments today, in areas such as biotechnology, will not hit the streets until 2015 or so. This is a source of much uncertainty, as the likelihood of biotechnology, and the new discoveries about the human genome, producing lots of fantastic treatments is currently unknown. If science happens to go up a dead end, even if only for a few years, then the cost to the large pharmaceutical companies ('Big Pharma') could be colossal – and terminal.

The net results of all this are not entirely satisfactory. First, drugs are relatively expensive, particularly in the United States. Pharmaceutical companies have to recover their massive R&D costs, which they do by defending their intellectual property rights. They take out patents on the drugs they develop, and either prevent others from making the same drugs or make them pay a licensing fee to do so. The result is that the company has an effective monopoly for the 20 years that the patent is in force. Unfortunately (for the company), that period of time is effectively less, because if the molecule is patented at an early stage of testing, then it may be 10 years or more before it can be sold. When the patent has run out, other drugs (called *generic* drugs), which are copies of the original drug (the *branded* drug), can be sold in competition. The costs of generic drugs are basically the costs of making them, so they can undercut the prices of branded drugs (whose costs include not only the cost of production but also the cost of development).

Secondly, because the pharmaceutical companies have to recover the very large development costs, the drugs that go into production are, by and large, the ones that they know will sell well, which means that they are generally aimed at those diseases and conditions that are suffered in the developed world. Tropical diseases, such as sleeping sickness and malaria, are not very exciting for Big Pharma, because the return on investment is not likely to be very high. This means that, although 90% of the burden of disease is carried by the developing world, that burden is addressed by only 3% of the R&D spend.[8] Of the 1500 or so drugs that have been launched since 1975, fewer than 20 are aimed specifically at tropical diseases.[9]

It is tempting to put this down to greed, and indeed many activists and non-government organisations do. However, it is important to understand that the creativity and innovatory powers of pharmaceutical companies, large and small, are responsible for the large number of drugs that we have to treat such an impressive range of conditions, and partially responsible for the giant strides in improvements in public health since the landmark discovery of penicillin. No profits, no innovation. No innovation, no great drugs. Even if it is the greed of pharmaceutical companies that drives their R&D and pricing policies, we need to understand that without this greed, we would not have the range and quality of drugs that we do.

The examples of banking and pharmaceuticals show that, with political willingness, industries which provide services that are too important to be neglected but need freedom to innovate can be lightly regulated, or nudged in the right direction, without curbing their ability to create new products. There is a lesson here for ICT, that the extraordinary outgrowth of innovation of the last two or three decades can continue while a level of access for all those people who need it is ensured. Any compromise reached will require a degree of cooperation between government and the industry, may well need sticks as well as carrots, and will almost certainly be messy and perverse in some respects. We should not expect theoretical or ideological purity when dealing with multi-billion-dollar industries, and the needs of countries large and small, rich and poor, democratic and authoritarian.

The digital divide

We have talked about the potential, and the evidence, for the digital divide in other chapters, particularly chapter 3. It has also become clear that the more important the services that ICT provides, and the more central its role in the lives of citizens, the more important it is in a just society that people get sufficient access to ICT to play their part in the democratic organisation of their society, to be able to achieve their reasonable preferences and pursue their conception of the good, and to avoid their voices being drowned out by the richer and more powerful. The nature of the digital divide (if any) that exists in societies, both global and local, and the extent to which that cuts some people off unfairly from essential services or spaces will determine the sorts of regulation required. If unfairness was rife, then we might be more prepared to shackle the creativity of the ICT industry than we would be if the harms were relatively small.

So how serious is the digital divide as a factor? We have looked at some representative areas, at a theoretical level, in this book, where we have decided that ICT has an important place in political life, both as problem and potential solution, as summarised in table 2.

It is probably already evident that the notion of the digital divide that we canvassed at the outset has undergone much subsequent alteration, refinement and deepening as we have proceeded through the various issues. Much of this has been implicit in our discussion. It is now time to make some of those changes explicit.

We began with the concept of the digital divide as being quite straightforward – a distinction between the information-haves and the information-have-nots. You either had access to ICT or you didn't. Empirical studies – especially the early ones – lent support to this

Table 2: Problems and potential of ICT

Chapter	Problems caused by ICT	Potential of ICT
5	Uneven growth between wired (developed) world and developing world.	Disseminating knowledge and information, both to aid local industry and to combat totalitarian dictatorships.
6	Replacement of citizenship with consumerism. Customisation of content reducing interaction with others.	Deliberative spaces. Freedom of online association tempering extremism.
7	Rush to modernisation. Potential for fraud in e-voting. Potential for disenfranchisement of those without access to ICT.	Online delivery of government services, bypassing inefficient or corrupt bureaucracies.
8	Invasions of privacy.	Privacy enhancing technologies. Sousveillance.

view, firming up the concept of the dichotomous divide. Access to ICT was seen to vary within the advanced industrial countries of the world in line with other cleavages, such as income group, gender, race, age, ethnicity and educational levels. Those who were being excluded from access to ICT were usually those who were also excluded from social activities on other grounds as well.

At the outset of our concern over an emerging digital divide the problem looked simple, and so did the solution. If the problem was a lack of access to ICT, then the solution was to place computers strategically so that those in excluded groups would have access. Bingo! Problem solved. This type of thinking undoubtedly drove government initiatives such as the giving away of reconditioned computers to less affluent households and the emphasis on local IT centres.

As we have proceeded, however, our treatment of the digital divide has become more nuanced. As we have considered the different dimensions to the rise of digital technology our understanding of the divide has altered, becoming more complex. Note, for example, how the assumptions underlying the simple notion of a digital divide have been systematically challenged. At the outset the conceptualisation of the problem was largely in terms of access to computing hardware. Whether some individual or group was excluded was measured by whether they had physical access to a desktop computer. As we saw in the first chapter, the diverse range and uses of digital technology make this sort of simplification far too crude to be of any real use. Software, the Internet and the World Wide Web, physical network connections, mobile telephony, satellite and digital technology, and much more are all part of ICT. A lack of access to ICT might plausibly mean a lack of access to any one or more of these specific technologies, not just to beige computer boxes. Any attempts at solving the digital divide must take the diversity of ICT into account in some form lest they turn out to appear hopelessly naïve and misdirected. Similarly, even though the Internet is fairly indicative of things such as levels of technological proliferation, we should be wary once again of conflating Internet access and use with access to ICT in general. The Internet is not the whole story.

Even if we accept that the 'subject' of the digital divide is a group of different digital technologies – i.e. we answer the question 'Access to what?' – there remain other factors that complicate the issue further. One of these is the question of what 'access' itself means. As we saw in chapter 4, in the discussion about what 'universal access' might mean, 'access' admits of a variety of different interpretations. Remember, for instance, the example of the academic with all the latest electronic wizardry and computer gadgetry sat on his desk, compared with the person who has to take two bus rides in order to get a 30 minute slot on a rather dated desktop computer at the local library. Both could be said to have access to ICT. The level of access, however, is clearly different in both quantitative and qualitative terms.

Similarly, just having access can be woefully insufficient. The idea of reconditioning computers and giving them to families in deprived areas is arguably based on the idea that possession of a computer equals access. Unfortunately it does not. Reconditioned computers, however well meaning the intention, are worthless if the recipients do not have the desire, need or ability to use them. Dropping computers by parachute into the Bronx or the London Borough of Hackney is unlikely to solve the problem of the digital divide. This requires rectifying more difficult problems than the simple physical access to computers and other technology.

Take desire first. If people lack the desire to use ICT, then whatever technology they have formal access to will remain untouched. So if the Internet does not speak to their interests, they won't explore it. Similarly, if they lack the need – if there is nothing to benefit them from using the technology – then even if they have the desire and the ability, their access promotes nothing more than curiosity or intellectual stimulation. Part of the challenge of e-governance is to give citizens incentives to use the technological route, otherwise there is no need for them to change from traditional methods of accessing state services.

Finally, and probably most importantly, if individuals lack ICT skills, then even if they have the latest computer wizardry at their disposal they will not be able to access it in any meaningful sense. As we have seen, the ability to access and utilise ICT is increasing with each generation. Those of us in middle age are immigrants to the Network Society; some pick things up easier than others, and are more comfortable in that society. Those from the older generation have typically found it harder to adapt. The younger generations are natives (albeit first generation) of the Network Society and, by-and-large, fit easily into the technological framework. Knowing nothing else, their abilities are nurtured from the outset.

A recent survey carried out under the auspices of the Oxford Internet Institute has indicated that all those in the UK who want

Internet access now have it. This is an interesting fact for a number of reasons, not least the story it tells about proliferation spans. It is not unreasonable to assume, however, that out of those who say they do not want Internet access, there are many for whom such access is deemed to offer no real benefit, or who lack the skills necessary to make effective use of any access. The idea of not wanting something can hide many details.

At a minimum, then, access to ICT must include not only the physical dimension of individuals getting their hands on technology, but also the skills necessary for those individuals to make meaningful use of that technology. Once we add this to the previous point about the different types of technology encompassed under the ICT banner, we can see how multi-dimensional the idea of a digital divide really is. Things are far more complex – they vary along many more dimensions – than the simple question of whether someone has a computer or not.

As well as the complexity of what actually constitutes digital technology and the different understandings of the divide itself, there also remains the important feature of the knock-on effects or consequences of the digital divide. This adds another dimension to the deepening understanding of the distributional patterns of ICT. As we have seen in chapters 3–5, effective or meaningful access to ICT forms a central component of many types of human activity. Productive activity, political decision making, social activities and consumption opportunities are all affected in important ways by the level and type of access that individuals have to ICT. To the extent that individuals lack such meaningful access they are excluded from important social, political and economic activities. ICT and normal levels of social functioning are intimately bound together, and any understanding of the digital divide must echo the fact that meaningful participation in one's society is based, in part, upon effective access to ICT.

The understanding of the digital divide that we have been

operating with, then, is one that contains a number of divergent and overlapping elements. It encompasses many different types of technology, and involves different forms and levels of access. It also impacts on sundry areas of human society and the activities of individuals within that society. This is very different to the simple dichotomous notion of a digital divide with which we began. The increasingly complex nature of the problem has demanded a corresponding multi-layered, comprehensive and versatile response.

Prioritarianism revisited

We have argued that the ICT industry is a tender plant, and that regulation cannot be too strict or standards too severe. Indeed, so fast are its innovative cycles that the standards of ordinary software suffer.[10] Now when you install a piece of software on your computer you have to tick a licensing agreement that indemnifies the software producer against any harm you may incur because the software is crummy, which of course removes all incentives that the producer has to remove the bugs. One of the reasons for this is that because software is so complex nowadays, and has to work in such a range of environments, testing and debugging software to a decent standard takes so long that the product would be out of date before it hit the shelves.

On the other hand, we have noted that sometimes access to ICT is essential for a citizen, in which case in a just society that access should be engineered. We argued this in chapter 3, and in chapter 4 set out a framework by which fairness might be judged. That was, of course, a quite abstract framework, and now we have a greater understanding of the context, perhaps it is time to revisit the idea of prioritarianism. Given the context in which we are arguing, are we sure that the framework is appropriate for the domain in question?

Objections to the appropriateness of prioritarianism arise from two broad directions. One – that the distribution of ICT is not the subject of social justice and should be left to market forces – has operated as our point of departure throughout. We have argued that the new technologies form part of the basic goods that are necessary for normal levels of social functioning in our societies and therefore are the legitimate subject matter of debates about justice. Furthermore, even those who defend the free market in principle are usually committed to the idea of equality of opportunity (on grounds of either efficiency or ethics). From here, it is a short, and defensible, step to a prioritarian principle of distribution.

The second type of objection is one that views prioritarianism as nothing more than a defence of the status quo. Recall from our abstract discussion in chapter 4 that a policy that assigns priority in the distribution of a certain good to those who are likely to be the worst placed in that distribution is perfectly consistent with an unequal distribution. Priority and equality are, as we saw, not the same things. Yet, for some, this means that a prioritarian view sanctions all, or virtually all, inequalities. It provides an ethical foundation for the inequalities that currently exist. This would be agreeably ecumenical for defenders of priority. It would require that we change nothing.

Take a specific example: the provision of ICT and ICT training in schools. Governments around the world have begun to wake up to the fact that the best sites for developing a technology-literate populace are formal educational institutions. We have canvassed a number of policies from different countries that target such institutions as a method for bridging what they conceive to be a growing digital divide. Yet we have also noted how, even though universal access has been achieved in some cases, there are significant quantitative and qualitative differences in the levels of access. Some wealthier schools, or schools in wealthier catchment areas, may have vastly superior IT suites to those poorer ones down the road.

Similarly, the social background of students varies, and some may have computers at home whilst others do not. This differentially disadvantages the latter group even though access is supposedly universal.

A prioritarian principle that specified that inequalities are justified when those inequalities are to the benefit of all might be thought to sanction such a distribution of computing technology within schools. If, using our framework for thinking about such matters, we concluded that individuals could benefit differentially from the exercise of their talents, so long as those who were worst off were at their maximum possible level, then we might justify spending more on some schools than on others.

A recent academic article by Elizabeth Hendrix embraces this particular complaint in relation to the distribution of ICT across schools:

> This theory of justice, wherein, inequalities exist for just ends, especially for the least favored, is like an oxymoron in practice, *just injustice*, because in reality, the disadvantaged group remain marginalized.[11]

Here, then, anything other than equality is automatically seen as constituting an injustice. What's more, if correct, then a prioritarian distribution would be incapable of overcoming the social exclusion that it aimed to alleviate.

There are some deep confusions in this position, but it is worth examining it in a little more depth in order to draw out more details about prioritarian justice as it applies to ICT in schools.

Again, Hendrix writes:

> In regard to technology and schools, administrators and educators embrace John Rawls' theory of justice, wherein economic inequalities are embraced supposedly to benefit everyone, but in practice as well as in funding, justice and equality do not exist.[12]

Hendrix clearly thinks that prioritarian principles, such as Rawls's view, act as a mask for entrenched injustices, inequalities and partisan interests. There is some equivocation, however, as to whether this is intended as a critique of prioritarianism in principle or as a criticism of its practical applications. This is an important general point. However ideal, acceptable or well worked out a view might be, it is always susceptible to misapplication. When policy architects attempt to transfer a given principle into an actual working policy, with all the detail and interpretation that entails, the danger that the principle may be misapplied is always present. This could, of course, be either intentional or accidental. But objecting to the application of a principle as it is manifested in, say, a policy is very different to objecting to the principle itself. Think here, for example, of the offside rule in the game of football (soccer). The principle of not allowing a player to gain a significant advantage over the opposing team is often said to underpin the retention of the offside rule. However, from season to season, different permutations of the offside rule have been tried out by the footballing authorities (e.g. one season you had to be behind the penultimate defender, while the following season you could be level with but not in front of the defender). It is possible to object to specific manifestations (i.e. rules) of offside without actually objecting to the idea of having offsides in principle. It is also possible to object to offsides in principle, regardless of how it is manifested in practice.

Commentators such as Hendrix often blur this distinction. The above two quotations talk about 'practice' and 'reality' as though they differ (which they do) from principle. However, the objection can also operate at the level of principle: 'Rawls' notion that inequalities are acceptable as long as everyone benefits is unjust.'[13] It is crucial to keep these two types of objection separate. The case against prioritarianism largely collapses once this distinction is enforced.

Some other instances illustrate this general conflation. Hendrix rightly highlights the differences in qualitative and quantitative levels of access that seem to exist under the banners of 'universal' access or 'equal' opportunities. But, as we have already seen, prioritarianism does not support just any old level of access: it supports maximising the position of those who fare worst under a distribution of a given resource. Here, Hendrix writes:

> Echoing Rawls' theory of justice, the suburbanites [i.e. the wealthy] ask, 'So long as every child has a guarantee of education, what harm can it really be to let us spend a little more [on our own children]?'[14]

Such a position would be more reminiscent of the sufficiency view we criticised in chapter 4, rather than the prioritarian view that Rawls holds. The point of prioritarianism is not to guarantee that individuals surpass a minimum threshold of a given good, but that the position of the worst off is maximised. Commentators such as Hendrix worry that this type of view simply entrenches the advantages of suburban, white, wealthy students that already exist, that prioritarianism allows these inequalities within its parameters. But this is to twist the priority view out of all recognisable shape. Recall our discussion of the grounds for distributing goods. We have defended throughout the idea that arbitrary characteristics should not feature as legitimate grounds for distribution. To allow a principle that distributes according to social or racial position is a violation of this. It is also a very different principle to the priority view.

What observers such as Hendrix alert us to is the tendency of people (parents, teachers, policy makers) to enlist, and twist, ethical principles in support of their own partisan position. From the outset we have attempted to guard against the unjustified interference of partiality by placing various restrictions, checks and balances on our thinking about these matters. Claiming that something like Rawls's respected philosophical position is consistent with the existing unequal set of circumstances lends the latter a veneer of credibility. However, once we scratch the surface it becomes evident that the inequalities we witness are in no way consistent with, or underpinned by, such a normative position. Policies that distributed more ICTs to white suburban schools because they were white suburban schools, or which merely required that all schools have a minimum specified quantity of ICT resources, would fall foul of the criterion of the priority view. Clearly, those pupils who fare worst under such schemes have a legitimate complaint – on grounds of priority – that they are not benefiting to the maximum extent possible. To claim that a view such as Rawls's would support this is to misunderstand the very nature of that view.

Arguably, what often motivates this type of criticism is an unargued for assumption that justice requires equality. Any departure from that baseline is intuitively felt to be a departure from justice. We have dealt with this position at length. Maintaining equality in the face of a distribution that would make everyone better off falls foul of the levelling down objection and runs contrary to economic efficiency. The latter is an important consideration. Earlier we discussed the importance of research and design for the ICT industry. Heavy regulation stifles development, but the unfettered market does not always lead to developments in the right direction. A number of examples were given as illustrations of this point. Prioritarianism, as a guiding principle, allows economic and material incentives to operate whilst regulating some of those inequalities so as to raise the share of those at the bottom. In terms of research and design, companies would retain their ability to make profitable interventions in the market, but some of the revenues from their products would be redistributed to raise such things as levels of access to technology.

The priority view, if adopted as the guiding principle for legislating in the ICT field, would require some significant alterations and reconceptualisations of current practice. It does not provide a blanket justification for the current state of affairs; far from it. The priority view would have far-reaching structural consequences for the ICT industry and the Information Society. It would not leave things unchanged, and this, we have argued, is no bad thing. But neither is it a call to change everything. What sort of changes would such an approach mandate?

Prioritarian policies

The key factor in a prioritarian approach is that inequalities are allowed to exist so long as such inequalities work to the benefit of the worst off. Here is a simple example of the prioritarian idea in action in the regulation of the Internet. One growth area of the Internet is telephony: Voice Over Internet Protocol (VOIP) is a standard used to carry voice or, for that matter, video calls over the Internet as digital packets. For a traditional synchronous conversation, one needs speakers and a microphone (standard on most laptops), and a broadband connection to transfer the data to your interlocutor(s). It is much more flexible than conventional telephony, as it does not require a dedicated circuit at either end of the call, so voicemails can be stored in inboxes, forwarded to others and so on. In the US, VOIP had grown from a few tens of thousands of pioneers in early 2003 to about two million users by the first quarter of 2005. Because the number of users was so small, and the users themselves relatively clued up about what they were buying, American telecommunications regulators did not cover VOIP (the freedom with which VOIP providers were able to innovate and keep charges down no doubt helped the speedy growth).

However, as the number of users grew, average awareness of the technology inevitably declined. Tragic accidents and even deaths occurred as naïve customers dialled the emergency number 911, only to find that the VOIP network didn't provide a 911 service. On 19 May 2005, America's Federal Communications Commission (FCC) ruled that VOIP providers must handle emergencies. The move protected all VOIP users and raised standards to a level such that all telephone users had basic cover by critical infrastructure. At the same time, the FCC brought VOIP under a number of reasonable regulations, regarding such things as the reliability of the infrastructure, and the ability of the courts to intercept, monitor and intervene. All of this is perfectly sensible and hardly likely to jeopardise the innovative potential of the industry. Maintaining the material incentives for developing and improving the services has been retained whilst bringing certain regulations to bear that benefit everyone.

That light regulatory touch is essential for the Internet and the ICT industry. The Internet, for example, is run by not-for-profit bodies such as ICANN and the W3C, which specify rules and standards that are open and intended to provide a level surface on which people can build new ideas and ways of disseminating and acquiring knowledge.

Keeping that balance is hard. For example, in June 2005, ICANN (which doles out domain names) approved a new suffix, '.xxx', for pornographic sites (which are currently usually '.com' sites). If one set up a site called www.somethingrude.xxx, then people would know that it was pornographic (in the same way that they know that http://www.rsc.org.uk/ is a British non-commercial organisation – it's actually the Royal Shakespeare Company – and http://www.nottingham.ac.uk/ is a British university). That is good news for pornography users, who want to find sites efficiently, and non-users, who may want to censor sites to prevent them being downloaded, alike. However, this creation of a porn ghetto may well cause more confusion than intended. Different countries have different values. Indeed, it may be that many jurisdictions oppose the legitimisation of the pornography industry by tacitly accepting its web presence in this way. Even though the idea may have seemed like a good one – even though the idea of '.xxx' may work well – it shifts the regulation of the Internet away from the idea of its being a platform on which anyone can build towards the idea of its being a planned community with certain specified properties.

Attempts to steer ICT use have generally been counterproductive. We discussed the French Minitel system in chapter 4. It was a very successful system, at least in France, but had perverse side-effects – notably it restricted Internet uptake in France, because even though the Internet is superior, Minitel was pretty well adequate for a number of purposes, so many of its users failed to see any reason for switching. Recall Metcalfe's Law from chapter 2, that the value of a network increases proportionally to the square of the network's size. The Minitel network was very large, and at the time the society of Internet users was relatively small. The French are still behind on Internet use, which has helped with the anglophone domination of the web; this rankles with the francophone community, but it is really the fault of a centralised French system that attempted (successfully) to create a communications network just before the big technological breakthrough left it behind.

This has led to retaliation, but perhaps most bizarrely the French have declared war on the Google search engine. President Chirac has asked his Culture Minister and the head of the Bibliothèque Nationale to devise a French version of Google, this despite the fact that Google is a highly technical system developed by classic nerdy computer types (not guardians of culture) and that three-quarters of French Internet searches use Google (so there is hardly pressure from the grass roots for an alternative). Google is seen as an American cultural invasion. Why American, particularly? Because it uses the popularity of sites to rank them. The culture minister disputed that 'the only key to access our culture should be the automatic ranking by popularity, which has been behind Google's success'. The solution being floated is that sites should be ranked by a committee of experts – an extraordinary suggestion, given the number of sites to be ranked.[15] This is the sort of idiocy one gets into if one starts legislating without considering the technical qualities of the Internet. The one saving grace of the whole idea is that it will never get off the ground.

This sort of misguided paternalism is hard to avoid; there is a strong feeling that ICT has coarsened experience. The evidence for this is relatively scanty, however. Indeed, it has been argued that modern popular culture, from television to computer games, actually demands rather more emotional and logical intelligence to understand than earlier forms,[16] and that computer games actually teach us a great deal about simple notions of virtue that seem to have got lost in our relativist times.[17]

What, then, would a prioritarian approach do? We do not wish to be too prescriptive. After all, understanding the changing context of technology is the hardest thing. It is not actually that difficult to guess what technologies will appear over a five-year time frame, say; one can extrapolate from where research money is going now. But it is next to impossible to guess what technologies, in what packages and combinations, will really take off as medical equipment, consumer goods, fashion items or military hardware.

The prioritarian approach is intended to raise people's level of provision without necessarily equalising total provision or shifting resources from the wealthy. In the broad context of ICT, that means ensuring that the information-poor receive sufficient access to ICT without distorting the general ICT market too much. Massive disturbances to the market would be bad for two reasons. First, we do not want to stifle innovation. Secondly, the market actually works reasonably well. We know from experience that people are prepared to pay for techno-goods; mobile phones are not particularly cheap items, but even relatively poor people, in both the rich and the developing worlds, are prepared to sacrifice other goods to own them. We probably don't really know why this is so, and certainly few people predicted it before the technology had really bedded down; Metcalfe's Law no doubt had much to do with it, but it can't be the only explanation. Whatever the reason, it shouldn't be the government's job to put goods into the hands of people who were perfectly prepared to pay for them in the first place.

Given the aim of the prioritarian approach, to do enough to solve problems without engineering a complete solution, we might reconsider the last two columns of table 2 above: the problems caused by ICT and the potential. The prioritarian should wish to address the problems without undermining the potential. The worries of the first of these columns should be addressed while preserving the hopes expressed in the second. Prioritarianism and economic efficiency are, in this sense, compatible.

Globalisation and ICT

With respect to the issues raised about globalisation in chapter 5, in effect we are in a win–win situation. The problem to be addressed is the global digital divide, but addressing it is unlikely to shackle the potential of ICT in the developing world for disseminating knowledge and therefore increasing the power of those receiving it. Speeding up the developing world's access to ICT will in and of itself spread the benefits of ICT.

One happy point is that the initial move towards spreading ICT should be a one-off sunk cost – in equipment and, equally important, in training – which could be part of a foreign aid programme, such as those sponsored by the UK's Department for International Development; a governmental drive, such as the ICT programme followed by Chandrababu Naidu's government in Andhra Pradesh; or a charitable effort, such as the knowledge centre initiative of the M.S. Swaminathan Research Foundation around Pondicherry.

There is a limited quantity of aid funding, and many things for aid to do. But it does have to be noted that aid has been the focus of some stern examinations recently, as the people aid is aimed at rarely seem to be taken out of poverty. It may seem frivolous to spend money on computers rather than food, but in the long run it could well be a better-targeted expenditure.

With regard to the dissemination of knowledge to give political power, the main issue is with the governance of the Internet itself. The Internet is a source of power for repressed peoples, and it is surely important that the regulation of the Internet, and the creation of its standards, remain in the hands of committed democrats. The United Nations Secretary General has convened a Working Group on Internet Governance, mentioned in chapter 1, but as it contains representatives from Saudi Arabia, Cuba and China among others, one might be a tad sceptical about whether the free dissemination of knowledge is uppermost in all minds. On the other hand, if the system remains administered by not-for-profit organisations closely related to the United States, it is important that they do not impose too American an architecture on the Internet (which does not mean that Google should be reconfigured, but does mean that careful thought should be given to the setting up of domain name suffixes such as '.xxx').

The citizen and ICT

With regard to the issue of citizenship, and the way that the online world affects that, the position is somewhat more complex. For instance, customisation of content worried legal theorist Cass Sunstein, because it could create (indeed, on occasion, has created) vicious feedback loops tending to exacerbate extremism. But regulation of the Internet along the lines proposed by Sunstein is impractical, and the danger is that the real advantages of customisation and personalisation will be lost in the shuffle.

The Internet is, potentially, a fine space for discussion, deliberation and interaction. Certainly it is becoming an increasingly important source of information. Websites such as those of the BBC and al-Jazeera have established important brands, certain blogs have achieved importance and established newspapers have had to adapt.

At present, automatic filtering technology is in its relative infancy. It is certainly too soon to tell whether such technology will actively undermine the potential of ICT to support deliberation. It is a political question of whether the occasional explosion of extremist violence as a result of exposure to corrupting websites (e.g. the US school shootings, the development of nihilistic Islamic neo-fundamentalism) makes the repression of a potentially useful technology worthwhile. The Internet is currently a relatively rich political space in terms of the number of viewpoints served (certainly many more views than in other media, or in democratically elected chambers), if not so rich in the number of people actually using it to deliberate. This, combined with the difficulties of getting a policeable regulatory system, suggests that a sceptical wait-and-see policy may be the way forward here, and that the burden of proof about regulating the content of political websites should always be on the regulator.

Democracy and ICT

With respect to democracy, it is not clear what the benefits of e-voting are in general, though in some polities it has been important in improving electoral administration and reducing fraud and disenfranchisement. But there needs to be clear reason to move ahead beyond paper-based systems. We all saw what a mess the 2000 US presidential election was as a result of a poor piece of technology – the machines to punch voting cards that produced all the notorious hanging chads and pregnant chads. Normally the poor performance of such technology wouldn't have mattered, but when the election swung on a small number of electoral college votes, which in turn depended on just a few hundred voters in Florida, it mattered a lot.

But why bother trying out new systems anyway? Given that crosses on paper are cheap, usually unambiguous, easy to audit and simple to understand, why go beyond that basic technology?

In the event that the benefits of e-voting systems are proved (e.g. they are shown to be auditable, cheap and fair), then it needs also to be shown that their use does not privilege certain groups of voters over others. Will the system penalise rural voters? Will it put off the elderly? Indeed, as we argued in chapter 7, it is not clear that trying to increase the turnout of certain groups, such as the young, who fail to vote through apathy rather than a lack of access is a properly fair use of the technology.

Much better as a use of technology for government is the online delivery of government services, and the use of computers rather than clerks in offices as the interface between government and citizen (as, for example, with Andhra Pradesh's e-Seva system). The key here, once more, is to ensure that access is improved for people who have been denied it without privileging certain groups. It is also important to have a fall-back position – there are people who have been interacting with government via letters, filling in forms, etc., who are quite happy to continue to do so, and they should be able so to do. The Oxford Internet Institute survey that found 7% of Britons were refuseniks. These people cannot and should not be marginalised. Systems need to be built that are flexible enough to adapt to them, even if they are eccentric or misguided. Governmental systems exist for their citizens, not the other way around.

Privacy and ICT

ICT gives enormous scope for the invasion of our privacy. Indeed, the post-Enlightenment concept of privacy is under probably terminal pressure from the proliferation of ICT. We need to adapt to

that and balance our security needs against our privacy requirements.

There is a danger that, like the future, privacy will be unevenly
distributed. If the preservation of privacy depends on people buying
Privacy Enhancing Technologies (PETs) and keeping them up to date,
this will tend to benefit the rich and technologically adept, as
opposed to the poor, the uninformed and the casual user. It is
probably not reasonable to try to ensure privacy for the general public
in such a way (although that is not to say that PETs shouldn't be
available, only that there should be another strategy). It is important
that privacy is available for everyone without a giant cognitive
overhead.

It is very important to realise, and for politicians to communicate,
that our ideas of privacy will also have to change radically. People
wishing to preserve the level of privacy they enjoyed even twenty
years ago would have to deny themselves almost all communication
beyond speech and pen-and-paper. It is not clear that there is a
sustainable lifestyle for those who are obsessively private, at least in
the developed world. Governments should abstain from collecting
information as much as they can, but resting hopes for privacy on
such self-denying ordinances is Utopian in the extreme – especially
as we are surprisingly willing to donate valuable personal information, which we would never volunteer to a democratically elected
government, to unaccountable supermarkets and credit card
companies.

Governments, legal theorists and international agencies need to
find new rules to regulate this informational glut – indeed, there are
many initiatives underway in this field already. But the essential thing
is that no one is left behind, that no groups in society end up being
more transparent to the authorities than others. And, as ever, the aim
of the prioritarian should be to ensure protection for the weak first
and foremost.

Conclusions

There are a number of broad conclusions we should draw from our study. The first, which we have flagged up at a number of points in our inquiry, is still perhaps surprising. We hope the reader has noted how often, in our inquiries, we have had to consult the great masters of political philosophy, from Adam Smith to Karl Marx, and others in the long tradition of thinkers stretching back to Plato and Aristotle, such as Thomas Hobbes and David Hume. Not only that, but many of the more recent thinkers of the twentieth century have also loomed large, perhaps most notably John Rawls, who, though he lived to see the twenty-first century, did most of his important writing when the World Wide Web was but a gleam in Tim Berners-Lee's eye, and others such as Hannah Arendt, Ronald Coase and Marshall McLuhan. These thinkers feature at least as much as those present day sages whose specific writings about the Internet are so valuable, such as Laurence Lessig, Steve Fuller, Cass Sunstein and Manuel Castells.

What does that tell us? Well, it seems to hint at least that the Internet has not radically transformed human life and society. The old offline political problems of distribution, freedom, and the relation between the individual and society are all mirrored online. But as our discussions in the second half of the book have shown, the Internet has altered many of our offline assumptions – in particular, that information is hard to get hold of and difficult to read. The Internet has not changed the nature of power, but, if knowledge is power, what it has done is change the distribution of power. It is an instrument that is simultaneously democratic and Big Brotherish. The new political space bears a strong family resemblance to other, more traditional political spaces, but the resemblance is marked more in some respects than others. The Internet has not changed politics any more than it changed economics or commerce (despite what many late-twentieth-century commentators assumed); but, within the traditional paradigm of Plato and Aristotle, it has thrown up new problems and new issues to which policy makers should be alive.

The second conclusion is that ICT is so central to the conduct of democratic politics that distributional questions cannot be left to the market alone, although as we have argued strongly, particularly in this chapter, any regulation needs to be light in order that the industry's astonishing innovatory capacity remains untouched. It is also important not to go to the other extreme of insisting on egalitarian distributions of equipment, education or other types of access. The prioritarian framework we outlined in chapter 4 hits about the right level.

Finally, ICT is a fascinating industry, and the effect on all of us, particularly of the Internet, has been as dramatic as any other event in the last fifty years or so. It is important that as few people as possible are left behind, compared with both their fellow countrymen and worldwide. The temptation to muse on the possibilities and the difficulties of ICT's effect on society is naturally very strong in the political field. What our study has indicated is the importance of understanding how the technology works, what its properties really are, and what the relation is between the science fiction hype and the actual implemented machinery. A pinch of salt needs to be taken with some of the wilder claims, but equally patience has to be shown to some systems of promise.

One of the hardest tasks is getting a system to work as it should. Debugging and testing take up a huge percentage of development cost, while maintenance of an implemented system or database is another costly overhead. Security issues often loom large, and it is unfortunate that there are many people online who wish to sabotage systems just for the hell of it. New types of cybercrime are coming into fashion every day, while some of the old types are being displaced online. If, given all that, a system does not work perfectly, or falls short of a theoretical ideal, we shouldn't be surprised, or cynical, or over-critical. If we let the perfect be the enemy of the good, we will fail to harness the potential of ICT to improve the conduct of our politics. To think about ICT and politics without knowing how either works, and without understanding the failings of each, is to deny ourselves the possibility of improving our deliberations, increasing the depth of our consultation and, ultimately, restoring the legitimacy that many feel that Western democracies have recently lost.

Notes

Chapter 1

1. Thomas Hobbes, *Leviathan* (London: Penguin, 1985 [1651]).
2. Bernard Crick, *In Defence of Politics* (London: Weidenfeld & Nicolson, 1962).
3. Hannah Arendt, *The Human Condition* (Chicago: University of Chicago Press, 1958), pp. 52–3.
4. Arendt, *The Human Condition*, p. 50.
5. See Karl Marx, *On the Jewish Question* (1843).
6. William J. Baumol, *The Free-Market Innovation Machine: Analyzing the Growth Miracle of Capitalism* (Princeton: Princeton University Press, 2002), p. 134.
7. Adam Smith, *An Inquiry into the Nature and Causes of the Wealth of Nations*, ed. R.H. Campbell and A.S. Skinner (Indianapolis: Liberty Fund, 1981), vol. 1, I.i.11, pp. 23–24. Footnote omitted.
8. See Albert O. Hirschman, *Exit, Voice, and Loyalty: Responses to Decline in Firms, Organizations, and States* (Cambridge, MA: Harvard University Press, 1970).
9. Nathan Myhrvold, 'Software in the Driver's Seat', available at http://bostonreview.mit.edu/BR18.6/debatemitch.html.
10. Whilst libraries and filing cabinets are largely apolitical features in the contemporary world, historically speaking, this claim is untrue. Libraries were incredibly politically problematic. They were seen as forms of control, regulating the reading of the working class and so forth. Even the history of the filing cabinet is checkered with political dimensions. We thank Mark Neocleous for raising this point.
11. Kieron O'Hara and Tom Scutt, 'Groundwork for the Virtual Metaphysics of Online Morals: Virtue and its Representation in Computer Games', forthcoming.
12. For the historical impact of the political pamphlet, see Don Herzog, *Poisoning the Minds of the Lower Orders* (Princeton: Princeton University Press, 1998).

13. Laurence Lessig, *Code, and Other Laws of Cyberspace* (New York: Basic Books, 1999).
14. Report of the Working Group on Internet Governance, available at http://www.wgig.org/docs/WGIGREPORT.pdf.
15. Paul Twomey, 'Hands Off the Internet', *New Scientist*, 12 November 2005.
16. 'A Peace of Sorts', *The Economist*, 19 November 2005.

Chapter 2

1. David Hume, *A Treatise of Human Nature*, ed. L.A. Selby-Bigge (Oxford: Clarendon Press, 1978 [1739]).
2. One of the most dispiriting things about political writing is how few writers understand capitalism, even when capitalism is their main topic.
3. Charles Jonscher, *WiredLife* (London: Bantam Press, 1999), p. 248.
4. Though even there, some scientists think they can exploit quantum effects for computing purposes, in so-called quantum computing.
5. 'Blitz' chess is played under extremely tight time limits – usually five minutes for each of the two players to make all of their moves. Such short time limits tend to favour the processing power of computers (because of their speed in calculation) over the human player's reliance on their chess intuition (built up through repeated play).
6. Filleted from Bill Wall, 'Computer Chess History', available at http://www.geocities.com/SiliconValley/Lab/7378/comphis.htm.
7. Ronald Coase, 'The Nature of the Firm', in *The Nature of the Firm: Origins, Evolution and Development*, ed. Oliver E. Williamson and Sidney G. Winter (Oxford University Press, Oxford, 1993). For those interested in these issues, all the papers in this collection are worth reading.
8. Oliver Williamson, *Markets and Hierarchies* (New York: Free Press, 1975).
9. Chris Hand, 'Television Ownership in Britain and the Coming of ITV: What Do the Statistics Show?', available at http://www.rhul.ac.uk/Media-Arts/staff/Television%20Ownership.pdf.
10. For various individual and collective responses to the actions of firms,

organisations and states, see e.g. Albert O. Hirschman, *Exit, Voice, and Loyalty: Responses to Decline in Firms, Organizations, and States* (Cambridge, MA: Harvard University Press, 1970).

11. Peter Lyman, Hal R. Varian, Kirsten Swearingen, Peter Charles, Nathan Good, Laheem Lamar Jordan and Joyojeet Pal, 'How Much Information? 2003', available at http://www.sims.berkeley.edu/research/projects/how-much-info-2003/.

12. Audrey Gillan, 'Shocking Images Revealed at Britain's "Abu Ghraib trial"', *The Guardian*, 19 January 2005.

13. Lyman *et al.*, 'How Much Information? 2003'.

14. Plato, *Phaedrus*, in *Plato: Complete Works*, ed. John M. Cooper with D.S. Hutchinson (Indianapolis: Hackett, 1997), pp. 506–56; Eric A. Havelock, *Preface to Plato* (Oxford: Basil Blackwell, 1963).

15. Marshall McLuhan, *The Gutenberg Galaxy* (Toronto: University of Toronto Press, 1962).

16. Lyman *et al.*, 'How Much Information? 2003'.

17. Tim Berners-Lee, James Hendler and Ora Lassila, 'The Semantic Web', *Scientific American*, May 2001.

18. They are, honest – whatever publishers might tell you.

19. Definitions of 'grid computing' can vary from person to person. In particular, the director of SETI, David Anderson, does not accept the description for SETI, because the setup is very task specific and centrally controlled (one disputed definition of grid computing says that grids should be generic and without a central controlling system). However, we are not interested in the best or most precise definition; our aim is merely to point out the prevailing technological trends, one of which is the harnessing of distributed computers to work together on a common problem.

20. Yochai Benkler, 'Sharing Nicely: on Shareable Goods and the Emergence of Sharing as a Modality of Economic Production', *Yale Law Journal*, 114, 2004.

21. McLuhan, *The Gutenberg Galaxy*, p. 5.

22. Kevin Warwick, *I, Cyborg* (London: Century, 2002); Donna Haraway, 'A Manifesto for Cyborgs: Science, Technology and Socialist Feminism in the 1980s', *Socialist Review*, 80, 1985, pp. 65–108; Susan Greenfield, *Tomorrow's People: How 21st Century Technology is Changing the Way We Think and Feel* (London: Allen Lane, 2003).

Chapter 3

1. See e.g. http://pubs.socialistreviewindex.org.uk/sr186/letters.htm.
2. Peter Hyman, *1 Out of 10: From Downing Street Vision to Classroom Reality* (London: Vintage, 2005).
3. John Rawls, *A Theory of Justice* (Oxford: Oxford University Press, 1972), p. 92.
4. Rawls, *A Theory of Justice*, pp. 90–1.
5. http://www.foresight.gov.uk.
6. This list is taken from GB Office of Science and Technology, *Progress Through Partnership: Technology Foresight Report 8: IT and Electronics* (London: HMSO, 1995).
7. Figures from Manuel Castells, 'The Informational City is a Dual City: Can it be Reversed?', in *High Technology and Low-Income Communities: Prospects for the Positive Use of Advanced Information Technology*, ed. D.A. Schon, B. Sanyal and W.J. Mitchell (Cambridge, MA: MIT Press, 1999), pp. 33–4. For a comprehensive statistical analysis of job creation rates, unemployment rates and changes in the forms of employment during the latter quarter of the twentieth century, see Manuel Castells, *The Information Age: Economy, Society and Culture, vol. 1: The Rise of the Network Society* (Boston, MA: Blackwell, 1996), esp. ch. 4.
8. Steve Fuller, *Knowledge Management Foundations* (Woburn, MA: Butterworth-Heinemann, 2002).
9. Castells, 'The Informational City is a Dual City', p. 32.
10. For more on this see Castells, *The Rise of Network Society*, pp. 202–80.
11. Castells, 'The Informational City is a Dual City', p. 33.
12. See Will Hutton, *The State We're In* (London: Vintage, 1996), esp. pp. 105–12.
13. P. Hall, 'Changing Geographies: Technology and Income', in Schon *et al.*, *High Technology and Low-Income Communities*, p. 58.
14. *Global Employment Trends for Youth 2004* (International Labour Office, Geneva).
15. On the deleterious effects of migration from the cities, see J. Rifkin, *The End of Work: The Decline of the Global Labour Force and the Dawn of the Post-Market Era* (New York: Tarcher/Putnam, 1995).
16. Hall, 'Changing Geographies: Technology and Income', p. 59.
17. Pippa Norris, *Digital Divide*, p. 68.

18. List drawn from T. Burchardt, J. Le Grand and D. Piachaud, 'Social Exclusion in Britain 1991–1995', *Social Policy and Administration*, 33, 1999, pp. 227–44.

Chapter 4

1. W.J. Mitchell, 'Equitable Access to the Online World', in Schon *et al.*, *High Technology and Low-Income Communities*, p. 153.
2. International Telecommunications Union, Draft Declaration of Principles, WSIS, 21 March 2003, B.21, http://www.itu.int/dms_pub/itu-s/md/03/wsis/doc/S03-WSIS-DOC-0004!!MSW-E.doc.
3. Policy Action Team 15, Social Exclusion Unit, *Closing the Digital Divide: Information and Communication Technologies in Deprived Areas* (London: Department for Trade and Industry, 2000), para. 11. Emphasis added.
4. On the way that private education undermines equality of opportunity and the efficiency of the market, see Adam Swift, *How Not to be a Hypocrite: School Choice for the Morally Perplexed Parent* (London: Routledge, 2003).
5. Of course, this is not the case in all fields. In the UK, for example, it is, in effect, still possible to buy one's child a place at university. This is achieved by purchasing an education at a private school which is superior to that provided by state schools. The superior education purchased at such institutions helps to shift one's child further up the queue for university places (beyond what they would have attained without such special educational resources). This defeats equality of opportunity for university places by allowing things other than merit to enter the equation. Similarly, in the US it is possible to buy significant levels of political influence via such routes as campaign financing. Further examples abound.
6. The origin of the term 'meritocracy' is also instructive. Michael Young originally coined the term in his 1958 book *Rise of the Meritocracy*. Interestingly, Young intended the term in a pejorative sense. Young's future world is one where an individual's social position is determined by his or her IQ plus his or her level of effort. Such a system is portrayed in the

book to be so unpalatable that the masses overthrow the political elite which has become disconnected from public opinion.

7. James Fishkin, *Justice, Equal Opportunity, and the Family* (New Haven: Yale University Press, 1984), p. 37. See also A. Swift and G. Marshall, 'Meritocratic Equality of Opportunity: Economic Efficiency, Social Justice, or Both?', *Policy Studies*, 18, 1997.

8. Rawls, *A Theory of Justice*, p. 73.

	Group A	Group B	Total
Distribution 1	100	125	225
Distribution 2	99	99	198

9. A numerical representation may help illustrate this point. Consider the following table (the numbers are merely representational).
Where two possible groups exist in society (A and B), the principle of equality would recommend, as in one way at least better, Distribution 2 as opposed to Distribution 1, even though this would make everyone worse off.

10. David Estlund, 'Democratic Theory', in *Oxford Handbook of Contemporary Philosophy*, ed. Frank Jackson and Michael Smith (Oxford: Oxford University Press, forthcoming).

11. On the inadequacy of this type of clashing of principles view, see David Stevens, 'Crossing Moral No-Man's Land', *Res Publica*, 9, 2003, pp. 303–14.

12. See Vilfredo Pareto, *Manual of Political Economy* (London: Macmillan, 1972 [1906]).

13. For a statement of the sufficiency view, see Harry Frankfurt, *The Importance of What We Care About* (Cambridge: Cambridge University Press, 1988). For an astute synopsis of the various egalitarian positions and the problems that beset them, including the sufficiency view, see Christopher Woodard, 'Egalitarianism', *Philosophical Books*, 46, 2005, pp. 97–112. We draw on Woodard's piece in this section.

14. *Young People in Canada: Their Health and Well-Being* (Public Health Agency of Canada, 2004), ch. 2, available at http://www.phac-aspc.gc.ca/dca-dea/publications/hbsc-2004/chapter_2_e.html.

15. For a free-market view of the ICT industry, see Robert E. Litan and William A. Niskanen, *Going Digital!* (Washington, DC: Brookings Institution Press, 1998).

16. Although not everyone's intuitions are the same in these regards, for most it is more morally disturbing that some people have too little of some resource, rather than the fact that there is inequality between the 'filthy' rich and the just 'plain' rich.

17. The term is borrowed from Derek Parfit's Lindley Lecture 'Equality or Priority?', delivered at the University of Kansas in 1991. The full version of this lecture can be found in Matthew Clayton and Andrew Williams, eds, *The Ideal of Equality* (London: Palgrave Macmillan, 2002). References to Parfit are from this volume. The previous example of blinding the sighted is also from Parfit's piece.

18. Parfit, 'Equality or Priority?', p. 104. Emphasis in original.

19. Bedtime stories are widely acknowledged by empirical studies as a factor determining levels of educational attainment amongst children.

20. Indeed, it has a long and venerable history in political philosophy.

Chapter 5

1. In 1998 there were a mind-blowing 2822 academic papers published on globalisation, a staggering 589 new books and countless newspaper articles (www.globalisationguide.org).

2. Tony Woodley, 'The Underbelly of Globalisation', *The Guardian*, 7 February 2004.

3. George Monbiot, *The Age of Consent: A Manifesto for a New World Order* (London: Flamingo, 2003), pp. 8–9.

4. Jagdish Bhagwati, *In Defense of Globalization* (New York: Oxford University Press, 2004), pp. 3–4.

5. The most prominent critic here is Naomi Klein, *No Logo* (London: Flamingo, 2000). See also Kieron O'Hara, *Trust: From Socrates to Spin* (Cambridge: Icon, 2004), pp. 146–54.

6. Philippe Roger, *The American Enemy: The History of French Anti-Americanism* (Chicago: University of Chicago Press, 2005).

7. Olivier Roy, *Globalized Islam: The Search for a New Ummah* (New York: Columbia University Press, 2004).

8. Amy Chua, *World On Fire: How Exporting Free-Market Democracy Breeds Ethnic Hatred and Global Instability* (London: William Heinemann, 2003).

9. And in more academic contexts, too. John Gray, *False Dawn: The Delusions of Modern Capitalism* (London: Granta, 2002).

10. Manuel Castells, 'Information Technology and Global Capitalism', in *On the Edge: Living With Global Capitalism*, eds Will Hutton and Anthony Giddens (London: Vintage, 2001), p. 53.

11. David Manasian, 'Caught in the Net', *The Economist*, 23 January 2003.

12. For an excellent reconstruction of Marx's view see G.A. Cohen's, *Karl Marx's Theory of History: A Defence* (Oxford: Clarendon Press, 1978).

13. William J. Baumol, *The Free-Market Innovation Machine: Analyzing the Growth Miracle of Capitalism* (Princeton: Princeton University Press, 2002), pp. 123–5.

14. Even enthusiastic right-wing commentators sometimes get carried away with technological determinism in the Marxist style, such as Thomas Friedman, *The Lexus and the Olive Tree* (London: HarperCollins, 2000).

15. Castells, 'Information Technology and Global Capitalism', p. 54.

16. Simon Jeffery, 'What is Globalisation', *The Guardian*, 31 October 2002.

17. Though it has also increased the security risks, as containers are hard to search. Some 15,000,000 containers are on the move every day, and only 2% of them are ever inspected at ports. Post-September 11 screening of containers in the USA nearly crippled the Detroit motor industry. See 'When Trade and Security Clash', *The Economist*, 4 April 2002.

18. John Smutniak, 'Financial WMD?', *The Economist*, 22 January 2004.

19. Ulrich Beck, *Risk Society* (London: Sage, 1992).

20. Michael Ignatieff, 'Is Nothing Sacred? The Ethics of Television', in *The Warrior's Honor: Ethnic War and the Modern Conscience* (London: Chatto & Windus, 1998), pp. 9–33.

21. See e.g. *NHS Direct in England: Report by the Comptroller and Auditor General* (London: Stationery Office, 2002), available at http://www.nao.org.uk/publications/nao_reports/01-02/0102505.pdf.

22. Ben Edwards, 'Men and Machines', *The Economist*, 11 November 2004.

23. Thomas Sargeant and François Velde, *The Big Problem of Small Change* (Princeton: Princeton University Press, 2002).

24. Bhagwati, *The Defense of Globalization*, pp. 11–12.

NOTES

25. See Justin Rosenberg, *The Follies of Globalisation Theory* (London: Verso, 2000), esp. ch. 2.
26. Ibid., pp. 19–20.
27. Ibid., p. 32. Interestingly, the Westphalian model of international relations is a particularly European view. If such a state of affairs did ever exist, then it did so only in a specific part of the world. Many non-European areas of the globe have never conceived of their political affairs in such state-centric, spatially organised and autonomously acting ways.
28. Will Hutton, 'Anthony Giddens and Will Hutton in Conversation', in their *On the Edge*, p. 3.
29. See Karl Marx and Friedrich Engels, *The Communist Manifesto* (London: Penguin Books, 1967 [1848]), esp. part I.
30. Cf. e.g. Kishore Mahbubani, *Can Asians Think? Understanding the Divide Between East and West*, revised and expanded edition (South Royalton, VT: Steerforth Press, 2002).
31. Jon Guice and Kyle Eischen, 'Information Technology for Development: From Charity to Sustainability', *Development*, 45(4), 2002, pp. 29–34, at p. 30.
32. Assuming, of course, that fish stocks in his area have not been depleted by overfishing or via the environmentally hazardous dumping of chemicals.
33. Thomas Pogge, *World Poverty and Human Rights* (Oxford: Blackwell, 2002), p. 9. Pogge also lists other oft-cited reasons for being unconcerned about global poverty, including the claim that relieving poverty will only cause more deaths in the long run. The thought here is that saving those who are currently starving will cause there to be more starving people in ten years' time. Better that some die now rather than more die later. Again, however, this ignores the possibility of aid being used to provide an infrastructure of self-support. As Pogge notes, this is the surest method of actually lowering birth rates to a sustainable level, and hence guarding against poverty and famine. We draw upon Pogge's views in the following sections.
34. John Rawls, *A Theory of Justice* (Oxford: Oxford University Press, 1972), p. 7.
35. Although, admittedly, this is something that Rawls himself seems to deny. See his *The Law of Peoples* (Cambridge, MA.: Harvard University

Press, 1999). This claim is strikingly incongruous with respect to every other part of Rawls's position, as several commentators have pointed out, and should probably be rejected. See David Stevens, 'Reasonableness and Inequality in Rawls's Defence of Global Justice', *Acta Politica*, 38, 2003, pp. 231–53, for one such rebuttal of Rawls's view on this.

36. Allen Buchanan, *Justice, Legitimacy, and Self-Determination: Moral Foundations for International Law* (Oxford: Oxford University Press, 2004), p. 83.
37. See note 3 above.
38. Guice and Eischen, 'Information technology for development'.
39. Ibid., pp. 30–2.
40. Described with some candour in Sevanti Ninan, 'Introduction', in *Plain Speaking*, N. Chandrababu Naidu with Sevanti Ninan (New Delhi: Viking, 2000), pp. xx–xxiii.
41. Even now, with Manmohan Singh as Prime Minister of India, the difficulties of weaning communities from free power can seem overwhelming. Kanwar Yogendra, 'Manmohan: Free Power to Farmers is an Obstacle', *The Hindu*, 29 May 2005.
42. Naidu, *Plain Speaking*.
43. K. Srinivasulu, 'Political Articulation and Policy Discourse in the 2004 Election in Andhra Pradesh' (Governance and Policy Spaces Project Working Paper 1, 2004).
44. *Andhra Pradesh: Vision 2020*, available at http://www.aponline.gov.in/quick%20links/vision2020/vision2020.html, p. 1.
45. Naidu, *Plain Speaking*.
46. Srinivasulu, *Policy Articulation and Policy Discourse*.
47. *Andhra Pradesh: Vision 2020*, pp. 8–9.
48. http://www.aponline.gov.in/apportal/index.asp.
49. 'e-Seva Centres Becoming Popular', *The Hindu*, 23 July 2002. As Rameesh Kailasam points out, however, the tedium of the queues was nothing to the hours-long waits that one had to endure under the old low-tech system.
50. 'Government by Computer', *The Economist*, 20 March 2003.
51. Luke Harding and John Vidal, 'This is the Path to Disaster', *The Guardian*, 7 July 2001.
52. Srinivasulu, *Policy Articulation and Policy Discourse*.

53. Randeep Ramesh, 'Prophets of Cyberabad Face Rural Backlash', *The Guardian*, 10 May 2004.

54. Ramesh, 'Prophets of Cyberabad'.

55. The TDP and their coalition partners the Hindu nationalist BJP together took 39.66% of the vote. Since the election defeat, interestingly, part of Naidu's attempts to rebuild the TDP's position has included accusations that Reddy has failed to stop the rash of suicides. 'Chandrababu Naidu Vows to Rebuild Telugu Desam Party', *The Hindu*, 29 May 2005.

56. George Monbiot, 'This is What We Paid For', *The Guardian*, 18 May 2004.

57. 'The Bangalore Paradox', *The Economist*, 23 April 2005.

58. Srinivasulu, *Policy Articulation and Policy Discourse*.

59. 'Five More eSeva Centres to be Set Up', *The Hindu*, 7 January 2005.

60. 'The Bangalore Paradox'.

61. K. Venkateshwalu, 'Cyber Campaign against Ship-breaking Units', *The Hindu*, 7 April 2005.

62. Kyle Eischen, 'Building a "Soft Region" on Hard Legacies: The Development of an Informational Society in Andhra Pradesh, India' (Center for Global, International and Regional Studies, University of California, Santa Cruz, Working Paper WP#2000–3, December 2000).

63. Kieron O'Hara, *Plato and the Internet* (Cambridge: Icon Books, 2002).

64. Kieron O'Hara, 'Ontologies and Technologies: Knowledge Representation or Misrepresentation?', *SIGIR Forum*, 38, 2004, available at http://www.acm.org/sigir/forum/2004D/ohara_sigirforum_2004d.pdf.

65. Ikujiro Nonaka and Hirotaka Takeuchi, *The Knowledge-Creating Company: How Japanese Companies Create the Dynamics of Innovation* (New York: Oxford University Press, 1995).

66. Steve Fuller, *Knowledge Management Foundations* (Woburn, MA: Butterworth-Heinemann, 2002).

67. Eischen, 'Building a "Soft Region" on Hard Legacies', p. 8.

68. Leonard Waverman, Meloria Meschi and Melvyn Fuss, 'The Impact of Telecoms on Economic Growth in Developing Countries', in 'Africa: The Impact of Mobile Phones' (Vodafone Policy Paper no. 2), pp. 10–23, available at http://www.vodafone.com/assets/files/en/AIMP17032005.pdf.

69. *National Alliance for Mission 2007: Every Village a Knowledge Centre* (M.S. Swaminathan Research Foundation, 2004).
70. 'Behind the Digital Divide', *The Economist*, 12 March 2005.
71. 'Behind the Digital Divide'.

Chapter 6

1. Adam Smith, *An Inquiry into the Nature and Causes of the Wealth of Nations*, ed. R.H. Campbell and A.S. Skinner (Indianapolis: Liberty Fund, 1981), vol. 2, V.i.f.50, p. 782.
2. Ibid., V.i.f.61, p. 788.
3. Ibid., V.i.g.12, p. 795. Footnote omitted.
4. Alexander Hamilton, James Madison and John Jay, *The Federalist Papers* (New York: Mentor, 1961), no. 84, pp. 514–15.
5. Kieron O'Hara, *After Blair: Conservatism Beyond Thatcher* (Cambridge: Icon, 2005), pp. 5–31.
6. Ian Gilmour, *Dancing With Dogma* (London: Simon & Schuster, 1992).
7. David Willetts, *Modern Conservatism* (Harmondsworth: Penguin, 1992). See also O'Hara, *After Blair*, pp. 171–250.
8. John Gray, 'The Undoing of Conservatism', in *Enlightenment's Wake: Politics and Culture at the Close of the Modern Age* (London: Routledge, 1995), pp. 87–119.
9. A good, though inevitably partial, review of the literature is Barry Smart, *Economy, Culture and Society* (Buckingham: Open University Press, 2003).
10. There are many articles to choose from here, but see e.g. Polly Toynbee, 'Shoppers, not Citizens', *The Guardian*, 1 April 2005.
11. On the different virtues necessary for liberalism and for democracy, see Meira Levinson, *The Demands of Liberal Education* (Oxford: Oxford University Press, 1999), esp. ch. 4.
12. Thomas Christiano, *The Rule of the Many: Fundamental Issues in Democratic Theory* (Oxford: Westview Press, 1996), p. 84.
13. Joshua Cohen, 'Deliberation and Democratic Legitimacy', in *Deliberative Democracy*, ed. James Boheman and William Rehg (Cambridge, MA: MIT Press, 1997), p. 72.

14. Christiano, *The Rule of the Many*, p. 169.
15. Of course aims and means are not always easily separable, and may in fact be intrinsically bound together. This is a feature that needs to be acknowledged when considering calls for more 'direct' forms of democratic decision making, especially at the local level. We return to this consideration in chapter 7.
16. Richard Paul, *Critical Thinking* (Rohnert Park, CA: Sonoma State University, 1990), p. 189.
17. Eamonn Callan, *Creating Citizens: Political Education and Liberal Democracy* (Oxford: Oxford University Press, 1997), p. 26.
18. John Dryzek, *Deliberative Democracy and Beyond* (Oxford: Oxford University Press, 2000), p. 1.
19. Gordon Graham, *The Internet: A Philosophical Inquiry* (London: Routledge, 1999), p. 83. Graham's overtly pessimistic view has been discussed elsewhere. See Kieron O'Hara, 'Democracy and the Internet', *Ends and Means*, 4, 2000, available at http://www.abdn.ac.uk/philosophy/cpts/article9.hti; Kieron O'Hara and L. Crow, 'Review of Graham', *International Studies in the Philosophy of Science*, 15, 2001.
20. Cass Sunstein, *Republic.com* (Princeton: Princeton University Press, 2001).
21. There was an interesting set of papers about the new possibilities that the Semantic Web provides for personalisation in an American Association for Artificial Intelligence Workshop on Semantic Web Personalization, which are available at http://maya.cs.depaul.edu/~mobasher/swp04/accepted.html
22. Nicholas Negroponte, *Being Digital* (London: Hodder & Stoughton, 1995).
23. Sunstein, *Republic.com*, p. 31. Emphasis in original.
24. Ibid., pp. 65–80; Graham, *The Internet: A Philosophical Inquiry*, p. 83.
25. Graham, ibid., pp. 37–8.
26. Sir J. Daniel, 'Can You Get My Hard Nose in Focus? Universities, Mass Education and Appropriate Technology', in *The Knowledge Web: Learning and Collaborating on the Net*, ed. Marc Eisenstadt and Tom Vincent (London: Kogan Page, 1998), pp. 21–9.
27. Sunstein, *Republic.com*, pp. 169–84.
28. Ibid., pp. 141–66.
29. Speech by Rupert Murdoch to the American Society of Newspaper

Editors, 13 April 2005, available at http://www.newscorp.com/news/ news_247.html.

30. A point we owe to Mark Neocleous.

31. Sunstein, *Republic.com*, p. 64.

32. Cf. Sunstein, *Republic.com*, pp. 186ff.

33. C. Goble, S. Bechhofer, L. Carr, D. De Roure and W. Hall, 'Conceptual Open Hypermedia = the Semantic Web?' (Second International Workshop on the Semantic Web, Hong Kong, 2001), available at http://sunsite.informatik. rwth-aachen.de/Publications/CEUR-WS/ Vol-40/Goble-et-al.pdf.

34. Nancy Rosenblum, *Membership and Morals: The Personal Uses of Pluralism in America* (Princeton: Princeton University Press, 1998).

35. Most notably recently in a work bemoaning the demise of such associations, Robert Putnam, *Bowling Alone* (New York: Simon & Schuster, 2000).

36. Alexis De Tocqueville, *Democracy in America* (London: Everyman's Library, 1994 [1848]), vol. 2, p. 115. Tocqueville is entirely convinced of the role of secondary associations as seedbeds of civic virtue, and of the laws and institutions of democracy as shaping the feelings and characters of citizens. Thus, he writes (p. 110): 'Among the laws that rule human societies there is one which seems to be more precise and clear than all others. If men are to remain civilized or to become so, the art of associating together must grow and improve in the same ratio in which the equality of condition is increased.'

37. Kieron O'Hara, *Trust: From Socrates to Spin* (Cambridge: Icon, 2004), pp. 260–2.

38. An argument recently made in the modern context by Sam Harris, *The End of Faith: Religion, Terror and the Future of Reason* (London: Free Press, 2005).

39. Smith, *Wealth of Nations*, 2, V.i.g.2, pp. 789–90.

40. Ibid., p. 790.

41. For Hume's view, see David Hume, *History of England*, 1778, iii, pp. 30–1.

42. Smith, *Wealth of Nations*, 2, V.i.g., p. 798.

43. Ibid., p. 793.

44. 'US School Shootings', *The Guardian*, 22 March 2005.

45. Joseph Conrad, *The Secret Agent* (Harmondsworth: Penguin), p. 74.

46. We use the term 'neo-fundamentalist' carefully, following sociologist

Olivier Roy. Islamic terrorists are not fundamentalists (in the sense that Christian fundamentalists are fundamentalists) in that they don't base their philosophy on a literal interpretation of canonical texts. Partly this is because Islam is a much less centralised religion than Christianity, but it is also because many of the neo-fundamentalists' ideas are actually relatively radical. In common with a general move throughout the world from organised religion to religiosity (i.e. the pursuit of one's personal ideas of religion), the neo-fundamentalists stretch orthodox Islamic thinking to the limits. See Olivier Roy, *Globalized Islam: The Search for a New Ummah* (New York: Columbia University Press, 2004).

47. Cf. e.g. Phil Marfleet, 'Islamic Political Thought', in *New Political Thought: An Introduction*, ed. Adam Lent (London: Lawrence & Wishart, 1998), pp. 89–111.

48. See e.g. 'Should the West Always be Worried if Islamists Win Elections?', *The Economist*, 30 April 2005.

49. Tariq Ramadan, *Islam, the West and the Challenges of Modernity* (Leicester: The Islamic Foundation, 2001).

50. Gilles Kepel, *The War for Muslim Minds: Islam and the West* (Cambridge, MA: Belknap Press, 2004); Olivier Roy, *The Failure of Political Islam* (Cambridge, MA: Harvard University Press, 1995).

51. Andrew Sparrow, 'Mosque Demonstrators Say Voting Is a Sin', *Daily Telegraph*, 20 April 2005.

52. Roy, *Globalized Islam*, p. 247.

53. Ibid., p. 240. See http://www.islaam.com/Scholars.aspx.

54. Roy, *Globalized Islam*, p. 169.

55. Ibid.

56. 'The World Through Their Eyes', *The Economist*, 24 February 2005.

57. Ibid.

58. Shibley Telhami, 'Finding the Right Media for the Message in the Middle East', testimony to the Senate Foreign Relations Committee, 29 April 2004, available at http://www.brookings.edu/views/testimony/telhami/20040429.htm.

59. Shibley Telhami, Keynote Address to the Cambridge Arab Media Project, The Media and Political Change in the Arab World, 29–30 September 2004, reprinted in *Transnational Broadcasting Studies*, 13.

Chapter 7

1. See Benjamin Constant, *Political Writings*, ed. B. Fontana (Cambridge: Cambridge University Press, 1998).
2. Paul Rahe, *Republics Ancient and Modern, Volume One: The Ancient Regime in Classical Greece* (Chapel Hill: University of North Carolina Press, 1994), p. 44.
3. John Locke, *Second Treatise on Civil Government* (1689), ch. 6. An easily accessible version is available in David Wootton's *John Locke: Political Writings* (London: Penguin, 1993). The quoted passage is from p. 289 of Wootton's edition.
4. Kieron O'Hara, *Plato and the Internet* (Cambridge: Icon, 2002).
5. Rebecca T. Mercuri and L. Jean Camp, 'The Code of Elections', *Communications of the ACM*, 47(10), 2004, pp. 53–7.
6. Douglas W. Jones, 'Auditing Elections', *Communications of the ACM*, 47(10), 2004, pp. 46–50.
7. Jones, 'Auditing Elections'.
8. 'Good Intentions, Bad Technology', *The Economist*, 22 January 2004.
9. Kieron O'Hara, *The Referendum Roundabout* (London: Imprint, forthcoming).
10. H.D.F. Kitto, *The Greeks* (Harmondsworth: Penguin, 1951), pp. 134–5.
11. *Thucydides, The Peloponnesian War*, I, 89–117.
12. Ibid., III, 36.
13. Ibid., III, 37.
14. Ibid., III, 41–48.
15. Ibid., VI, 1.
16. Ibid., V, 116. For the Melian affair in general, see V, 84–116.
17. See Barbara Beck, 'Voting as a Way of Life', *The Economist*, 12 February 2004, to which this discussion is much indebted.
18. For many of the points in this section, we are indebted to David Jefferson, Aviel D. Rubin, Barbara Simons and David Wagner, 'Analyzing Internet Voting Security', *Communications of the ACM*, 47(10), 2004, pp. 59–64.
19. Richard Stenger, 'Constituent Puts Vote Up for Sale on eBay', CNN.com, 16 August 2000, available at http://archives.cnn.com/2000/TECH/computing/08/16/internet.vote/; 'E-democracy as Voter Tries to Auction Ballot Online', *The Guardian*, 9 June 2004; Tim Richardson, 'eBay

Deletes "Buy my Vote" Auctions', *The Register*, 7 April 2005, available at http://www.theregister.co.uk/ 2005/04/07/ebay_votes/.

20. Anthony Di Franco, Andrew Petro, Emmett Shear and Vladimir Vladimirov, 'Small Vote Manipulations Can Swing Elections', *Communications of the ACM*, 47(10), 2004, pp. 43–5.

21. Stephan Shakespeare, 'How e-Democracy Can Help Deliver Better Public Services', in *Viral Politics: Communication in the New Media Era*, ed. Anthony Painter and Ben Wardle (London: Politico's, 2001), pp. 72–92, at p. 76.

22. Jefferson *et al.*, 'Analyzing Internet Voting Security'.

23. David Batty, 'Call to Give 16-year-olds the Vote', *The Guardian*, 4 May 2005. For an excellent rebuttal of most of the points raised in favour of lowering the voting age, see Tak Wing Chan and Matthew Clayton, 'Should the Voting Age be Lowered to 16? Normative and Empirical Considerations', available at http://www.sociology.ox.ac.uk/swps/ 2004–06.pdf. Forthcoming in *Political Studies*.

24. Laura Smith and Tania Branigan, 'Two Thirds of First-time Voters Care about Key Issues, but Still Will Not Vote', *The Guardian*, 3 May 2005.

25. Jennifer McCoy, 'What Really Happened in Venezuela?', *The Economist*, 2 September 2004.

26. 'The Next Round', *The Economist*, 10 June 2004.

27. 'Debates and Dilemmas', *The Economist*, 16 September 2004.

28. Michael Cross, 'Traditional Systems Get Our Vote', *The Guardian*, 20 April 2005.

29. Julian Padget, 'e-Government and e-Democracy in Latin America', *IEEE Intelligent Systems*, January/February 2005, pp. 94–6.

30. Jefferson *et al.*, 'Analyzing Internet Voting Security'.

31. Kieron O'Hara, *Trust: From Socrates to Spin* (Cambridge: Icon Books, 2004), pp. 207–14.

32. Padget, 'e-Government and e-Democracy in Latin America'.

33. O'Hara, *Trust*, pp. 250–3.

34. Geoff Mulgan, 'My Time in the Engine Room', *The Guardian*, 23 April 2005. The claim made by Mulgan, who was a policy wonk in Tony Blair's office, is actually more plausible – he says it was a new way of talking to the public. But the plausibility is bought at the cost of subconsciously revealing the one-way nature of the 'conversation'.

35. Catherine Bennett, 'Blair's Big Silence is Deafening', *The Guardian*, 18 November 2004.
36. Painter and Wardle, *Viral Politics*.
37. Anthony Painter and Ben Wardle, 'Introduction', in *Viral Politics*, pp. vii–xv, at p. ix.
38. Kate McCarthy and Andrew Saxton, 'Labour: the e-Campaign is Born', in Painter and Wardle, *Viral Politics*, pp. 129–41.
39. Justin Jackson, 'e-Campaigning: Active and Interactive', in Painter and Wardle, *Viral Politics*, pp. 142–53.
40. Cross, 'Traditional Systems Get Our Vote'.
41. Rupert Murdoch, speech to the American Society of Newspaper Editors, 13 April 2005, available at http://www.newscorp.com/news/news247.html.
42. http://www.compranet.gob.mx/.
43. Padget, 'e-Government and e-Democracy in Latin America'.
44. Ted Becker, 'Rating the Impact of New Technologies on Democracy', *Communications of the ACM*, 44(1), 2001, pp. 39–43.
45. Joachim Åström, 'Should Democracy Online Be Quick, Strong or Thin?' *Communications of the ACM*, 44(1), 2001, pp. 49–51.

Chapter 8

1. 'The No-computer Virus', *The Economist*, 30 April 2005.
2. Ibid.
3. Ross Koppel, Joshua P. Metlay, Abigail Cohen, Brian Abaluck, A. Russell Localio, Stephen E. Kimmel and Brian L. Strom, 'Role of Computerized Physician Order Entry Systems in Facilitating Medication Errors', *Journal of the American Medical Association*, 293, 2005, pp. 1197–1203.
4. Non-trivial. See 'Clinical Data Standards Explained', California Health Care Foundation fact sheet, November 2004, available at http://www.chcf.org/documents/ClinicalDataStandardsExplained.pdf.
5. 'Niggles and Nerves', *The Economist*, 21 May 2005.
6. For surveys of these issues, and the technical solutions available at the time of writing, see the papers collected in Robin Mansell and Brian S. Collins, eds, *Trust and Crime in Information Societies* (Cheltenham: Edward Elgar, 2005).

NOTES

7. 'Mobile Phones Begin to Outnumber People', *Netimperative*, 6 May 2005, available at http://www.netimperative.com/2005/05/6/phones_outnumber_people.
8. Not including drinks, only if three other meals are bought, offer applies to the cheapest meal.
9. One free night is included in a stay of not less than three nights in a twin room for two people with shower but no bath, stay not including a Saturday.
10. Costing a maximum of $5.00.
11. See e.g. Annik Pardailhé-Galabrun, *The Birth of Intimacy* (Cambridge: Polity Press, 1991); Patricia Meyer Spacks, *Privacy: Concealing the Eighteenth-Century Self* (Chicago: University of Chicago Press, 2003).
12. See e.g. Christine Sypnowich, 'The Civility of Law: between Public and Private', in *Public and Private: Legal, Political and Philosophical Perspectives*, ed. Maurizio Passerin d'Entrèves and Ursula Vogel (London: Routledge, 2000), pp. 93–116, at pp. 94–5.
13. 'Can They Can Spam?', *The Economist*, 12 March 2004.
14. Others, such as postmodernists, claim that the notion of privacy isn't even coherent. We won't spend any time evaluating such claims.
15. A somewhat different, but more detailed, argument to this effect is presented by Sypnowich, 'The Civility of Law'.
16. Beate Rössler, *The Value of Privacy* (Cambridge: Polity Press, 2005).
17. As argued, for instance, by Hillel Steiner, 'The "Public–Private" Demarcation', in d'Entrèves and Vogel, *Public and Private*, pp. 19–27 and Dario Castiglione, 'Public Reason, Private Citizenship', in ibid., pp. 28–50, in their different ways.
18. For more on the reasons behind Microsoft's less-than-sparkling record on computer security, see Kieron O'Hara, *Trust: From Socrates to Spin* (Cambridge: Icon Books, 2004), pp. 104–6.
19. 'Bug Trouble', *The Economist*, 2 September 2004.
20. http://www.w3.org/P3P/.
21. Cf. Charles D. Raab, 'The Future of Privacy Protection', in Mansell and Collins, *Trust and Crime in Information Societies*, pp. 282–318, at pp. 300–1.
22. 'Move Over Big Brother', *The Economist*, 2 December 2004.
23. David Brin, *The Transparent Society: Will Technology Force us to Choose Between Privacy and Freedom?* (New York: Perseus, 1998).

24. Marshall McLuhan, *The Gutenberg Galaxy* (Toronto: University of Toronto Press, 1962).

25. Kieron O'Hara, *Plato and the Internet* (Cambridge: Icon Books, 2002).

26. 'Know Thine Enemy', *The Economist*, 5 May 2005.

27. 'Free Speech and Witch Hunts', *The Economist*, 11 August 2005.

28. Raab, 'The Future of Privacy Protection', pp. 289–90.

29. William H. Dutton and Adrian Shepherd, 'Confidence and Risk on the Internet', in Mansell and Collins, *Trust and Crime in Information Societies*, pp. 207–44, at p. 230.

Chapter 9

1. 'Data with a Human Touch', *The Economist*, 11 June 2005.

2. William J. Baumol, *The Free-Market Innovation Machine: Analyzing the Growth Miracle of Capitalism* (Princeton: Princeton University Press, 2002).

3. Robert E. Litan and William A. Niskanen, *Going Digital!* (Washington, DC: Brookings Institution Press and Cato Institute, 1998).

4. http://flexdisplay.asu.edu/.

5. Kenneth J. Arrow, 'Economic Welfare and the Allocation of Resources for Invention', in *Science Bought and Sold: Essays in the Economics of Science*, ed. Philip Mirowski and Esther Mirjam-Sent (Chicago: University of Chicago Press, 2002), pp. 165–80.

6. For more details on the banking industry, see David Shirreff, 'Open Wider', *The Economist*, 21 May 2005, and other articles by that author in the same issue, to which this review is indebted. The importance of maintaining trust in the banking system is discussed in Kieron O'Hara, *Trust: From Socrates to Spin* (Cambridge: Icon Books, 2004), pp. 127–30.

7. Shereen El Feki, 'Testing Times', *The Economist*, 18 June 2005.

8. 'Hale and Healthy', *The Economist*, 14 April 2005.

9. Shereen El Feki, 'Alternative Medicine', *The Economist*, 18 June 2005.

10. Cf. O'Hara, *Trust*, pp. 103–4.

11. Elizabeth Hendrix, 'Permanent Injustice: Rawls' Theory of Justice and the Digital Divide', *Educational Technology and Society*, 8, 2005, p. 64. Emphasis in original.

12. Hendrix, 'Permanent Injustice', p. 63.

NOTES

13. Hendrix, 'Permanent Injustice', p. 67.
14. Hendrix, 'Permanent Injustice', p. 65. Quoting Jonathan Kozol, *Savage Inequalities: Children in America's Schools* (New York: Harper Perrenial, 1991), p. 222.
15. 'Google à la française', *The Economist*, 31 March 2005.
16. Steven Johnson, *Everything Bad is Good for You: How Today's Popular Culture is Actually Making Us Smarter* (New York: Riverhead, 2005).
17. Kieron O'Hara and Tom Scutt, 'Virtue in Computer Games', in *The Two Moralities*, ed. Digby Anderson (London: Social Affairs Unit, 2005).
18. Oxford Internet Survey, 2003, available at http://www.oii.ox.ac.uk/research/?rq=oxis/oxis2003_results.

Index

Locators in brackets refer to notes

INDEX

INDEX

INDEX